TACITUS

V

LCL 322

TACITUS

THE ANNALS

WITH AN ENGLISH TRANSLATION BY
JOHN JACKSON

BOOKS XIII–XVI

HARVARD UNIVERSITY PRESS
CAMBRIDGE, MASSACHUSETTS
LONDON, ENGLAND

First published 1937
Reprinted 1951, 1956, 1962, 1969, 1981, 1991, 1994

ISBN 0-674-99355-1

Printed in Great Britain by St Edmundsbury Press Ltd,
Bury St Edmunds, Suffolk, on acid-free paper.
Bound by Hunter & Foulis Ltd, Edinburgh, Scotland.

CONTENTS

THE ANNALS OF TACITUS

BOOK XIII

AB EXCESSU DIVI AUGUSTI

P. CORNELII TACITI

LIBER XIII

I. Prima novo principatu mors Iunii Silani pro-
consulis Asiae ignaro Nerone per dolum Agrippinae
paratur, non quia ingenii violentia exitium inrita-
verat, segnis et dominationibus aliis fastiditus, adeo
ut Gaius Caesar pecudem auream eum appellare
solitus sit: verum Agrippina fratri eius L. Silano
necem molita ultorem metuebat, crebra vulgi fama
anteponendum esse vixdum pueritiam egresso Neroni et imperium per scelus adepto virum aetate
composita, insontem, nobilem et, quod tunc spectaretur, e Caesarum posteris: quippe et Silanus divi
Augusti abnepos erat. Haec causa necis. Ministri fuere P. Celer eques Romanus et Helius libertus,
rei familiari principis in Asia impositi. Ab his pro-
consuli venenum inter epulas datum est apertius,
quam ut fallerent. Nec minus properato Narcissus
Claudii libertus, de cuius iurgiis adversus Agrippinam
rettuli, aspera custodia et necessitate extrema ad

---

[1] So Diogenes τὸν ἀμαθῆ πλούσιον πρόβατον εἶπε χρυσόμαλλον
(D. Laert. VI. 2, 47).

[2] Once the affianced husband of Octavia: see XII. 3 sqq.

[3] Their grandmothers, Julia and the elder Agrippina, had
been sisters: see vol: ii. p. 240.

[4] See XII. 57, 65.

THE ANNALS OF
TACITUS
BOOK XIII

I. THE first death under the new principate, that
of Junius Silanus, proconsul of Asia, was brought
to pass, without Nero's cognizance, by treachery on
the part of Agrippina. It was not that he had provoked his doom by violence of temper, lethargic as
he was, and so completely disdained by former des-
potisms that Gaius Caesar usually styled him " the
golden sheep ";[1] but Agrippina, who had procured the
death of his brother Lucius Silanus,[2] feared him as
a possible avenger, since it was a generally expressed
opinion of the multitude that Nero, barely emerged
from boyhood and holding the empire in consequence
of a crime, should take second place to a man of
settled years, innocent character, and noble family,
who—a point to be regarded in those days—was
counted among the posterity of the Caesars: for
Silanus, like Nero, was the son of a great-grandchild
of Augustus.[3] Such was the cause of death: the
instruments were the Roman knight, Publius Celer,
and the freedman Helius, who were in charge of
the imperial revenues in Asia. By these poison was
administered to the proconsul at a dinner, too openly
to avoid detection. With no less speed, Claudius'
freedman Narcissus, whose altercations with Agrippina I have already noticed,[4] was forced to suicide by
a rigorous confinement and by the last necessity,

3

mortem agitur, invito principe, cuius abditis adhuc
vitiis per avaritiam ac prodigentiam mire congruebat.

II. Ibaturque in caedes, nisi Afranius Burrus et
Annaeus Seneca obviam issent. Hi rectores impera-
toriae iuventae et, rarum in societate potentiae,
concordes, diversa arte ex aequo pollebant, Burrus
militaribus curis et severitate morum, Seneca praeceptis eloquentiae et comitate honesta, iuvantes in
vicem, quo facilius lubricam principis aetatem, si
virtutem aspernaretur, voluptatibus concessis retinerent. Certamen utrique unum erat contra
ferociam Agrippinae, quae cunctis malae dominationis cupidinibus flagrans habebat in partibus Pallantem, quo auctore Claudius nuptiis incestis et
adoptione exitiosa semet perverterat. Sed neque
Neroni infra servos ingenium, et Pallas tristi adrogantia modum liberti egressus taedium sui moverat.
Propalam tamen omnes in eam honores cumula-
bantur, signumque more militiae petenti tribuno
dedit optimae matris. Decreti et a senatu duo
lictores, flaminium Claudiale, simul Claudio cen-
sorium funus et mox consecratio.

III. Die funeris laudationem eius princeps exorsus
est, dum antiquitatem generis, consulatus ac

---

[1] In command of the praetorian cohort on guard at the
palace.

much against the will of the emperor, with whose still hidden vices his greed and prodigality were in admirable harmony.

II. The tendency, in fact, was towards murder, had not Afranius Burrus and Seneca intervened. Both guardians of the imperial youth, and—a rare occurrence where power is held in partnership—both in agreement, they exercised equal influence by contrasted methods; and Burrus, with his soldierly interests and austerity, and Seneca, with his lessons in eloquence and his self-respecting courtliness, aided each other to ensure that the sovereign's years of temptation should, if he were scornful of virtue, be restrained within the bounds of permissible indulgence. Each had to face the same conflict with the overbearing pride of Agrippina; who, burning with all the passions of illicit power, had the adherence of Pallas, at whose instigation Claudius had destroyed himself by an incestuous marriage and a fatal adoption. But neither was Nero's a disposition that bends to slaves, nor had Pallas, who with his sullen arrogance transcended the limits of a freedman, failed to awaken his disgust. Still, in public, every compliment was heaped upon the princess; and when the tribune,[1] following the military routine, applied for the password, her son gave: "The best of mothers." The senate, too, accorded her a pair of lictors and the office of priestess to Claudius, to whom was voted, in the same session, a public funeral, followed presently by deification.

III. On the day of the obsequies, the prince opened his panegyric of Claudius. So long as he rehearsed the antiquity of his family, the consulates and the

triumphos maiorum enumerabat, intentus ipse et
ceteri; liberalium quoque artium commemoratio et
nihil regente eo triste rei publicae ab externis
accidisse pronis animis audita: postquam ad pro-
videntiam sapientiamque flexit, nemo risui temperare,
quamquam oratio a Seneca composita multum cultus
praeferret, ut fuit illi viro ingenium amoenum et
temporis eius auribus adcommodatum. Adnotabant
seniores, quibus otiosum est vetera et praesentia
contendere, primum ex iis, qui rerum potiti essent,
Neronem alienae facundiae eguisse. Nam dictator
Caesar summis oratoribus aemulus; et Augusto
prompta ac profluens quae[1] deceret principem eloquentia fuit. Tiberius artem quoque callebat, qua
verba expenderet, tum validus sensibus aut consulto
ambiguus. Etiam Gai Caesaris turbata mens vim
dicendi non corrupit. Nec in Claudio, quotiens
meditata dissereret,[2] elegantiam requireres. Nero
puerilibus statim annis vividum animum in alia
detorsit: caelare, pingere, cantus aut regimen
equorum exercere; et aliquando carminibus pangen-
dis inesse sibi elementa doctrinae ostendebat.

IV. Ceterum peractis tristitiae imitamentis curiam
ingressus et de auctoritate patrum et consensu
militum praefatus, consilia sibi et exempla capessendi
egregie imperii memoravit. Neque iuventam armis
civilibus aut domesticis discordiis imbutam; nulla

---

[1] quae] quaeque *Ernesti.*
[2] dissereret *Puteolanus :* dissererentur.

---

[1] An impressive catalogue of his literary labours, Greek and
Latin, is given by Suetonius (*Claud.* 41 sq.). The most regret-
able loss is, no doubt, that of the eight rolls of an autobio-
graphy, composed *magis inepte quam ineleganter.*

triumphs of his ancestors, he was taken seriously by himself and by others. Allusions, also, to his literary attainments[1] and to the freedom of his reign from reverses abroad had a favourable hearing. But when the orator addressed himself to his foresight and sagacity, no one could repress a smile; though the speech, as the composition of Seneca, exhibited the degree of polish to be expected from that famous man, whose pleasing talent was so well suited to a contemporary audience. The elderly observers, who make a pastime of comparing old days and new, remarked that Nero was the first master of the empire to stand in need of borrowed eloquence. For the dictator Caesar had rivalled the greatest orators; and Augustus had the ready and fluent diction appropriate to a monarch. Tiberius was, in addition, a master of the art of weighing words— powerful, moreover, in the expression of his views, or, if ambiguous, ambiguous by design. Even Caligula's troubled brain did not affect his power of speech; and, when Claudius had prepared his harangues, elegance was not the quality that was missed. But Nero, even in his childish years, turned his vivacious mind to other interests: he carved, painted, practised singing or driving, and occasionally in a set of verses showed that he had in him the rudiments of culture.

IV. However, when the mockeries of sorrow had been carried to their close, he entered the curia; and, after an opening reference to the authority of the Fathers and the unanimity of the army, stated that "he had before him advice and examples pointing him to an admirable system of government. Nor had his youth been poisoned by civil war or family strife:

7

odia, nullas iniurias nec cupidinem ultionis adferre. Tum formam futuri principatus praescripsit, ea maxime declinans. quorum recens flagrabat invidia. Non enim se negotiorum omnium iudicem fore, ut clausis unam intra domum accusatoribus et reis paucorum potentia grassaretur; nihil in penatibus suis venale aut ambitioni pervium; discretam domum et rem publicam. Teneret antiqua munia senatus, consulum tribunalibus Italia et publicae provinciae adsisterent: illi patrum aditum praeberent, se mandatis exercitibus consulturum.

V. Nec defuit fides, multaque arbitrio senatus constituta sunt: ne quis ad causam orandam mercede aut donis emeretur, ne designatis quaestoribus edendi gladiatores necessitas esset. Quod quidem adversante Agrippina, tamquam acta Claudii subverterentur, obtinuere patres, qui in Palatium ob id vocabantur, ut adstaret additis a tergo foribus velo discreta, quod visum arceret, auditus non adimeret. Quin et legatis Armeniorum causam gentis apud Neronem orantibus escendere suggestum imperatoris et praesidere simul parabat, nisi ceteris pavore defixis Seneca admonuisset, venienti matri occurreret. Ita specie pietatis obviam itum dedecori.

---

[1] Deputations from Italy or the public—*i.e.* senatorial—provinces, wishing to approach the senate, were in the first place to secure the authorization of the consuls. For the traditional procedure, see Liv. XXIX. 16.

[2] Stationed in the imperial provinces.

[3] See XI. 7–8. The exact terms of the present decree are unknown.

[4] See XI. 22.

[5] II. 37 n.

he brought to his task no hatreds, no wrongs, no desire for vengeance." He then outlined the character of the coming principate, the points which had provoked recent and intense dissatisfaction being specially discountenanced:—" He would not constitute himself a judge of all cases, secluding accusers and defendants within the same four walls and allowing the influence of a few individuals to run riot. Under his roof would be no venality, no loophole for intrigue: the palace and the state would be things separate. Let the senate retain its old prerogatives! Let Italy and the public provinces take their stand before the judgement-seats of the consuls, and let the consuls grant them access to the Fathers:[1] for the armies delegated to his charge[2] he would himself be responsible."

V. Nor was the pledge dishonoured, and many regulations were framed by the free decision of the senate. No advocate was to sell his services as a pleader for either fee or bounty;[3] quaestors designate were to be under no obligation to produce a gladiatorial spectacle.[4] The latter point, though opposed by Agrippina as a subversion of the acts of Claudius, was carried by the Fathers, whose meetings were specially convened in the Palatium,[5] so that she could station herself at a newly-added door in their rear, shut off by a curtain thick enough to conceal her from view but not to debar her from hearing. In fact, when an Armenian deputation was pleading the national cause before Nero, she was preparing to ascend the emperor's tribunal and to share his presidency, had not Seneca, while others stood aghast, admonished the sovereign to step down and meet his mother: an assumption of filial piety which averted a scandal.

VI. Fine anni turbidis rumoribus prorupisse rursum Parthos et rapi Armeniam adlatum est, pulso Radamisto, qui saepe regni eius potitus, dein profugus, tum quoque bellum deseruerat. Igitur in urbe sermonum avida, quem ad modum princeps vix septemdecim annos egressus suscipere eam molem aut propulsare posset, quod subsidium in eo, qui a femina regeretur, num proelia quoque et obpugnationes urbium et cetera belli per magistros administrari possent, anquirebant. Contra alii melius evenisse disserunt, quam si invalidus senecta et ignavia Claudius militiae ad labores vocaretur, servilibus iussis obtemperaturus. Burrum tamen et Senecam multarum rerum experientia cognitos; et imperatori quantum ad robur deesse, cum octavo decumo aetatis anno Cn. Pompeius, nono decumo Caesar Octavianus civilia bella sustinuerint? Pleraque in summa fortuna auspiciis et consiliis quam telis et manibus geri. Daturum plane documentum, honestis an secus amicis uteretur, si ducem amota invidia egregium quam si pecuniosum et gratia subnixum per ambitum deligeret.

VII. Haec atque talia vulgantibus, Nero et iuventutem proximas per provincias quaesitam supplendis Orientis legionibus admovere legionesque ipsas

---

[1] XII. 44–47, 50–51.

[2] Actually, in 84 B.C., at the age of twenty-three (Plut. *Pomp.* 6). Tacitus follows the erroneous reckoning, censured by Velleius Paterculus (II. 53), which deducted five years from the age of Pompey.

[3] In 44 B.C.

VI. At the close of the year, rumour brought the disturbing news that the Parthians had again broken out and were pillaging Armenia after expelling Radamistus;[1] who, often master of the kingdom, then a fugitive, had now once more abandoned the struggle. It followed that in a city with such an appetite for gossip the question was asked, " how a prince who had barely passed his seventeenth birthday would be able to sustain or repel such a menace. What hope was there in a youth swayed by a woman? Were even battles, the assault of cities, the other operations of war, capable of being handled through the agency of pedagogues? " Others held, in opposition, that " fortune had been kinder than if it were Claudius, incapacitated by age and by apathy, who was now being summoned to the labours of a campaign in which he would certainly have taken his orders from his slaves. But Burrus and Seneca were well known for their great experience of affairs—and how far short of maturity was the emperor, when Pompey in his eighteenth year[2] and Octavian in his nineteenth[3] had been equal to the strain of civil war? In the case of the head of the state, he accomplished more through his auspices and by his counsels than with the sword and the strong arm. He would give a plain indication whether the friends around him were honourable or the reverse, if he ignored jealousies and appointed an outstanding general in preference to an intriguer commended by a long purse and court favour."

VII. In the midst of these popular discussions, Nero gave orders that both the recruits levied in the adjacent provinces to keep the eastern legions at strength were to be moved up, and the legions

propius Armeniam collocari iubet, duosque veteres reges Agrippam et *Ant*iochum expedire copias, quis Parthorum fines ultro intrarent, simul pontes per amnem Euphratem iungi; et minorem Armeniam Aristobulo, regionem Sophenen Sohaemo cum insignibus regiis mandat. Exortusque in tempore aemulus Vologesi filius Vardanes: et abscessere Armenia Parthi, tamquam differrent bellum.

VIII. Sed apud senatum omnia in maius celebrata sunt sententiis eorum, qui supplicationes et diebus supplicationum vestem principi triumphalem, utque ovans urbem iniret, effigiemque [1] eius pari magnitudine ac Martis Ultoris eodem in templo censuere, praeter suetam adulationem laeti, quod Domitium Corbulonem retinendae Armeniae praeposuerat videbaturque locus virtutibus patefactus. Copiae Orientis ita dividuntur, ut pars auxiliarium cum duabus legionibus apud provinciam Suriam et legatum eius Quadratum Ummidium remaneret, par civium sociorumque numerus Corbuloni esset, additis cohortibus alisque, quae *in* [2] Cappadocia hiemabant.

---

[1] effigiemque *Nipperdey :* effigiesque.
[2] <in> *Bekker.*

---

[1] Herod Agrippa II.—the Agrippa of *Acts* xxv. sq.—son of Herod Agrippa I. (XII. 23 n.).
[2] Antiochus Epiphanes IV. king of Commagene (II. 42 n.) and part of Cilicia; *servientium regum ditissimus* (*Hist.* II. 81). Like Agrippa and Sohaemus, he supported Vespasian in the Civil War, and sided with Rome against the Jews.
[3] XI. 9 n.
[4] A strip of territory along the south-western frontier of Armenia.
[5] See II. 64 n. and III. 18.
[6] Cn. Domitius Corbulo, half-brother of the accuser P. Suillius Rufus and of Caligula's wife Caesonia; consul (*suffectus*)

themselves stationed closer to Armenia; while the two veteran kings, Agrippa[1] and Antiochus,[2] prepared their forces, so as to take the initiative by crossing the Parthian frontier: at the same time bridges were to be thrown over the Euphrates, and Lesser Armenia[3] was assigned to Aristobulus, the district of Sophene[4] to Sohaemus, each receiving royal insignia. Then, in the nick of time, a rival to Vologeses appeared in the person of his son Vardanes; and the Parthians, wishing apparently to postpone hostilities, evacuated Armenia.

VIII. But in the senate the whole incident was magnified in the speeches of the members, who proposed that there should be a national thanksgiving; that on the days of that thanksgiving the emperor should wear the triumphal robe; that he should enter the capital with an ovation; and that he should be presented with a statue of the same size as that of Mars the Avenger,[5] and in the same temple. Apart from the routine of sycophancy, they felt genuine pleasure at his appointment of Domitius Corbulo[6] to save Armenia: a measure which seemed to have opened a career to the virtues. The forces in the East were so divided that half the auxiliaries, with two legions, remained in the province of Syria under its governor Ummidius Quadratus, Corbulo being assigned an equal number of citizen and federate troops, with the addition of the auxiliary foot and horse wintering in Cappadocia. The allied

in 39 A.D.; legatus of Lower Germany in 47 A.D. (XI. 18 sqq.); proconsul of Asia shortly after 50 A.D. His eastern campaigns are related in this and the two following books. In 67 A.D., he was summoned to Greece by Nero and forestalled his execution by suicide.

Socii reges, prout bello conduceret, parere iussi : sed
studia eorum in Corbulonem promptiora erant. Qui
ut *instaret* [1] famae, quae in novis coeptis validissima
est, itinere propere confecto apud Aegeas civitatem
Ciliciae obvium Quadratum habuit, illuc progressum,
ne, si ad accipiendas copias Suriam intravisset
Corbulo, omnium ora in se verteret, corpore ingens,
verbis magnificis et super experientiam sapientiamque
etiam specie inanium validus.

IX. Ceterum uterque ad Vologesen regem nuntiis
monebant, pacem quam bellum mallet datisque
obsidibus solitam prioribus reverentiam in populum
Romanum continuaret. Et Vologeses, quo bellum
ex commodo pararet, an ut aemulationis suspectos
per nomen obsidum amoveret, tradit nobilissimos ex
familia Arsacidarum. Accepitque eos centurio Insteius ab Ummidio missus, forte priore [2] de causa
adito rege. Quod postquam Corbuloni cognitum est,
ire praefectum cohortis Arrium Varum et reciperare
obsides iubet. Hinc ortum inter praefectum et
centurionem iurgium ne diutius externis spectaculo
esset, arbitrium rei obsidibus legatisque, qui eos
ducebant, permissum. Atque illi recentem gloria [3]
et inclinatione [4] quadam etiam hostium Corbulonem
praetulere. Unde discordia inter duces, querente

---

[1] <instaret> *Haase* (cl. *Agr.* 18, 4).
[2] priore] prior ea *Muretus, al.*
[3] recentem gloria *Med.*[1] : recentem gloriam *Med.*
[4] inclinatione *Med.*[1] : inclinationem *Med.*

---

[1] Now Ayás, on the northern shore of the Gulf of Alexan-
dretta.
[2] Distinguished later as a partisan of Vespasian (*Hist.* III.
6, 16, 52 etc.).

kings were instructed to take their orders from either, as the exigencies of the war might require: their sympathies, however, leaned to the side of Corbulo. Anxious to strengthen that personal credit which is of supreme importance at the beginning of an enterprise, Corbulo made a rapid journey, and at the Cilician town of Aegeae [1] was met by Quadratus; who had advanced so far, in the fear that, should his rival once have entered Syria to take over his forces, all eyes would be turned to this gigantic and grandiloquent soldier, hardly more imposing by his experience and sagacity than by the glitter of his unessential qualities.

IX. However, each by courier recommended King Vologeses to choose peace in preference to war, and, by giving hostages, to continue that respectful attitude towards the Roman nation which had been the rule with his predecessors. Vologeses, either to prepare for war at his convenience or to remove suspected rivals under the style of hostages, handed over the most distinguished members of the Arsacian family. They were received by Ummidius' envoy, the centurion Insteius, who happened to have an interview with the king in connection with some previous affair. As soon as the fact came to the knowledge of Corbulo, he ordered Arrius Varius,[2] the prefect of a cohort, to set out and take over the hostages. An altercation followed between the prefect and the centurion, and, not to prolong the scene under foreign eyes, the decision was left to the hostages and the envoys escorting them. They preferred Corbulo, on the strength of his recent glory and of that half-liking which he inspired even in his enemies. The consequence was an estrange-

Ummidio praerepta quae suis consiliis patravisset,
testante contra Corbulone non prius conversum regem
ad offerendos obsides, quam ipse dux bello delectus
spes eius ad metum mutaret. Nero quo componeret
diversos, sic evulgari iussit: ob res a Quadrato et
Corbulone prospere gestas laurum fascibus imperatoriis addi. Quae in alios consules egressa coniunxi.

X. Eodem anno Caesar effigiem Cn. Domitio patri
et consularia insignia Asconio Labeoni, quo tutore
usus erat, petivit a senatu; sibique statuas argento
vel auro solidas adversus offerentis prohibuit. Et
quamquam censuissent patres, ut principium anni
inciperet mense Decembri, quo ortus erat Nero,
veterem religionem kalendarum Ianuariarum in-
choando anno retinuit. Neque recepti sunt inter
reos Carrinas Celer senator servo accusante, aut
Iulius Densus equester,[1] cui favor in Britannicum
crimini dabatur.

XI. Claudio Nerone L. Antistio consulibus cum
in acta principum iurarent magistratus, in sua acta
collegam Antistium iurare prohibuit, magnis patrum
laudibus, ut iuvenilis animus levium quoque rerum

---

[1] equester] eques R. *Muretus.*

---

[1] The twelve, logically assigned by the senate to Augustus
on his acceptance of a life-consulate in 19 B.C., and retained by
his successors.

[2] The emperor. For his colleague, see chap. 53, with XIV.
58 and XVI. 10.

ment between the generals; Ummidius complaining that he had been robbed of the results achieved by his policy, Corbulo protesting that the king had been converted to the course of offering hostages, only when his own appointment as commander in the field changed his hopes into alarm. Nero, to compose the quarrel, gave orders for a proclamation to the effect that, in view of the successes attained by Quadratus and Corbulo, laurels were being added to the imperial fasces.[1]—These incidents I have narrated in sequence, though they ran into the following consulate.

X. In the same year, Nero applied to the senate for a statue to his father Gnaeus Domitius, and for consular decorations for Asconius Labeo, who had acted as his guardian. At the same time he vetoed an offer of effigies in solid gold or silver to himself; and, although a resolution had been passed by the Fathers that the new year should begin in December, the month which had given Nero to the world, he retained as the opening day of the calendar the first of January with its old religious associations. Nor were prosecutions allowed in the cases of the senator Carrinas Celer, who was accused by a slave, and of Julius Densus of the equestrian order, whose partiality for Britannicus was being turned into a criminal charge.

XI. In the consulate of Claudius Nero [2] and Lucius Antistius, while the magistrates were swearing allegiance to the imperial enactments, the prince withheld his colleague Antistius from swearing to his own: a measure which the senate applauded warmly, in the hope that his youthful mind, elated by the fame attaching even to small things, would

A.V.C. 808 = A.D 55

gloria sublatus maiores continuaret. Secutaque
lenitas in Plautium Lateranum, quem ob adulterium
Messalinae ordine demotum reddidit senatui, clementiam suam obstringens crebris orationibus, quas
Seneca testificando, quam honesta praeciperet, vel
iactandi ingenii voce principis vulgabat.

XII. Ceterum infracta paulatim potentia matris
delapso Nerone in amorem libertae, cui vocabulum
Acte fuit, simul adusmptis in conscientiam *M.*[1]
Othone et Claudio Senecione, adulescentulis decoris,
quorum Otho familia consulari, Senecio liberto
Caesaris patre genitus. Ignara matre, dein frustra
obnitente, penitus inrepserant[2] per luxum et ambigua
secreta, ne senioribus quidem principis amicis
adversantibus, muliercula nulla cuiusquam iniuria
cupidines principis explente, quando uxore ab
Octavia, nobili quidem et probitatis spectatae, fato
quodam, an quia praevalent inlicita, abhorrebat,
metuebaturque, ne in stupra feminarum inlustrium
prorumperet, si illa libidine prohiberetur.

XIII. Sed Agrippina libertam aemulam, nurum
ancillam aliaque eundem in modum muliebriter
fremere, neque paenitentiam filii aut satietatem

[1] <M.> *Ritter.*
[2] inrepserant *Lipsius :* inrepserat.

---

[1] XI. 36.
[2] His *De clementia* was written about this time, when Nero
was *duodevicesimum egressus annum* (I. 9).
[3] She was a native of Asia Minor, and appears to have been
genuinely attached to Nero, whose funeral she arranged in
conjunction with his two old nurses (Suet. *Ner.* 50). For the
unfounded theory that she was a Christian, see Lightfoot,
Philippians, p. 21.

proceed forthwith to greater. There followed, in fact, a display of leniency towards Plautius Lateranus,[1] degraded from his rank for adultery with Messalina, but now restored to the senate by the emperor, who pledged himself to clemency in a series of speeches, which Seneca, either to attest the exalted qualities of his teaching or to advertise his ingenuity, kept presenting to the public by the lips of the sovereign.[2]

XII. For the rest, maternal authority had weakened little by little. For Nero had slipped into a love affair with a freedwoman by the name of Acte,[3] and at the same time had taken into his confidence Marcus Otho [4] and Claudius Senecio,[5] two handsome youths; the former of consular family, the latter a son of one of the imperial freedmen. At first, without the knowledge of his mother, then in defiance of her opposition, they had crept securely into the prince's favour as the partners of his dissipation and of his questionable secrets; while even his older friends showed no reluctance that a girl of that standing should gratify, without injury to anyone, the cravings of the emperor: for, whether from some whim of fate or because the illicit is stronger than the licit, he abhorred his wife Octavia, in spite of her high descent and proved honour; and there was always the risk that, if he were checked in this passion, his instincts would break out at the expense of women of rank.

XIII. But Agrippina, true to her sex, vented her spleen against " her competitor the freedwoman," " her daughter-in-law the waiting-maid," with more in the same vein. She declined to await the

opperiri, quantoque foediora exprobrabat, acrius accendere, donec vi amoris subactus exueret obsequium in matrem seque Senecae permitteret, ex cuius familiaribus Annaeus Serenus simulatione amoris adversus eandem libertam primas adulescentis cupidines velaverat praebueratque nomen, ut quae princeps furtim mulierculae tribuebat, ille palam largiretur. Tum Agrippina versis artibus per blandimenta iuvenem adgredi, suum potius cubiculum ac sinum offerre contegendis quae prima aetas et summa fortuna expeterent : quin et fatebatur intempestivam severitatem et suarum opum, quae haud procul imperatoriis aberant, copias tradebat, ut nimia nuper coercendo filio, ita rursum intemperanter demissa. Quae mutatio neque Neronem fefellit, et proximi amicorum metuebant orabantque cavere insidias mulieris semper atrocis, tum et falsae.

Forte illis diebus Caesar inspecto ornatu, quo principum coniuges ac parentes effulserant, deligit vestem et gemmas misitque donum matri nulla parsimonia, cum praecipua et cupita aliis prior deferret. Sed Agrippina non his instrui cultus suos, sed ceteris arceri proclamat et dividere filium, quae cuncta ex ipsa haberet.

---

[1] *Haec tibi scribo, is qui Annaeum Serenum, carissimum mihi, tam immodice flevi ut (quod minime velim) inter exempla sim eorum quos dolor vicit,* Sen. *Ep.* 63.—Much younger than Seneca, he was *praefectus vigilum,* and died, with some of his tribunes and centurions, through eating poisonous *fungi* at a dinner (Plin. *H.N.* 23, 96).

repentance, or satiety, of her son, and the fouler she
made her imputations, the more she fanned the flame;
till at last, conquered by the force of his infatuation,
he threw off his filial obedience and put himself in
the hands of Seneca, whose friend Annaeus Serenus[1]
had screened his adolescent desires by feigning an
intrigue with the same freedwoman, and had been
so liberal with his name that the gifts covertly
bestowed on the girl by the emperor were, to the
eye of the world, lavished upon her by Serenus.
Agrippina now reversed her methods, attacked the
prince with blandishments, and offered her bedroom
and its privacy to conceal the indulgences claimed
by his opening manhood and sovereign rank. She
even confessed her mistimed harshness, and—with
an exaggerated humility as marked in its turn as her
late excessive severity in repressing her son—offered
to transfer to him her private resources, which were
not greatly less than those of the sovereign. The
change did not escape the attention of Nero, and
roused the alarm of his intimates, who begged him
to be on his guard against the machinations of a
woman, always ruthless, and now, in addition, false.

During these days, as chance would have it, the
Caesar, who had been inspecting the apparel which
had once glittered on wives and matrons of the
imperial family, selected a dress and jewels and sent
them as a gift to his mother. Parsimony in the action
there was none, for he was bestowing unasked some
of the most valuable and coveted articles. But
Agrippina protested loudly that the present was
designed less to enrich her wardrobe than to deprive
her of what remained, and that her son was dividing
property which he held in entirety from herself.

XIV. Nec defuere qui in deterius referrent. Et
Nero infensus iis, quibus superbia muliebris innite-
batur, demovet Pallantem cura rerum, quis a Claudio
impositus velut arbitrium regni agebat; ferebaturque
degrediente eo magna prosequentium multitudine
non absurde dixisse, ire Pallantem, ut eiuraret.
Sane pepigerat Pallas, ne cuius facti in praeteritum
interrogaretur paresque rationes cum re publica
haberet. Praeceps posthac Agrippina ruere ad
terrorem et minas, neque principis auribus abstinere,
quo minus testaretur adultum iam esse Britannicum,
veram dignamque stirpem suscipiendo patris imperio,
quod insitus et adoptivus per iniurias matris exerceret.
Non abnuere se, quin cuncta infelicis domus mala
patefierent, suae in primis nuptiae, suum veneficium:
id solum dis et sibi provisum, quod viveret privignus.
Ituram cum illo in castra; audiretur hinc Germanici
filia, inde debilis rursus[1] Burrus et exul Seneca,
trunca scilicet manu et professoria lingua generis
humani regimen expostulantes. Simul intendere
manus, aggerere probra, consecratum Claudium,
infernos Silanorum manis invocare et tot inrita
facinora.

[1] [rursus] *Acidalius, Muretus.*

---

[1] His position as *libertus a rationibus* (XI. 29 n.).
[2] A high magistrate, on laying down his office, took a formal
oath *se nihil contra leges fecisse* (Plin. *Pan.* 65), and was
attended on the occasion by a retinue of friends. Here the
consul or praetor is replaced by an ex-slave, the friends by a
regiment of satellites, the oath by the far-sighted stipulation
mentioned in the next sentence.
[3] That of the praetorians.
[4] XII. 8; XIII. 1.

XIV. Persons were not lacking to report her words with a more sinister turn; and Nero, exasperated against the supporters of this female arrogance, removed Pallas from the charge[1] to which he had been appointed by Claudius, and in which he exercised virtual control over the monarchy. The tale went that, as he left the palace with an army of attendants, the prince remarked not unhappily that Pallas was on the way to swear himself out of office.[2] He had, in fact, stipulated that there should be no retrospective inquiry into any of his actions, and that his accounts with the state should be taken as balanced. At once, Agrippina rushed headlong into a policy of terror and of threats, and the imperial ears were not spared the solemn reminder that " Britannicus was now of age— Britannicus, the genuine and deserving stock to succeed to his father's power, which an interloping heir by adoption now exercised in virtue of the iniquities of his mother. She had no objection to the whole dark history of that unhappy house being published to the world, her own marriage first of all, and her own resort to poison: one sole act of foresight lay to the credit of Heaven and herself—her stepson lived. She would go with him to the camp.[3] There, let the daughter of Germanicus be heard on the one side; on the other, the cripple Burrus and the exile Seneca, claiming, forsooth, by right of a maimed hand and a professorial tongue the regency of the human race!" As she spoke, she raised a threatening arm, and, heaping him with reproaches, invoked the deified Claudius, the shades of the dead Silani,[4] and all the crimes committed to no effect.

23

XV. Turbatus his Nero et propinquo die, quo
quartum decumum aetatis annum Britannicus exple-
bat, volutare secum modo matris violentiam, modo
ipsius indolem, *levi* quidem experimento nuper
cognitam, quo tamen favorem late quaesivisset.
Festis Saturno diebus inter alia aequalium ludicra
regnum lusu sortientium evenerat ea sors Neroni.
Igitur ceteris diversa nec ruborem adlatura : ubi
Britannico iussit exsurgeret progressusque in medium
cantum aliquem inciperet, inrisum ex eo sperans
pueri sobrios quoque convictus, nedum temulentos
ignorantis, ille constanter exorsus est carmen, quo
evolutum eum sede patria rebusque summis signi-
ficabatur. Unde orta miseratio manifestior, quia
dissimulationem nox et lascivia exemerat. Nero
intellecta invidia odium intendit; urguentibusque
Agrippinae minis, quia nullum crimen neque iubere
caedem fratris palam audebat, occulta molitur
pararique venenum iubet, ministro Pollione Iulio
praetoriae cohortis tribuno, cuius cura attinebatur
damnata veneficii nomine Locusta, multa scelerum
fama. Nam ut proximus quisque Britannico neque
fas neque fidem pensi haberet, olim provisum erat.
Primum venenum ab ipsis educatoribus accepit,
tramisitque exsoluta alvo parum validum, sive tem-
peramentum inerat, ne statim saeviret. Sed Nero

---

[1] The point was of importance, as he would then assume the
toga virilis.

[2] Ἐν Σατορναλίοις λέλογχε βασιλεύς· ἔδοξε γὰρ παῖξαι ταύτην
τὴν παιδιάν. προστάσσει " σὺ πίε, σὺ κέρασον, σὺ ᾆσον, σὺ
ἄπελθε, σὺ ἐλθέ "(Epict. *Diss.* I. 25, 8).

[3] XII. 66 n.

XV. Perturbed by her attitude, and faced with the approach of the day on which Britannicus completed his fourteenth year,[1] Nero began to revolve, now his mother's proclivity to violence, now the character of his rival,—lately revealed by a test which, trivial as it was, had gained him wide sympathy. During the festivities of the Saturnalia, while his peers in age were varying their diversions by throwing dice for a king, the lot had fallen upon Nero. On the others he imposed various orders, not likely to put them to the blush: but, when he commanded Britannicus to rise, advance into the centre, and strike up a song[2]—this, in the hope of turning into derision a boy who knew little of sober, much less of drunken, society—his victim firmly began a poem hinting at his expulsion from his father's house and throne. His bearing awoke a pity the more obvious that night and revelry had banished dissimulation. Nero, once aware of the feeling aroused, redoubled his hatred; and with Agrippina's threats becoming instant, as he had no grounds for a criminal charge against his brother and dared not openly order his execution, he tried secrecy and gave orders for poison to be prepared, his agent being Julius Pollio, tribune of a praetorian cohort, and responsible for the detention of the condemned poisoner Locusta,[3] whose fame as a criminal stood high. For that no one about the person of Britannicus should regard either right or loyalty was a point long since provided for. The first dose the boy received from his own tutors, but his bowels were opened, and he passed the drug, which either lacked potency or contained a dilution to prevent immediate action. Nero, however,

lenti sceleris inpatiens minitari tribuno, iubere supplicium veneficae, quod, dum rumorem respiciunt, dum parant defensiones, securitatem morarentur. Promittentibus dein tam praecipitem necem, quam si ferro urgueretur, cubiculum Caesaris iuxta decoquitur virus cognitis antea venenis rapidum.

XVI. Mos habebatur principum liberos cum ceteris idem aetatis nobilibus sedentes vesci in aspectu propinquorum propria et parciore mensa. Illic epulante Britannico, quia cibos potusque eius delectus ex ministris gustu explorabat, ne omitteretur institutum aut utriusque morte proderetur scelus, talis dolus repertus est. Innoxia adhuc ac praecalida et libata gustu potio traditur Britannico; dein, postquam fervore aspernabatur, frigida in aqua adfunditur venenum, quod ita cunctos eius artus pervasit, ut vox pariter et spiritus raperentur. Trepidatur a circumsedentibus, diffugiunt imprudentes : at quibus altior intellectus, resistunt defixi et Neronem intuentes. Ille ut erat reclinis et nescio similis, solitum ita ait per comitialem morbum, quo prima ab infantia adflictaretur Britannicus, et redituros paulatim visus sensusque. At Agrippinae is pavor, ea consternatio mentis, quamvis vultu premeretur,

---

[1] First on a kid, which lived five hours; then, after improvements, on a young pig, which was *statim exanimatus* (Suet. *Ner.* 33).

[2] Their elders reclined. The custom was observed at the courts both of Augustus and of Claudius—under Tiberius and Caligula the case did not arise—and Suetonius' memory fails him when he notices a " belief " that Titus, *iuxta cubans*, also tasted the poisoned wine and narrowly escaped the consequences.

impatient of so much leisure in crime, threatened the tribune and ordered the execution of the poisoner, on the ground that, with their apprehensions of scandal and their preparations for defence, they were delaying his release from anxiety. They now promised that death should be as abrupt as if it were the summary work of steel; and a potion—its rapidity guaranteed by a previous test of the ingredients[1]—was concocted hard by the Caesar's bedroom.

XVI. It was the regular custom that the children of the emperors should take their meals in sight of their relatives,[2] seated with other nobles of their age at a more frugal table of their own. There Britannicus dined; and, as his food, solid and liquid, was tried by a taster chosen from his attendants, the following expedient was discovered, to avoid either changing the rule or betraying the plot by killing both master and man. A drink, still harmless, very hot, and already tasted, was handed to Britannicus; then, when he declined it as too warm, cold water was poured in, and with it the poison; which ran so effectively through his whole system that he lost simultaneously both voice and breath. There was a startled movement in the company seated around, and the more obtuse began to disperse; those who could read more clearly sat motionless, their eyes riveted on Nero. He, without changing his recumbent attitude or his pose of unconsciousness, observed that this was a usual incident, due to the epilepsy with which Britannicus had been afflicted from his earliest infancy: sight and sensation would return by degrees. But from Agrippina, in spite of her control over her features, came a flash of such terror

27

emicuit, ut perinde ignaram fuisse *atque* Octaviam sororem Britannici constiterit : quippe sibi supremum auxilium ereptum et parricidii exemplum intellegebat. Octavia quoque, quamvis rudibus annis, dolorem, caritatem, omnis adfectus abscondere didicerat. Ita post breve silentium repetita convivi laetitia.

XVII. Nox eadem necem Britannici et rogum coniunxit, proviso ante funebri paratu, qui modicus fuit. In campo tamen Martis sepultus est adeo turbidis imbribus, ut vulgus iram deum portendi crediderit adversus facinus, cui plerique etiam [1] hominum ignoscebant, antiquas fratrum discordias et insociabile regnum aestimantes. Tradunt plerique eorum temporum scriptores, crebris ante exitium diebus illusum isse pueritiae Britannici Neronem, ut iam non praematura neque saeva mors videri queat, quamvis inter sacra mensae, ne tempore quidem ad complexum sororum dato, ante oculos inimici properata sit in illum supremum Claudiorum sanguinem, stupro prius quam veneno pollutum. Festinationem exsequiarum edicto Caesar defendit, ita [2] maioribus institutum referens, subtrahere oculis acerba funera neque laudationibus aut pompa detinere. Ceterum

[1] etiam] tamen *Heinsius, Halm.*
[2] ita *Halm :* id a *Med.*[1], id *Med.*

---

[1] In the Mausoleum of Augustus (I. 8 n.).
[2] Whose ethical code might be expected to be more rigid, since they lack the true Olympian impartiality *erga bona malaque* noted at XVI. 33. But the text does not inspire complete confidence.

and mental anguish that it was obvious she had been as completely in the dark as the prince's sister Octavia. She saw, in fact, that her last hope had been taken—that the precedent for matricide had been set. Octavia, too, youth and inexperience notwithstanding, had learned to hide her griefs, her affections, her every emotion. Consequently, after a short silence, the amenities of the banquet were resumed.

XVII. The same night saw the murder of Britannicus and his pyre, the funeral apparatus—modest enough—having been provided in advance. Still, his ashes were buried in the Field of Mars,[1] under such a tempest of rain that the crowd believed it to foreshadow the anger of the gods against a crime which, even among men,[2] was condoned by the many who took into account the ancient instances of brotherly hatred and the fact that autocracy knows no partnership. The assertion is made by many contemporary authors that, for days before the murder, the worst of all outrages had been offered by Nero to the boyish years of Britannicus: in which case, it ceases to be possible to regard his death as either premature or cruel, though it was amid the sanctities of the table, without even a respite allowed in which to embrace his sister, and under the eyes of his enemy, that the hurried doom fell on this last scion of the Claudian house, upon whom lust had done its unclean work before the poison. The hastiness of the funeral was vindicated in an edict of the Caesar, who called to mind that " it was a national tradition to withdraw these untimely obsequies from the public gaze and not to detain it by panegyrics and processions. However, now

et sibi amisso fratris auxilio reliquas spes in re publica
sitas, et tanto magis fovendum patribus populoque
principem, qui unus superesset e familia summum ad
fastigium genita.

XVIII. Exim largitione potissimos amicorum auxit.
Nec defuere qui arguerent viros gravitatem adsever-
antis, quod domos, villas, id temporis quasi praedam
divisissent. Alii necessitatem adhibitam credebant
a principe, sceleris sibi conscio et veniam sperante,
si largitionibus validissimum quemque obstrinxisset.
At matris ira nulla munificentia leniri, sed amplecti
Octaviam, crebra cum amicis secreta habere, super
ingenitam avaritiam undique pecunias quasi in
subsidium corripiens, tribunos et centuriones comiter
excipere, nomina et virtutes nobilium, qui etiam tum
supererant, in honore habere, quasi quaereret ducem
et partis. Cognitum id Neroni, excubiasque militaris, quae ut coniugi imperatoris olim, tum ut matri
servabantur, et Germanos nuper eundem *in* [1] honorem custodes additos degredi iubet. Ac ne coetu
salutantium frequentaretur, separat domum matremque transfert in eam, quae Antoniae fuerat, quotiens
ipse illuc ventitaret, saeptus turba centurionum et
post breve osculum digrediens.

XIX. Nihil rerum mortalium tam instabile ac

[1] nuper eundem in *Boetticher :* super eundem.

[1] The Claudian house, of which he was a member by adoption and on the mother's side by descent.
[2] See XV. 58 n.
[3] Claudius' mother—the grandmother of Agrippina.

that he had lost the aid of his brother, not only were his remaining hopes centred in the state, but the senate and people themselves must so much the more cherish their prince as the one survivor of a family [1] born to the heights of power."

XVIII. He now conferred bounties on his chief friends. Nor were accusers wanting for the men of professed austerity, who at such a moment had partitioned town and country houses like so much loot. Others believed that compulsion had been applied by the emperor, conscience-struck by his crime but hopeful of pardon, if he could lay the powerful under obligation by a display of liberality. But his mother's anger no munificence could assuage. She took Octavia to her heart; she held frequent and private interviews with her friends; while with even more than her native cupidity she appropriated money from all sources, apparently to create a fund for emergencies. Tribunes and centurions she received with suavity; and for the names and virtues of the nobility—there was a nobility still—she showed a respect which indicated that she was in quest of a leader and a faction. Nero knew it, and gave orders to withdraw the military watch, which she had received as the wife, and retained as the mother, of the sovereign, along with the Germans [2] lately assigned to her as a bodyguard for the same complimentary motive. That her levées should not be frequented by a crowd of visitants, he made his own establishment separate, installed his mother in the house once belonging to Antonia,[3] and, at his visits to her new quarters, came surrounded by a throng of centurions and left after a perfunctory kiss.

XIX. Nothing in the list of mortal things is so

31

fluxum est quam fama potentiae non sua vi nixae.
Statim relictum Agrippinae limen : nemo solari, nemo
adire praeter paucas feminas, amore an odio incertas.
Ex quibus erat Iunia Silana, quam matrimonio C. Sili
a Messalina depulsam supra rettuli, insignis genere
forma lascivia, et Agrippinae diu percara, mox
occultis inter eas offensionibus, quia Sextium Africanum nobilem iuvenem a nuptiis Silanae deterru-
erat Agrippina, inpudicam et vergentem annis
dictitans, non ut Africanum sibi seponeret, sed ne
opibus et orbitate Silanae maritus poteretur. Illa
spe ultionis oblata parat accusatores ex clientibus
suis, Iturium et Calvisium, non vetera et saepius iam
audita deferens, quod Britannici mortem lugeret aut
Octaviae iniurias evulgaret, sed destinavisse eam
Rubellium Plautum, per maternam originem pari ac
Nero gradu a divo Augusto, ad res novas extollere
coniugioque eius et iam imperio [1] rem publicam
rursus invadere. Haec Iturius et Calvisius Atimeto
Domitiae Neronis amitae liberto, aperiunt. Qui
laetus oblatis (quippe inter Agrippinam et Domitiam
infensa aemulatio exercebatur) Paridem histrionem,
libertum et ipsum Domitiae, impulit ire propere
crimenque atrociter deferre.

---

[1] et iam imperio *J. F. Gronovius :* etiam perio *Med.*, et
imperio *Nipperdey.*

---

[1] XI. 12.
[2] Son of Rubellius Blandus and Drusus' daughter Julia
(VI. 27) ; therefore great-grandson of Tiberius, and great-great-
grandson of Tiberius' adoptive father Augustus, to whom Nero
stood in the same relationship by direct descent on the
mother's side.—See XIV. 22 ; 57 sqq.
[3] Sister of Messalina's mother. Her husband Crispus Pas-
sienus (VI. 20 n.) had divorced her in order to marry Agrippina,
whence, no doubt, the feud.

unstable and so fleeting as the fame attached to a power not based on its own strength. Immediately Agrippina's threshold was forsaken: condolences there were none; visits there were none, except from a few women, whether out of love or hatred is uncertain. Among them was Junia Silana, driven by Messalina from her husband Silanus, as I related above.[1] Eminent equally in blood, beauty, and voluptuousness, she was long the bosom friend of Agrippina. Then came a private quarrel between the pair: for Agrippina had deterred the young noble Sextius Africanus from marriage with Silana by describing her as a woman of no morals and uncertain age; not with the intention of reserving Africanus for herself, but to keep a wealthy and childless widow from passing into the possession of a husband. With the prospect of revenge presenting itself, Silana now suborned two of her clients, Iturius and Calvisius, to undertake the accusation; her charge being not the old, oft-heard tale that Agrippina was mourning the death of Britannicus or publishing the wrongs of Octavia, but that she had determined to encourage Rubellius Plautus[2] into revolution—on the maternal side he was a descendant of the deified Augustus in the same degree as Nero—and as the partner of his couch and then of his throne to make her way once more into the conduct of affairs. The charges were communicated by Iturius and Calvisius to Atimetus, a freedman of Nero's aunt Domitia.[3] Overjoyed at this windfall— for competition was bitter between Agrippina and Domitia—Atimetus incited the actor Pallas, also a freedman of Domitia, to go on the instant and present the charge in the darkest colours.

33

XX. Provecta nox erat et Neroni per vinolentiam
trahebatur, cum ingreditur Paris, solitus alioquin id
temporis luxus principis intendere, sed tunc compositus ad maestitiam, expositoque indicii ordine
ita audientem exterret, ut non tantum matrem
Plautumque interficere, sed Burrum etiam demovere
praefectura destinaret, tamquam Agrippinae gratia
provectum et vicem reddentem. Fabius Rusticus
auctor est, scriptos esse ad Caecinam Tuscum codicillos, mandata ei praetoriarum cohortium cura, sed
ope Senecae dignationem Burro retentam : Plinius
et Cluvius nihil dubitatum de fide praefecti referunt ;
sane Fabius inclinat ad laudes Senecae, cuius amicitia
floruit. Nos consensum auctorum secuturi, quae [1]
diversa prodiderint, sub nominibus ipsorum trademus.
Nero trepidus et interficiendae matris avidus non
prius differri potuit, quam Burrus necem eius promit-
teret, si facinoris coargueretur : sed cuicumque,
nedum parenti defensionem tribuendam ; nec accusatores adesse, sed vocem unius ex inimica domo
adferri : reputaret tenebras et vigilatam convivio
noctem omniaque temeritati et inscitiae propiora.

XXI. Sic lenito principis metu et luce orta itur ad

---

[1] quae *G :* qui *Med.,* <si> qui *Halm. (after Walther).*

---

[1] " The most eloquent of the moderns, as Livy of the
ancients " (*Agr.* 10); generally identified with the *vir saeculo-
rum memoria dignus* of Quint. X. 1, 104; apparently a legatee,
along with Tacitus and the younger Pliny, under the will of
Dasumius (*C.I.L.* VI. p. 1350).

[2] See the note on XII. 43.

[3] M. Cluvius Rufus, consul (*suffectus*) under Caligula, and
present at his murder (Jos. *A.J.* XIX. 1, 13); accompanied
Nero to Greece, acting (in succession to Gallio) as his herald
(D. Cass. LXIII. 14); legatus of Hispania Tarraconensis
under Galba (*Hist.* I. 8) afterwards a prominent Vitellian;

XX. The night was well advanced, and Nero was protracting it over his wine, when Paris—accustomed ordinarily about this hour to add life to the imperial debauch, but now composed to melancholy—entered the room, and by exposing the indictment in detail so terrified his auditor that he decided not merely to kill his mother and Plautus but even to remove Burrus from his command, on the ground that he owed his promotion to Agrippina and was now paying his debt. According to Fabius Rusticus,[1] letters patent to Caecina Tuscus, investing him with the charge of the praetorian cohorts, were actually written, but by the intervention of Seneca the post was saved for Burrus. Pliny[2] and Cluvius[3] refer to no suspicion of the prefect's loyalty; and Fabius certainly tends to overpraise Seneca, by whose friendship he flourished. For myself, where the authorities are unanimous, I shall follow them: if their versions disagree, I shall record them under the names of their sponsors.—Unnerved and eager for the execution of his mother, Nero was not to be delayed, until Burrus promised that, if her guilt was proved, death should follow. "But," he added, " any person whatsoever, above all a parent, would have to be allowed the opportunity of defence; and here no accusers were present; only a solitary voice, and that borne from the house of an enemy. Let him take into consideration the darkness, the wakeful night spent in conviviality, the whole of the circumstances, so conducive to rashness and unreason."

XXI. When the emperor's fears had been thus

regarded by Mommsen, in opposition to Nissen, as Tacitus' principal source in the *Histories*.

Agrippinam, ut nosceret obiecta dissolveretque vel
poenas lueret. Burrus iis mandatis Seneca coram
fungebatur; aderant et ex libertis arbitri sermonis.
Deinde a Burro, postquam crimina et auctores
exposuit, minaciter actum. Et Agrippina, ferociae
memor, " Non miror " inquit " Silanam, numquam
edito partu, matrum adfectus ignotos habere; neque
enim perinde a parentibus liberi quam ab inpudica
adulteri mutantur. Nec si Iturius et Calvisius
adesis omnibus fortunis novissimam suscipiendae
accusationis operam anui rependunt, ideo aut mihi
infamia parricidii aut Caesari conscientia subeunda
est. Nam Domitiae inimicitiis gratias agerem, si
benevolentia mecum in Neronem meum certaret:
nunc per concubinum Atimetum et histrionem Paridem quasi scaenae fabulas componit.[1] Baiarum
suarum piscinas extollebat, cum meis consiliis adoptio
et proconsulare ius et designatio consulatus et cetera
apiscendo imperio praepararentur. Aut exsistat
qui cohortis in urbe temptatas, qui provinciarum
fidem labefactatam, denique servos vel libertos ad
scelus corruptos arguat. Vivere ego Britannico
potiente rerum poteram? Ac si Plautus aut quis
alius rem publicam iudicaturus obtinuerit, desunt
scilicet mihi accusatores, qui non verba impatientia

---

[1] *The words* nunc . . . componit *were plausibly transposed
by Nipperdey to follow* praepararentur *below.*

calmed, at break of day a visit was paid to Agrippina;
who was to listen to the charges, and rebut them or
pay the penalty. The commission was carried out
by Burrus under the eye of Seneca: a number of
freedmen also were present as witnesses to the
conversation. Then, after recapitulating the charges
and their authors, Burrus adopted a threatening
attitude. Agrippina summoned up her pride:—
" I am not astonished," she said, " that Silana, who
has never known maternity, should have no knowledge of a mother's heart: for parents do not change
their children as a wanton changes her adulterers.
Nor, if Iturius and Calvisius, after consuming the
last morsel of their estates, pay their aged mistress
the last abject service of undertaking a delation, is
that a reason why my own fair fame should be
darkened by the blood of my son or the emperor's
conscience by that of his mother? For as to Domitia
—I should thank her for her enmity, if she were
competing with me in benevolence to my Nero,
instead of staging this comedy with the help of her
bedfellow Atimetus and her mummer Paris. In the
days when my counsels were preparing his adoption,
his proconsular power, his consulate in prospect, and
the other steps to his sovereignty, she was embel-
lishing the fish-ponds of her beloved Baiae.—
Or let a man stand forth to convict me of tam-
pering with the guards in the capital—of shaking
the allegiance of the provinces—or, finally, of seduc-
ing either slave or freedman into crime! Could
I have lived with Britannicus on the throne? And
if Plautus or another shall acquire the empire and
sit in judgement, am I to assume there is a dearth of
accusers prepared to indict me, no longer for the

caritatis aliquando incauta, sed ea crimina obiciant, quibus nisi a filio absolvi non possim." Commotis qui aderant ultroque spiritus eius mitigantibus, conloquium filii exposcit; ubi nihil pro innocentia, quasi diffideret, nec *de* [1] beneficiis, quasi exprobraret, disseruit, sed ultionem in delatores et praemia amicis obtinuit.

XXII. Praefectura annonae Faenio Rufo, cura ludorum, qui a Caesare parabantur, Arruntio Stellae, Aegyptus Ti.[2] Balbillo permittuntur. Suria P. Anteio destinata, set variis mox artibus elusus, ad postremum in urbe retentus est. At Silana in exilium acta, Calvisius quoque et Iturius relegantur; de Atimeto supplicium sumptum, validiore apud libidines principis Paride, quam ut poena adficeretur. Plautus ad praesens silentio transmissus est.

XXIII. Deferuntur dehinc consensisse Pallas ac Burrus, ut Cornelius Sulla claritudine generis et adfinitate Claudii, cui per nuptias Antoniae gener erat, ad imperium vocaretur. Eius accusationis auctor extitit Paetus quidam, exercendis apud aerarium sectionibus famosus et tum vanitatis manifestus. Nec tam grata Pallantis innocentia quam gravis superbia fuit: quippe nominatis libertis eius, quos conscios

---

¹ <de> *Acidalius*.   ² Ti. *Labus :* C.

---

[1] He was, however, executed later (67 A.D.) by Nero as a professional rival (Suet. *Ner.* 54; D. Cass. LXIII. 18). His only connection with the more famous Paris of the Flavian period is the name, which was common on the stage.

[2] Chap. 47 n.

occasional hasty utterances of an ill-regulated love, but for guilt from which only a son can absolve?" The listeners were moved, and ventured an attempt to calm her transports, but she demanded an interview with her son. There she neither spoke in support of her innocence, as though she could entertain misgivings, nor on the theme of her services, as though she would cast them in his teeth, but procured vengeance upon her accusers and recognition for her friends.

XXII. The prefectship of the corn supply was awarded to Faenius Rufus; the supervision of the Games, now in preparation by the Caesar, to Arruntius Stella; Egypt, to Tiberius Balbillus. Syria was marked out for Publius Anteius; but later, by one subterfuge or another, his claims were eluded, and finally he was kept in Rome. Silana, on the other side, was driven into exile; Calvisius and Iturius, also, were relegated; on Atimetus the death penalty was inflicted, Paris being too powerful a figure in the debaucheries of the emperor to be liable to punishment.[1] Plautus, for the moment, was passed over in silence.

XXIII. Information was next laid that Pallas and Burrus had agreed to call Cornelius Sulla[2] to the empire, on the strength of his distinguished race and his connection with Claudius, whose son-in-law he had become by his marriage with Antonia. The accusation was fathered by a certain Paetus, notorious for the systematic purchase of confiscated estates from the treasury, and now plainly guilty of falsehood. But the innocence of Pallas gave less pleasure than his arrogance evoked disgust: for when the freedmen were named whose complicity he was

haberet, respondit nihil umquam se domi nisi nutu aut manu significasse, vel si plura demonstranda essent, scripto usum, ne vocem consociaret. Burrus quamvis reus inter iudices sententiam dixit. Exiliumque accusatori inrogatum et tabulae exustae sunt, quibus oblitterata aerarii nomina [1] retrahebat.

XXIV. Fine anni statio cohortis adsidere ludis solita demovetur, quo maior species libertatis esset, utque miles theatrali licentiae non permixtus incorruptior ageret et plebes daret experimentum, an amotis custodibus modestiam retineret. Urbem princeps lustravit ex responso haruspicum, quod Iovis ac Minervae aedes de caelo tactae erant.

XXV. Q. Volusio P. Scipione consulibus otium foris, foeda domi lascivia, qua Nero itinera urbis et lupanaria et deverticula veste servili in dissimulationem sui compositus pererrabat, comitantibus qui raperent venditioni exposita et obviis vulnera inferrent, adversus ignaros adeo, ut ipse quoque exciperet ictus et ore praeferret. Deinde ubi Caesarem esse, qui grassaretur, pernotuit augebanturque iniuriae adversus viros feminasque insignis, et quidam

---

[1] nomina *J. F. Gronovius*: monimenta.

---

[1] Since he was a knight, the trial must have been held, not in the Senate, but in the private court of the emperor.

alleged to have used, he replied that, under his own roof, he had never intimated an order but by a nod or a motion of the hand; or, if more explanation was needed, he had used writing, so as to avoid all interchange of speech. Burrus, though on his trial, recorded his vote among the judges.[1] Sentence of banishment was passed on the prosecutor, and the account books, by help of which he was resuscitating forgotten claims of the treasury, were burned.

XXIV. At the end of the year, the cohort usually present on guard at the Games was withdrawn; the objects being to give a greater appearance of liberty, to prevent the troops from being corrupted by too close contact with the licence of the theatre, and to test whether the populace would continue its orderly behaviour when its custodians were removed. A lustration of the city was carried out by the emperor at the recommendation of the soothsayers, since the temples of Jupiter and Minerva had been struck by lightning.

XXV. The consulate of Quintus Volusius and Publius Scipio was marked by peace abroad and by disgraceful excesses at home, where Nero—his identity dissembled under the dress of a slave—ranged the streets, the brothels, and the wine-shops of the capital, with an escort whose duties were to snatch wares exhibited for sale and to assault all persons they met, the victims having so little inkling of the truth that he himself took his buffets with the rest and bore their imprints on his face. Then, it became notorious that the depredator was the Caesar; outrages on men and women of rank increased; others, availing themselves of the licence once accorded, began with impunity, under the

A.v.c. 809 = A.D. 56

41

permissa semel licentia sub nomine Neronis inulti propriis cum globis eadem exercebant, in modum captivitatis nox agebatur; Iuliusque Montanus senatorii ordinis, sed qui nondum honorem capessisset, congressus forte per tenebras cum principe, quia vi attemptantem acriter reppulerat, deinde adgnitum oraverat, quasi exprobrasset, mori adactus est. Nero tamen [1] metuentior in posterum milites sibi et plerosque gladiatores circumdedit, qui rixarum initia modica et quasi privata sinerent: si a laesis validius ageretur, arma inferebant.   Ludicram quoque licentiam et fautores histrionum velut in proelia convertit inpunitate et praemiis atque ipse occultus et plerumque coram prospectans, donec discordi populo et gravioris motus terrore non aliud remedium repertum est, quam ut histriones Italia pellerentur milesque theatro rursum adsideret.

XXVI. Per idem tempus actum in senatu de fraudibus libertorum, efflagitatumque ut adversus male meritos revocandae libertatis ius patronis daretur. Nec deerant qui censerent, sed consules relationem incipere non ausi ignaro principe, perscripsere tamen ei consensum senatus.   Ille an auctor constitutionis fieret, . . .[2] ut inter paucos et sententiae diversos,[3]

---

[1] tamen *Petersen :* tū *or* aū.   . . . *Andresen.*
[3] diversos *Lipsius :* adversos.

---

[1] The text is past restoration, but the discussion takes place at a private council in the palace.

name of Nero, to perpetrate the same excesses with their own gangs; and night passed as it might in a captured town. Julius Montanus, a member of the senatorial order, though he had not yet held office, met the emperor casually in the dark, and, because he repelled his offered violence with spirit, then recognized his antagonist and asked for pardon, was forced to suicide, the apology being construed as a reproach. Nero, however, less venturesome for the future, surrounded himself with soldiers and crowds of gladiators, who were to stand aloof from incipient affrays of modest dimensions and semi-private character: should the injured party behave with too much energy, they threw their swords into the scale. Even the licence of the players and of the theatrical claques he converted into something like pitched battles by waiving penalties, by offering prizes, and by viewing the riots himself, sometimes in secret, very often openly; until, with the populace divided against itself and still graver commotions threatened, no other cure appeared but to expel the actors from Italy and to have the soldiers again take their place in the theatre.

XXVI. About the same time, the senate discussed the iniquities of freedmen, and a demand was pressed that, in dealing with an undeserving case, the former owner should be allowed the right of annulling the emancipation. The proposal did not lack supporters; but the consuls were not bold enough to put the motion without the cognizance of the emperor, though they advised him in writing of the feeling of the senate. Nero was doubtful whether to assume responsibility for the measure, as his advisers were few and their opinions conflicting.[1] Some were

quibusdam coalitam libertate inreverentiam eo prorupisse frementibus, ut ne aequo *quidem* [1] cum
patronis iure agerent, patientiam eorum insultarent [2]
ac verberibus manus ultro intenderent, impune [3]
vel poenam suam ipsi suadentes.[4] Quid enim aliud
laeso patrono concessum, quam ut centesimum ultra
lapidem in oram Campaniae libertum releget?
Ceteras actiones promiscas et pares esse : tribuendum
aliquod telum, quod sperni nequeat. Nec grave
manu missis per idem obsequium retinendi libertatem, per quod adsecuti sint : at criminum manifestos
merito ad servitutem retrahi, ut metu coerceantur,
quos beneficia non mutavissent.

XXVII. Disserebatur contra : paucorum culpam
ipsis exitiosam esse debere, nihil universorum iuri
derogandum ; quippe late fusum id corpus. Hinc
plerumque tribus, decurias, ministeria magistratibus
et sacerdotibus, cohortis etiam in urbe conscriptas ;
et plurimis equitum, plerisque senatoribus non
aliunde originem trahi : si separarentur libertini,
manifestam fore penuriam ingenuorum. Non frustra

---

[1] ut ne aequo <quidem> *Hiller :* vine an aequo.
[2] patientiam . . . insultarent *Ruperti :* sententiam . . .
consultarent.
[3] impune *Muretus :* impulere.
[4] ipsi suadentes *Madvig :* dissuadentes. *Med., alii alia.
The whole passage, however, is hopeless.*

---

[1] The gayest and, to the delinquent, most desirable part of
Italy, beginning conveniently at the hundred and seventh
milestone. The penalty was therefore as Gilbertian as Trimal-
chio's " relegation " of his hall-porter from Cumae to Baiae
(Petr. *Sat.* 53).
[2] Their only importance now was that they qualified for the
corn-dole.

indignant that " insolence, grown harder with
liberty, had reached a point where freedmen were no
longer content to be equal before the law with their
patrons, but mocked their tameness and actually
raised their hands to strike, without punishment—or
with a punishment suggested by themselves! For
what redress was allowed to an injured patron,
except to relegate his freedman beyond the hun-
dredth milestone to the beaches of Campania?[1]
For anything else, the law-courts were open to both
on equal terms ; and some weapon which it would
be impossible to despise ought to be put into the
hands of the freeborn. It would be no great burden
to a manumitted slave to keep his freedom by the
same obedience which had earned it : on the other
hand, notorious offenders deserved to be brought
back to their bondage, so that fear might coerce
those whom kindness had not reformed."

XXVII. It was urged on the other side that " the
guilt of a few persons ought to be fatal only to themselves : the rights of the class at large ought to
suffer no detriment. For the body in question was
widely extended. From it the tribes,[2] the decuries,[3]
the assistants of the magistrates and priests were
very largely recruited ; so also the cohorts[4] enrolled
in the capital ; while the origin of most knights and
of many senators was drawn from no other source.
If the freed were set apart, the paucity of the free
would be apparent ! It was not without reason that

---

[3] Guilds of magistrates' assistants—scribes, lictors, etc.
The *ministeria* include those not organized in decuries—order-
lies (*accensi*), criers (*calatores*), etc.

[4] Not the " urban cohorts " (IV. 5 n.), but the night-watch
and fire-brigade (*vigiles*) : see XI. 35 n.

maiores, cum dignitatem ordinum dividerent, libertatem in communi posuisse. Quin et manu mittendi
duas species institutas, ut relinqueretur paenitentiae
aut novo beneficio locus. Quos vindicta patronus
non liberaverit, velut vinclo servitutis attineri. Di-
spiceret quisque merita tardeque concederet, quod
datum non adimeretur. Haec sententia valuit,
scripsitque Caesar senatui, privatim expenderent
causam libertorum, quotiens a patronis arguerentur :
in commune nihil derogarent. Nec multo post
ereptus amitae libertus Paris quasi iure civili, non
sine infamia principis, cuius iussu perpetratum
ingenuitatis iudicium erat.

XXVIII. Manebat nihilo minus quaedam imago
rei publicae. Nam inter Vibullium praetorem et plebei
tribunum Antistium ortum certamen, quod inmodestos
fautores histrionum et a praetore in vincla ductos
tribunus omitti iussisset. Conprobavere patres,
incusata Antistii licentia. Simul prohibiti tribuni
ius praetorum et consulum praeripere aut vocare ex
Italia, cum quibus lege agi posset. Addidit L. Piso
designatus consul, ne quid intra domum pro potestate
adverterent, neve multam ab iis dictam quaestores

---

[1] I. Formal and complete emancipation, effected (a) " by the
wand " (*vindicta*), the name coming from the wand laid on the
slave's head during the ceremony ; (b) by causing the slave to
be enrolled as a citizen by the Censor (*censu*) ; (c) by will (*testamento*). II. Informal and incomplete emancipation, effected
(a) by a verbal declaration in the presence of witnesses (*inter
amicos*) ; (b) by a written and countersigned declaration (*per
epistulam*) ; (c) by inviting the slave to his master's table
(*convivio*).

[2] Paris had paid Domitia 10,000 sesterces for his freedom,
and reclaimed the sum on the ground that he was of ingenuous

our ancestors, when distinguishing the position of the orders, made freedom the common property of all. Again, two forms of manumission[1] had been instituted, so as to leave room for a change of mind or a fresh favour. All, whose patron had not liberated them by the wand, were still, it might be said, held by the bond of servitude. The owner must look carefully into the merits of each case, and be slow in granting what, once given, could not be taken away." This view prevailed, and the Caesar wrote to the senate that they must consider individually all cases of freedmen accused by their patrons: no general rights were to be abrogated.—Nor was it long before his aunt was robbed of her freedman Paris, outwardly by process of civil law,[2] and not without discredit to the sovereign, by whose order a verdict of ingenuous birth had been procured.

XXVIII. There remained none the less some shadow of the republic. For a dispute arose between the praetor Vibullius and the plebeian tribune Antistius, because the tribune had ordered the release of some disorderly claqueurs thrown into prison by the praetor. The Fathers approved the arrest, and censured the liberty taken by Antistius. At the same time, the tribunes were forbidden to encroach on praetorian and consular jurisdiction or to summon litigants from Italian districts, should a civil action be possible there.[3] Lucius Piso, the consul designate, added a proposal that their official powers of punishment should not be exercised under their own roofs: fines inflicted by them were not to

birth: in view of his influence with the emperor, only one verdict was possible (*Dig.* XII. 4, 3, 5).

[3] The sentence has not been satisfactorily elucidated.

aerarii in publicas tabulas ante quattuor menses referrent; medio temporis contra dicere liceret, deque eo consules statuerent. Cohibita artius et aedilium potestas statutumque, quantum curules, quantum plebeii pignoris caperent vel poenae inrogarent. Et Helvidius Priscus tribunus plebei adversus Obultronium Sabinum aerarii quaestorem contentiones proprias exercuit, tamquam ius hastae adversus inopes inclementer augeret.[1] Dein princeps curam tabularum publicarum a quaestoribus ad praefectos transtulit.

XXIX. Varie habita ac saepe mutata eius rei forma. Nam Augustus senatui permisit deligere praefectos; deinde ambitu suffragiorum suspecto, sorte ducebantur ex numero praetorum qui praeessent. Neque id diu mansit, quia sors deerrabat ad parum idoneos. Tunc[2] Claudius quaestores rursum imposuit, iisque. ne metu offensionum segnius consulerent, extra ordinem honores promisit: sed deerat robur aetatis eum primum magistratum capessentibus. Igitur Nero praetura perfunctos et experientia probatos delegit.

XXX. Damnatus isdem consulibus Vipsanius Laenas ob Sardiniam provinciam avare habitam. Absolutus Cestius Proculus repetundarum, Cretensi-

---

[1] augeret] ageret *Ricklefs.*
[2] tunc] tum *Nipperdey.*

---

[1] See XII. 49 n. Which of the brothers (?) is meant, it is impossible to say: there are difficulties in the way of both identifications.

[2] The senatorial treasury—administered under the republic by quaestors, in the early years of Augustus, by prefects; then, from 23 B.C. to 44 A.D., by praetors. Claudius restored the quaestors, who were now (56 A.D.) permanently replaced by prefects.

be entered in the public accounts by the treasury-quaestors until four months had elapsed; in the interval, protests were to be allowable, the decision lying with the consuls. The powers of the aedileship were also narrowed, and statutory limits were fixed, up to which the curule or plebeian aediles, as the case might be, could distrain or fine. The tribune Helvidius Priscus [1] prosecuted a private quarrel with the treasury-quaestor, Obultronius Sabinus, by alleging that he was carrying his right of sale to merciless lengths against the poor. The emperor then transferred the charge of the public accounts from the quaestors to prefects.

XXIX. The organization of this department [2] had been variable and often modified. Augustus left the choice of prefects to the senate; then, as illicit canvassing was apprehended, the men to occupy the post were drawn by lot from the whole body of praetors. This also was a short-lived expedient, as the lot tended to stray to the unfit. Next, Claudius reinstated the quaestors, and—lest their zeal should be blunted by the fear of making enemies—guaranteed them promotion outside the usual order.[3] But, as this was their first magistracy, they wanted the stability of mature years: Nero, therefore, filled the office with ex-praetors who had stood the test of experience.

XXX. In the same consulate, Vipsanius Laenas was found guilty of malversation in his province of Sardinia; Cestius Proculus was acquitted on a

[3] Their term of office was three years, instead of one as previously, and at its expiry they passed immediately to the praetorship, without a preliminary tribunate or aedileship.

bus [1] accusantibus. Clodius Quirinalis, quod praefectus remigum, qui Ravennae haberentur, velut in-
fimam nationum Italiam luxuria saevitiaque adflicta-
visset, veneno damnationem anteiit. Caninius
Rebilus, ex primoribus peritia legum et pecuniae magnitudine, cruciatus aegrae senectae misso per venas
sanguine effugit, haud creditus sufficere ad constantiam sumendae mortis, ob libidines muliebriter
infamis. At L. Volusius egregia fama concessit, cui
tres et nonaginta anni spatium vivendi praecipuaeque
opes bonis artibus inoffensa tot imperatorum amicitia [2]
fuit.

XXXI. Nerone iterum L. Pisone consulibus pauca
memoria digna evenere, nisi cui libeat laudandis
fundamentis et trabibus, quis molem amphitheatri
apud campum Martis Caesar extruxerat, volumina
implere, cum ex dignitate populi Romani repertum
sit res inlustres annalibus, talia diurnis urbis actis
mandare. Ceterum coloniae Capua atque Nuceria
additis veteranis firmatae sunt, plebeique congiarium
quadringeni nummi viritim dati, et sestertium
quadringentiens aerario inlatum est ad retinendam
populi fidem. Vectigal quoque quintae et vicensimae
venalium mancipiorum remissum, specie magis quam

---

[1] Cretensibus *Nipperdey*: credentibus.
[2] amicitia *Lipsius*: malitia.

---

[1] A rather acid allusion to the interests of the elder Pliny.
The " beam " which aroused his admiration—*e larice, longa
pedes CXX, bipedali crassitudine aequalis*—is described at *H.N.*
XVI. 40, 200, and no doubt received appropriate notice in
his History.—For the " urban gazette," see III. 3 n.

[2] A wooden structure, erected in less than a year (Suet.
Ner. 12 init.).

[3] Imposed by Augustus, fifty years earlier, to defray the
expenses of his *vigiles* (XI. 35 n.). The " remission " was

charge of extortion brought by the Cretans. Clodius Quirinalis, who, as commandant of the crews stationed at Ravenna, had by his debauchery and ferocity tormented Italy, as though Italy were the most abject of the nations, forestalled his sentence by poison. Caninius Rebilus, who in juristic knowledge and extent of fortune ranked with the greatest, escaped the tortures of age and sickness by letting the blood from his arteries; though, from the unmasculine vices for which he was infamous, he had been thought incapable of the firmness of committing suicide. In contrast, Lucius Volusius departed in the fullness of honour, after enjoying a term of ninety-three years of life, a noble fortune virtuously gained, and the unbroken friendship of a succession of emperors.

XXXI. In the consulate of Nero, for the second time, and of Lucius Piso, little occurred that deserves remembrance, unless the chronicler is pleased to fill his rolls with panegyrics of the foundations and the beams [1] on which the Caesar reared his vast amphitheatre [2] in the Campus Martius; although, in accordance with the dignity of the Roman people, it has been held fitting to consign great events to the page of history and details such as these to the urban gazette. Still, the colonies of Capua and Nuceria were reinforced by a draft of veterans; the populace was given a gratuity of four hundred sesterces a head; and forty millions were paid into the treasury to keep the public credit stable. Also, the tax of four per cent. on the purchase of slaves [3] was remitted more in appearance than in effect: for, as payment

A.V.O. 810 = A.D. 57

purely formal, the tax being henceforward collected from the foreign dealer instead of the Roman purchaser.

51

vi, quia cum venditor pendere iuberetur, in partem pretii emptoribus adcrescebat. Et edixit[1] Caesar, ne quis magistratus aut procurator in provincia, *quam*[2] obtineret, spectaculum gladiatorum aut ferarum aut quod aliud ludicrum ederet. Nam ante non minus tali largitione quam corripiendis pecuniis subiectos adfligebant, dum, quae libidine deliquerant, ambitu propugnant.

XXXII. Factum et senatus consultum ultioni iuxta et securitati, ut si quis a suis servis interfectus esset, ii quoque, qui testamento manu missi sub eodem tecto mansissent, inter servos supplicia penderent. Redditur ordini Lurius Varus[3] consularis, avaritiae criminibus olim perculsus. Et Pomponia Graecina insignis femina, *A.*[4] Plautio, quem ovasse de Britannis rettuli, nupta ac superstitionis externae rea, mariti iudicio permissa. Isque prisco instituto propinquis coram de capite famaque coniugis cognovit et insontem nuntiavit.[5] Longa huic[6] Pomponiae aetas et continua tristitia fuit. Nam post Iuliam Drusi filiam dolo Messalinae interfectam per quadraginta annos

---

[1] Et edixit *Andresen*: et dixit *Med.*, edixit *vulg.*
[2] <quam> *Madvig.*
[3] Varus *Nipperdey :* Varius.   [4] <A.> *Nipperdey.*
[5] nuntiavit] pronuntiavit *Muretus.*
[6] huic] hinc *Neue.*

---

[1] Apparently a daughter of Ovid's friend, Pomponius Graecinus, and niece of Pomponius Flaccus (II. 32, 41, 66; VI. 27).

[2] Under the year 47 A.D., therefore in the lost beginning of Book XI.

[3] Christianity, as was first suggested by Lipsius; since whose day the catacombs have furnished inscriptions of Pomponii Bassi and a Pomponius Graecinus. The date of the trial would be approximately that of the Epistle to the Romans.

was now required from the vendor, the buyers found
the amount added as part of the price. The Caesar,
too, issued an edict that no magistrate or procurator
should, in the province for which he was responsible,
exhibit a gladiatorial spectacle, a display of wild
beasts, or any other entertainment. Previously,
a subject community suffered as much from the
spurious liberality as from the rapacity of its governors, screening as they did by corruption the offences
they had committed in wantonness.

XXXII. There was passed, also, a senatorial
decree, punitive at once and precautionary, that, if
a master had been assassinated by his own slaves,
even those manumitted under his will, but remaining
under the same roof, should suffer the penalty among
the rest. The consular Lurius Varus, sentenced
long before under charges of extortion, was restored
to his rank. Pomponia Graecina,[1] a woman of high
family, married to Aulus Plautius—whose ovation
after the British campaign I recorded earlier[2]—and
now arraigned for alien superstition,[3] was left to the
jurisdiction of her husband.[4] Following the ancient
custom, he held the inquiry, which was to determine
the fate and fame of his wife, before a family council,
and announced her innocent. Pomponia was a
woman destined to long life and to continuous grief:
for after Julia,[5] the daughter of Drusus, had been
done to death by the treachery of Messalina, she
survived for forty years, dressed in perpetual mourn-

---

[4] Her creed, as was often the case later, gave rise to a charge
of immorality, on which she was tried and acquitted by the
family council (cf. II. 50 fin.), presided over by her husband.

[5] See III. 29, V. 6 n., VI. 27; and, for her family connection
with the Pomponii, II. 43 fin. Messalina's motives for removing her are uncertain; her agent was Suillius (chap. 43).

non cultu nisi lugubri, non animo nisi maesto egit;
idque illi imperitante Claudio inpune, mox ad gloriam
vertit.

XXXIII. Idem annus plures reos habuit, quorum
P. Celerem accusante Asia, quia absolvere nequibat
Caesar, traxit, senecta donec mortem obiret; nam
Celer interfecto, ut memoravi, Silano pro consule
magnitudine sceleris cetera flagitia obtegebat.
Cossutianum Capitonem Cilices detulerant macu-
losum foedumque et idem ius audaciae in provincia
ratum, quod in urbe exercuerat; sed pervicaci
accusatione conflictatus postremo defensionem omisit
ac lege repetundarum damnatus est. Pro Eprio
Marcello, a quo Lycii res repetebant, eo usque
ambitus praevaluit, ut quidam accusatorum eius exilio multarentur, tamquam insonti periculum fecissent.

XXXIV. Nerone tertium consule simul iniit consulatum Valerius Messala, cuius proavum, oratorem
Corvinum, divo Augusto, abavo Neronis, collegam in
eo magistratu fuisse pauci iam senum meminerant.
Sed nobili familiae honor auctus est oblatis in singulos annos quingenis sestertiis, quibus Messala
paupertatem innoxiam sustentaret. Aurelio quoque
Cottae et Haterio Antonino annuam pecuniam statuit
princeps, quamvis per luxum avitas opes dissipassent.

---

[1] Chap. 1.

[2] XI. 6 n.

[3] Ti. Clodius Eprius Marcellus, twice consul (*suffectus*) and
proconsul of Asia from 70 to 73 A.D.; one of the most brilliant
and venomous orators of the age. For his humble origins and
enormous influence, see *Dial.* 8; for his indictment of Thrasea,
XVI. 22 sqq.; for his duels with Helvidius Priscus, *Hist.* IV.
6 sqq., 43, *Dial.* 5; for his implication in the conspiracy of
Caecina Alienus and suicide, D. Cass. LXVI. 16.

ing and lost in perpetual sorrow; and a constancy unpunished under the empire of Claudius became later a title to glory.

XXXIII. The same year saw many on their trial. Publius Celer, one of the number, indicted by the province of Asia, the Caesar could not absolve: he therefore held the case in abeyance until the defendant died of old age; for in his murder (already recorded)[1] of the proconsul Silanus, Celer had to his credit a crime of sufficient magnitude to cover the rest of his delinquencies. A charge had been laid by the Cilicians against Cossutianus Capito,[2] a questionable and repulsive character, who had assumed that the same chartered insolence which he had exhibited in the capital would be permitted in a province. Beaten, however, by the tenacity of the prosecution, he finally threw up his defence, and was sentenced under the law of extortion. On behalf of Eprius Marcellus,[3] from whom the Lycians were claiming reparation, intrigue was so effective that a number of his accusers were penalized by exile, on the ground that they had endangered an innocent man.

XXXIV. With Nero a third time consul, Valerius Messala entered upon office as his colleague, his great-grandfather, the orator Corvinus, being remembered now by only a few of old men as associated in the same magistracy with the deified Augustus, grandfather of Nero in the third degree. The honour, however, of a noble family received some increment in a yearly subsidy of five hundred thousand sesterces, on which Messala might support an honest poverty. An annual stipend was also assigned by the emperor to Aurelius Cotta and Haterius Antoninus, though they had dissipated their family estates in profligacy.

A.V.C. 811 = A.D. 58

Eius anni principio mollibus adhuc initiis prolatatum inter Parthos Romanosque de obtinenda Armenia bellum acriter sumitur,[1] quia nec Vologeses sinebat fratrem Tiridaten dati a se regni expertem esse aut alienae id potentiae donum habere, et Corbulo dignum magnitudine populi Romani rebatur parta olim a Lucullo Pompeioque recipere. Ad hoc Armenii ambigua fide utraque arma invitabant, situ terrarum, similitudine morum Parthis propiores conubiisque permixti ac libertate ignota illuc magis ad servitium inclinantes.

XXXV. Sed Corbuloni plus molis adversus ignaviam militum quam contra perfidiam hostium erat : quippe Suria transmotae legiones, pace longa segnes, munia *castrorum* Romanorum [2] aegerrime tolerabant. Satis constitit fuisse in eo exercitu veteranos, qui non stationem, non vigilias inissent, vallum fossamque

---

[1] sumitur] resumitur *Heinsius.*
[2] castrorum Romanorum *Nipperdey* (castrorum *Boetticher*) : romanorum.

---

[1] In the third Mithridatic War (74–63 B.C.).
[2] The notice of eastern affairs in chaps. 6–9 closed in 55 A.D., some time after the arrival of Corbulo in Asia Minor. Now, under the annalistic year 58 A.D., the narrative is taken up and carried to the fall of Artaxata (chap. 41). Then, under the annalistic year 60 A.D., there is recorded in XIV. 23 sqq.— the whole account should be read consecutively—the capture of Tigranocerta, with the events culminating in the induction of Tigranes into his kingdom and the withdrawal of Corbulo and the legions. The question obviously arises :—Where are the events of 59 A.D. related ? In XIII. 36 sqq. or XIV. 23 sqq., or part in the former place, part in the latter ? According to the answer, three methods of dating are possible :— **Preparatory measures of Corbulo** (XIII. 35 *Sed Corbuloni . . . peditatu cohortium*) : (*a*) (Mommsen) 55–58 A.D. ; (*b*) (Furneaux)

In the beginning of the year, the war between
Parthia and Rome for the possession of Armenia,
feebly begun, and till now carried on in dilatory
fashion, was taken up with energy. For, on the one
hand, Vologeses declined to allow his brother Tiridates to be debarred from the kingdom, which he had
himself presented to him, or to hold it as the gift of
an alien power ; and, on the other, Corbulo considered
it due to the majesty of the Roman nation to recover
the old conquests of Lucullus and Pompey.[1] In
addition, the Armenians—whose allegiance was a
matter of doubt—were invoking the arms of both
powers; though by geographical position and
affinity of manners they stood closer to the Parthians,
were connected with them by inter-marriage, and, in
their ignorance of liberty, were more inclined to
accept servitude in that quarter.

XXXV.[2] Still, Corbulo's main difficulty was rather
to counteract the lethargy of his troops than to
thwart the perfidy of his enemies. For the legions
transferred from Syria showed, after the enervation
of a long peace, pronounced reluctance to undergo
the duties of a Roman camp. It was a well-known
fact that his army included veterans who had never
served on a picket or a watch, who viewed the ram-

55–57 A.D.; (c) (Egli, Henderson) 55–57 A.D. **Preliminary
winter in Armenia** (XIII. 35 *retentusque . . . ignoscebatur*):
(a) 58–59 A.D.; (b) 57–58 A.D., (c) 57–58 A.D. **Operations result-
ing in the fall of Artaxata** : (a) 59 A.D. ; (b) 58 A.D.; (c) 58 A.D.
and the early summer of 59 A.D. **March upon and fall of
Tigranocerta** : (a) 60 A.D. ; (b) 59 A.D.; (c) late summer of 59 A.D.
Other operations, arrival of Tigranes, withdrawal of Corbulo :
(a), (b), (c) 60 A.D.—One of the systems must be right : all, as
will be seen, are open to grave objections. In any case, the
narrative of Tacitus—who had Corbulo's own memoirs to draw
upon—is singularly unsatisfactory.

quasi nova et mira viserent, sine galeis, sine loricis, nitidi et quaestuosi, militia per oppida expleta. Igitur dimissis, quibus senectus aut valetudo adversa erat, supplementum petivit. Et habiti per Galatiam Cappadociamque dilectus, adiectaque ex Germania legio cum equitibus alariis et peditatu cohortium. Retentusque omnis exercitus sub pellibus, quamvis hieme saeva adeo, ut obducta glacie nisi effossa humus tentoriis locum non praeberet. Ambusti multorum artus vi frigoris et quidam inter excubias exanimati sunt. Adnotatusque miles, qui fascem lignorum gestabat, ita praeriguisse manus, ut oneri adhaerentes truncis brachiis deciderent. Ipse cultu levi, capite intecto, in agmine, in laboribus frequens adesse, laudem strenuis, solacium invalidis, exemplum omnibus ostendere. Dehinc quia duritiam caeli militiaeque multi abnuebant deserebantque, remedium severitate quaesitum est. Nec enim, ut in aliis exercitibus, primum alterumque delictum venia prosequebatur, sed qui signa reliquerat, statim capite poenas luebat. Idque usu salubre et misericordia melius apparuit : quippe pauciores illa castra deseruere quam ea, in quibus ignoscebatur.

XXXVI. Interim Corbulo legionibus intra castra habitis, donec ver adolesceret, dispositisque per idoneos locos cohortibus auxiliariis, ne pugnam priores auderent praedicit : curam praesidiorum Paccio

---

[1] So far the chapter has dealt with the preliminaries of 55–57/8 (58/9?) A.D. Now, without a word to mark the transition, the expeditionary force is found encamped in N. Armenia—probably on the Erzerum plateau—with its base at Trebizond (chap. 39 init.), and ready to move at the opening of the short campaigning season (June to September).

part and fosse as novel and curious objects, and who owned neither helmets nor breastplates—polished and prosperous warriors, who had served their time in the towns. Accordingly, after discharging those incapacitated by age or ill-health, he applied for reinforcements. Levies were held in Galatia and Cappadocia, and a legion from Germany was added with its complement of auxiliary horse and foot. The entire army was kept under canvas,[1] notwithstanding a winter of such severity that the ice-covered ground had to be dug up before it would receive tents. As a result of the bitter cold, many of the men had frost-bitten limbs, and a few died on sentinel-duty. The case was observed of a soldier, carrying a bundle of firewood, whose hands had frozen till they adhered to his load and dropped off from the stumps. Corbulo himself, lightly dressed and bare-headed, was continually among his troops, on the march or at their toils, offering his praise to the stalwart, his comfort to the weak, his example to all. Then, owing to the rigours of the climate and the service, recalcitrancy and desertion grew common, and the cure was sought in severity. For, contrary to the rule in other armies, mercy did not attend first and second offences, but the man who had left the standards made immediate atonement with his life. That the treatment was salutary and an improvement on pity was proved by experience, the camp showing fewer cases of desertion than those in which pardons were the rule.

XXXVI. In the interval, until spring matured, Corbulo detained the legions in camp and distributed the auxiliary cohorts at suitable points, with orders not to risk a battle unattacked: the charge of these

59

Orfito primi pili honore perfuncto mandat. Is
quamquam incautos barbaros et bene gerendae rei
casum offerri scripserat, tenere se munimentis et
maiores copias opperiri iubetur. Sed rupto imperio,
postquam paucae e proximis castellis turmae advenerant pugnamque imperitia poscebant, congressus
cum hoste funditur. Et damno eius exterriti qui
subsidium ferre debuerant, sua quisque in castra
trepida fuga rediere. Quod graviter Corbulo accepit
increpitumque Paccium et praefectos militesque
tendere extra vallum iussit; inque ea contumelia
detenti nec nisi precibus universi exercitus exsoluti
sunt.

XXXVII. At Tiridates super proprias clientelas
ope Vologesi [1] fratris adiutus, non furtim iam, sed
palam bello infensare Armeniam, quosque fidos nobis rebatur, depopulari, et si copiae contra ducerentur,
eludere hucque et illuc volitans plura fama quam
pugna exterrere. Igitur Corbulo quaesito diu
proelio frustra habitus et exemplo hostium circumferre
bellum coactus, dispertit vires, ut legati praefectique
diversos locos pariter invaderent; simul regem
Antiochum monet proximas sibi praefecturas petere.
Nam Pharasmanes interfecto filio Radamisto quasi
proditore, quo fidem in nos testaretur, vetus adversus

---

[1] Vologesi] Vologaesis *Nipperdey.*

---

[1] An ancient form of punishment (Polyb. VI. 38). The
scene of the incident is given by the MSS. of Frontinus (IV. 1,
21) as *ad castellum Initia.*
[2] For Antiochus of Commagene, see chap. 7 n.; for the
Armenian prefectures, XI. 9 n.; for Pharasmanes and Radamistus, VI. 32, XI. 8, XII. 44, XIII. 6.

garrison-posts he entrusted to Paccius Orfitus, who had held the rank of leading centurion. Orfitus, though he had sent a written despatch that the barbarians were off their guard and an opportunity presented itself for a successful action, was ordered to keep within his lines and wait for larger forces. However, on the advent from the neighbouring forts of a few squadrons inexperienced enough to clamour for battle, he violated orders, engaged the enemy, and was routed. His reverse, in turn, so demoralized the troops which ought to have come to his rescue that they beat a hasty retreat to their various stations. The incident tried Corbulo's temper; and, after a sharp reprimand to Paccius, he, his prefects, and his men, were ordered to bivouac outside the rampart;[1] and in that humiliating position they were kept, until released at the petition of the entire army.

XXXVII. But Tiridates—now supported, apart from his own vassals, by help from his brother Vologeses—began to harass Armenia, no longer by stealth but in open war, ravaging the communities which he considered loyal to ourselves, or, if force was brought against him, eluding contact and, as he flew hither and thither, disseminating a terror due more to rumour than to the sword. Corbulo, therefore, frustrated in his persevering quest for battle, and forced to imitate the enemy by carrying his arms from district to district, divided his strength, so that the legates and prefects might deliver a simultaneous attack at widely separate points: at the same time, he directed King Antiochus[2] to march upon the prefectures adjoining him. For Pharasmanes, who had put his son Radamistus to death as a traitor, was now prosecuting his old feud against the Arme-

Armenios odium promptius exercebat. Tuncque primum inlecti Moschi,[1] gens ante alias socia Romanis, avia Armeniae incursavit. Ita consilia Tiridati in contrarium vertebant, mittebatque oratores, qui suo Parthorumque nomine expostularent, cur datis nuper obsidibus redintegrataque amicitia, quae novis quoque beneficiis locum aperiret, vetere Armeniae possessione depelleretur. Ideo nondum ipsum Vologesen commotum, quia causa quam vi agere mallent: sin perstaretur in bello, non defore Arsacidis virtutem fortunamque saepius iam clade Romana expertam. Ad ea Corbulo, satis comperto Vologesen defectione Hyrcaniae attineri, suadet Tiridati precibus Caesarem adgredi: posse illi regnum stabile et res incruentas contingere, si omissa spe longinqua et sera praesentem potioremque sequeretur.

XXXVIII. Placitum dehinc, quia commeantibus in vicem nuntiis nihil in summam pacis proficiebatur, conloquio ipsorum tempus locumque destinari. Mille equitum praesidium Tiridates adfore sibi dicebat: quantum Corbuloni cuiusque generis militum adsisteret, non statuere, dum positis loricis et galeis in faciem pacis veniretur. Cuicumque mortalium, nedum veteri et provido duci, barbarae astutiae

[1] Moschi *Ritter :* Insochi.

---

[1] In the N.W. of Armenia, just south of the Pontic frontier. They are coupled by Herodotus (III. 94) with the Tibareni, and a speculative identification is with the "Tubal and Meshech" of Ezekiel xxvii. 13.

[2] VI. 36 n.

nians with a readiness meant as evidence of his
fidelity to ourselves; while the Moschi,[1] most loyal of
tribes to the Roman alliance, were now won over
for the first time, and raided the less accessible parts
of Armenia. The plans of Tiridates were thus being
completely reversed, and he began to send legations,
demanding, in his own name and that of Parthia,
" why, after his late grant of hostages, and the
renewal of a friendship meant to pave the way to
further kindnesses, he was being evicted from his
long-standing occupancy of Armenia. The only
reason why Vologeses himself had as yet made no
movement was that they both preferred to proceed
by argument rather than force. But, if war was
persisted in, the house of Arsaces would not be found
wanting in the valour and fortune which had several
times already been demonstrated by a Roman
disaster." Corbulo, who had sure information that
Vologeses was detained by the revolt of Hyrcania,[2]
rejoined by advising Tiridates to approach the
emperor with a petition:—" A stable throne and a
bloodless reign might fall to his lot, if he would
renounce a dim and distant hope in order to pursue
one which was within his grasp and preferable."

XXXVIII. Then, as these messages and counter-
messages were achieving nothing towards a definite
peace, it was decided to fix the time and place for
a personal interview. A guard of a thousand horsemen, Tiridates announced, would be present with
himself: as to the forces of all arms, which might
attend Corbulo, he made no stipulation, so long as
they came divested of cuirasses and helmets, in the
guise of peace. Any man whatever—and most of
all, a veteran and far-sighted leader—was bound to

patuissent: ideo artum inde numerum finiri et hinc maiorem offerri, ut dolus pararetur; nam equiti sagittarum usu exercito si detecta corpora obicerentur, nihil profuturam multitudinem. Dissimulato tamen intellectu rectius de iis, quae in publicum consulerentur, totis exercitibus coram dissertaturos respondit. Locumque delegit, cuius pars altera colles erant clementer adsurgentes accipiendis peditum ordinibus, pars in planitiem porrigebatur ad explicandas equitum turmas. Dieque pacto prior Corbulo socias cohortis et auxilia regum pro cornibus, medio sextam legionem constituit, cui accita per noctem aliis ex castris tria milia tertianorum permiscuerat, una cum aquila, quasi eadem legio spectaretur. Tiridates vergente iam die procul adstitit, unde videri magis quam audiri posset. Ita sine congressu dux Romanus abscedere militem sua quemque in castra iubet.

XXXIX. Rex sive fraudem suspectans, quia plura simul in loca ibatur, sive ut commeatus nostros Pontico mari et Trapezunte oppido adventantes interciperet, propere discedit. Sed neque commeatibus vim facere potuit, quia per montis ducebantur praesidiis nostris insessos, et Corbulo, ne inritum bellum

---

[1] If both Artaxata and Tigranocerta are to be taken as captured in 59 A.D., then it has to be assumed that the first campaign closes here, and that *discedit* is separated from *sed*, not merely by a full stop, but by an unmentioned winter. There then arises the further necessity of making a similar intercalation somewhere in the course of XIV. 23-26.

fathom the barbarian ruse and to reflect that the
motive for specifying a restricted number on one
side, while offering a larger on the other, was to
prepare an act of treachery; since, if unprotected
flesh and blood were to be exposed to a cavalry
trained in the use of the bow, numerical strength
would be of no avail. Feigning, however, to under-
stand nothing, he replied that discussions of a
national importance would be more fitly conducted
in presence of the whole armies; and chose a site,
one half of which consisted of gently sloping hills
suited for lines of infantry, while the other spread
out into a plain admitting the deployment of mounted
squadrons. First in the field on the appointed day,
Corbulo stationed on the flanks the allied infantry
and the auxiliaries furnished by the kings; in the
centre, the sixth legion, with which he had embodied
three thousand men of the third, summoned from
another camp during the night: a solitary eagle
produced on the spectator the impression of a
single legion. The day was already declining when
Tiridates took up his position at a distance from
which he was more visible than audible: the Roman
commander, therefore, without conference, ordered
his troops to draw off to their various camps.

XXXIX. The king, either suspecting a ruse from
the different directions in which our men were
simultaneously moving, or hoping to cut off the
supplies reaching us by way of the Euxine and the
town of Trapezus, left in haste.[1] Not only was he
powerless, however, to molest the supplies, since
they were convoyed over mountains occupied by
our posts, but Corbulo, to avoid a protracted and
fruitless campaign, and at the same time to reduce the

traheretur utque Armenios ad sua defendenda cogeret, excindere parat castella, sibique quod validissimum in ea praefectura, cognomento Volandum, sumit; minora Cornelio Flacco legato et Insteio Capitoni castrorum praefecto mandat. Tum circumspectis munimentis et quae expugnationi idonea provisis, hortatur milites, ut hostem vagum neque paci aut proelio paratum, sed perfidiam et ignaviam fuga confitentem exuerent sedibus gloriaeque pariter et praedae consulerent. Tum quadripertito exercitu hos in testudinem conglobatos subruendo vallo inducit, alios scalas moenibus admovere, multos tormentis faces et hastas incutere iubet. Libritoribus funditoribusque attributus locus, unde eminus glandis torquerent, ne qua pars subsidium laborantibus ferret pari undique metu.[1] Tantus inde ardor certantis exercitus fuit, ut intra tertiam diei partem nudati propugnatoribus muri, obices portarum subversi, capta escensu munimenta omnesque puberes trucidati sint, nullo milite amisso, paucis admodum vulneratis. Et inbelle vulgus sub corona venundatum, reliqua praeda victoribus cessit. Pari fortuna legatus ac praefectus usi sunt, tribusque una die castellis expugnatis cetera terrore et alia sponte incolarum in deditionem veniebant. Unde orta

---

[1] metu *Lipsius :* motu.

---

[1] Igdir, according to Henderson : in any case, south of the Araxes and west of Artaxata.

[2] I. 20 n. For Insteius, see chap. 9.

[3] The precise difference between the *libritores* and *funditores* is not known.

Armenians to the defensive, prepared to demolish their fortresses. The strongest in that satrapy was known as Volandum,[1] and he reserved it for himself: minor holds he left to the legionary commander Cornelius Flaccus and the camp-prefect[2] Insteius Capito. Then, after inspecting the defences and making suitable provision for the assault, he urged the troops " to force from his lair this shifting enemy, disposed neither for peace nor for battle but confessing his perfidy and his cowardice by flight, and to strike equally for glory and for spoil." He next divided the army into four bodies. One, massed in the tortoise formation, he led to undermine the rampart, another he ordered to advance the ladders to the walls, while a strong party were to discharge brands and spears from the military engines. The slingers of each type[3] were assigned a position from which to hurl their bullets at long range—the object being that, with danger threatening equally on all hands, pressure at one point should not be relieved by reinforcements from another. In the sequel, the army showed so much enthusiasm in action that before a third of the day was elapsed the walls had been cleared of defenders, the barricades in the gateways broken down, the fortifications taken by escalade, and the whole of the adult population put to the sword: all without the loss of one soldier, and with extremely few wounded. The mob of non-combatants was sold by auction; the rest of the spoils became the property of the victors. The legionary commander and the prefect enjoyed equal good fortune; and, with three forts carried by storm in one day, the rest capitulated, from panic, or, in some cases, by the voluntary act of the inhabitants.—All this

fiducia caput gentis Artaxata adgrediendi. Nec tamen proximo itinere ductae legiones, quae si amnem Araxen, qui moenia adluit, ponte transgrederentur, sub ictum dabantur: procul et latioribus vadis transiere.

XL. At Tiridates pudore et metu, ne, si concessisset obsidioni, nihil opis in ipso videretur, si prohiberet, inpeditis locis seque et equestres copias inligaret, statuit postremo ostendere aciem et dato die proelium incipere vel simulatione fugae locum fraudi parare. Igitur repente agmen Romanum circumfundit, non ignaro duce nostro, qui viae pariter et pugnae composuerat exercitum. Latere dextro tertia legio, sinistro sexta incedebat, mediis decumanorum delectis; recepta inter ordines impedimenta, et tergum mille equites tuebantur, quibus iusserat, ut instantibus comminus resisterent, refugos non sequerentur. In cornibus pedes sagittarius et cetera manus equitum ibat, productiore cornu sinistro per ima collium, ut, si hostis intravisset, fronte simul et sinu exciperetur. Adsultare ex diverso Tiridates, non usque ad ictum[1] teli, sed tum minitans, tum specie trepidantis, si laxare ordines et diversos

[1] ad ictum *Baiter :* addictum *Med.,* ad iactum *Med.*[2]

---

[1] *Vexilla* detached for special service, the main body staying in Syria.

inspired confidence for an attack upon the national capital of Artaxata. The legions, however, were not taken by the shortest road, since to use the bridge over the Araxes, which runs hard under the city walls, would have brought them within missile range: the crossing was effected at some distance, and by a wider ford.

XL. But Tiridates, divided between shame and the fear that, if he acquiesced in the siege, he would give the impression of being powerless to prevent it—while, if he intervened, he might entangle himself and his mounted troops on impossible ground—determined finally to display his forces drawn up for battle; then, if a day offered, either to begin an engagement or by a simulated flight to seek the opportunity for some ruse of war. He therefore suddenly attacked the Roman column from all quarters, but without surprising our commander, who had arranged his army as much for battle as for the road. On the right flank marched the third legion, on the left the sixth, with a chosen contingent of the tenth[1] in the centre: the baggage had been brought within the lines, and the rear was guarded by a thousand horse, whose instructions were to resist an attack at close quarters, but not to pursue, if it became a retreat. On the wings were the unmounted archers and the rest of the cavalry force, the left wing extending the further, along the foot of a range of hills, so that, if the enemy forced an entry, he could be met both in front and by an enveloping movement. On the other side, Tiridates launched desultory attacks, never advancing within javelin-cast, but alternately threatening action and simulating panic, in the hope of loosening the ranks

consectari posset. Ubi nihil temeritate solutum,
nec amplius quam decurio equitum audentius progressus et sagittis confixus ceteros ad obsequium
exemplo firmaverat, propinquis iam tenebris abscessit.

XLI. Et Corbulo castra in loco metatus, an expe-
ditis legionibus nocte Artaxata pergeret obsidioque
circumdaret agitavit, concessisse illuc Tiridaten ratus.
Dein postquam exploratores attulere longinquum
regis iter et Medi an Albani peterentur incertum,
lucem opperitur, praemissaque levis armatura, quae
muros interim ambiret oppugnationemque eminus
inciperet. Sed oppidani portis sponte patefactis se
suaque Romanis permisere, quod salutem ipsis tulit :
Artaxatis ignis inmissus deletaque et solo aequata
sunt, quia nec teneri *poterant*[1] sine valido praesidio
ob magnitudinem moenium, nec id nobis virium erat,
quod firmando praesidio et capessendo bello divi-
deretur, vel si integra et incustodita relinquerentur,
nulla in eo utilitas aut gloria, quod capta essent.
Adicitur miraculum velut numine oblatum : nam
cuncta Artaxatis tenus[2] sole inlustria fuere ; quod
moenibus cingebatur, repente ita atra nube co-

[1] ⟨poterant⟩ *Halm.*
[2] Artaxatis tenus *Acidalius :* extra tectis actenus.

---

[1] If Artaxata fell in the early summer of 59 A.D., then this
sentence bears its natural and indeed only possible meaning :
Corbulo enters the town and destroys it immediately. Then
(see XIV. 23) he crosses Armenia diagonally in the intense heat
and is in Tigranocerta by the autumn. If, on the other hand,
it fell in the late summer, whether of 58 A.D. or 59 A.D., Corbulo
evidently did not fire the town in order to winter among the
ashes, and Furneaux and Mommsen have no option but to set
aside the plain sense of the passage and refer *Artaxatis ignis
inmissus* to the opening of the campaigning season in 59 or 60
A.D. respectively.

and falling on them while separated. Then, as there
was no rash break of cohesion, and the only result
attained was that a decurion of cavalry, who advanced too boldly and was transfixed with a flight of
arrows, had confirmed by his example the obedience
of the rest, he drew off when darkness began to
approach.

XLI. Pitching his camp on the spot, Corbulo
revolved the problem whether he should leave the
baggage, move straight upon Artaxata with the
legions under cover of night, and invest the city, on
which he presumed Tiridates to have retired.   Later,
when scouts came in with the news that the king's
journey was a lengthy one, and that it was difficult
to say whether his destination was Media or Albania,
he waited for the dawn, but sent the light-armed
troops in advance to draw a cordon round the walls
in the interval and begin the attack from a distance.
The townsmen, however, opened the gates voluntarily, and surrendered themselves and their property
to the Romans. This promptitude ensured their
personal safety; Artaxata itself was fired,[1] demolished
and razed to the ground; for in view of the extent of
the walls it was impossible to hold it without a
powerful garrison, and our numbers were not such
that they could be divided between keeping a strong
retaining force and conducting a campaign; while,
if the place was to remain unscathed and unguarded,
there was neither utility nor glory in the bare fact
of its capture. In addition, there was a marvel,
sent apparently by Heaven: up to Artaxata, the
landscape glittered in the sunlight, yet suddenly
the area encircled by the fortifications was so
completely enveloped in a cloud of darkness and

opertum fulguribusque discretum est, ut quasi infensantibus deis exitio tradi crederetur. Ob haec consalutatus imperator Nero, et senatus consulto supplicationes habitae, statuaeque et arcus et continui consulatus principi, utque inter festos referretur dies, quo patrata victoria, quo nuntiata, quo relatum de ea esset, aliaque in eandem formam decernuntur, adeo modum egressa, ut C. Cassius de ceteris honoribus adsensus, si pro benignitate fortunae dis grates agerentur, ne totum quidem annum supplicationibus sufficere disseruerit, eoque oportere dividi sacros et negotiosos dies, quis divina colerent et humana non impedirent.

XLII. Variis deinde casibus iactatus et multorum odia meritus reus, haud tamen sine invidia Senecae damnatur. Is fuit P. Suillius, imperitante Claudio terribilis ac venalis et mutatione temporum non quantum inimici cuperent demissus quique se nocentem videri quam supplicem mallet. Eius opprimendi gratia repetitum credebatur senatus consultum poenaque Cinciae legis adversum eos, qui pretio

---

[1] Egli's attempt to identify the "miracle" with the eclipse— not quite total—of 59 A.D. (XIV. 12), which is known from Pliny to have been observed by Corbulo in Armenia (*H.N.* II. 70, 180), is invalidated by two circumstances: in the first place, whatever is here described, the description is not that of an eclipse; in the second, the eclipse itself occurred at a date (Apr. 30), when it would have been barely possible for the legions to have left Erzerum and totally impossible for them to have reached Artaxata.

[2] By the victorious troops (II. 18 n.).   [3] XII. 11 n.

[4] The word *deinde* is by far the strongest argument for Furneaux' chronology: for, as he and Nipperdey insist, it is a definite statement that the impeachment of Suillius in 58 A.D. was subsequent to the debate in the senate with regard to the celebrations of the fall of Artaxata.

parted from the outside world by lightning flashes
that the belief prevailed that it was being con-
signed to its doom by the hostile action of the
gods.[1]—For all this, Nero was hailed as *Imperator*,[2]
and in obedience to a senatorial decree, thanksgivings
were held; statues and arches and successive consulates were voted to the sovereign; and the days on
which the victory was achieved, on which it was
announced, on which the resolution concerning it was
put, were to be included among the national festivals.
There were more proposals in the same strain, so
utterly extravagant that Gaius Cassius,[3] who had
agreed to the other honours, pointed out that, if
gratitude, commensurate with the generosity of
fortune, had to be shown to the gods, the whole year
was too short for their thanksgivings, and for that
reason a distinction ought to be made between holy
days proper and working days on which men might
worship Heaven without suspending the business
of earth.

XLII. And now[4] the hero of a chequered and
stormy career, who had earned himself a multitude
of hatreds, received his condemnation, though not
without some detriment to the popularity of Seneca.
This was Publius Suillius,[5] the terrible and venal
favourite of the Claudian reign, now less cast down
by the change in the times than his enemies could
wish, and more inclined to be counted a criminal
than a suppliant. For the sake, it was believed, of
crushing him, there had been revived an earlier decree
of the senate,[6] together with the penalties prescribed
by the Cincian law against advocates who had

---

[5] Half-brother, as it happened, of Corbulo (IV. 31 n.).
[6] XI. 5–7.

causas oravissent. Nec Suillius questu aut expro-
bratione abstinebat, praeter ferociam animi extrema
senecta liber et Senecam increpans infensum amicis
Claudii, sub quo iustissimum exilium pertulisset.
Simul studiis inertibus et iuvenum inperitiae suetum
livere iis, qui vividam et incorruptam eloquentiam
tuendis civibus exercerent. Se quaestorem Germanici, illum domus eius adulterum fuisse. An
gravius aestimandum sponte litigatoris praemium
honestae operae adsequi quam corrumpere cubicula
principum feminarum? Qua sapientia, quibus
philosophorum praeceptis intra quadriennium regiae
amicitiae ter miliens sestertium paravisset? Romae
testamenta et orbos velut indagine eius capi, Italiam
et provincias inmenso faenore hauriri: at sibi labore
quaesitam et modicam pecuniam esse. Crimen,
periculum, omnia potius toleraturum, quam veterem
ac domi[1] partam dignationem subitae felicitati
submitteret.

XLIII. Nec deerant qui haec isdem verbis aut versa
in deterius Senecae deferrent. Repertique accusatores direptos socios, cum Suillius provinciam Asiam
regeret, ac publicae pecuniae peculatum detulerunt.
Mox, quia inquisitionem annuam impetraverant,
brevius visum urbana crimina incipi, quorum obvii

---

[1] domi *Jac. Gronovius :* dō.

---

[1] In the first year of Claudius, the charge being one of
adultery with Germanicus' daughter Julia (XII. 8 n., D. Cass.
LX. 8).

[2] The question was asked by others than Suillius. Seneca's
reply is the *De vita beata* : see, for instance, chaps. 17 sq., 22 sq.

[3] By calling in a loan of 40,000,000 sesterces, he helped,
according to Dio (LXII. 2), to precipitate the British rebellion
of 61 A.D.

pleaded for profit. Suillius himself spared neither complaints nor objurgations, using the freedom natural not only to his fierce temper but to his extreme age, and assailing Seneca as "the embittered enemy of the friends of Claudius, under whom he had suffered his well-earned exile.[1] At the same time, since his only experience was of bookish studies and single-minded youths, he had a jaundiced eye for those who applied a living and unsophisticated eloquence to the defence of their fellow-citizens. He himself had been Germanicus' quaestor; Seneca, the adulterer under the prince's roof. To obtain as the voluntary gift of a litigant some reward for honourable service—was that an offence to be judged more harshly than the pollution of the couch of imperial princesses? By what branch of wisdom, by what rules of philosophy, had he acquired, within four years of royal favour, three hundred million sesterces?[2] In Rome his nets were spread for the childless and their testaments: Italy and the provinces were sucked dry by his limitless usury.[3] But he, Suillius, had his hard-earned and modest competence! He would suffer accusation, trial, everything, rather than stoop his old, homemade honour before this upstart success."

XLIII. There was no lack of auditors to report his remarks, word for word or with changes for the worse, to Seneca. Accusers were discovered, and they laid their charges—that the provincials had been plundered during Suillius' government of Asia, and that there had been embezzlement of public money. Then, as the prosecution had obtained a year for inquiries, it seemed shorter to begin upon his delinquencies at home, witnesses to

testes erant. Ii acerbitate accusationis Q. Pom-
ponium ad necessitatem belli civilis detrusum,
Iuliam Drusi filiam Sabinamque Poppaeam ad
mortem actas et Valerium Asiaticum, Lusium
Saturninum, Cornelium Lupum circumventos, iam
equitum Romanorum agmina damnata omnemque
Claudii saevitiam Suillio obiectabant. Ille nihil ex
his sponte susceptum, sed principi paruisse defende-
bat, donec eam orationem Caesar cohibuit, comper-
tum sibi referens ex commentariis patris sui nullam
cuiusquam accusationem ab eo coactam. Tum iussa
Messalinae praetendi et labare defensio: cur enim
neminem alium delectum, qui saevienti impudicae
vocem praeberet? Puniendos rerum atrocium
ministros, ubi pretia scelerum adepti scelera ipsa
aliis delegent. Igitur adempta bonorum parte (nam
filio et nepti pars concedebatur eximebanturque etiam
quae testamento matris aut *ab*[1] avia acceperant) in
insulas Balearis pellitur, non in ipso discrimine, non
post damnationem fractus animo; ferebaturque
copiosa et molli vita secretum illud toleravisse.
Filium eius Nerullinum adgressis accusatoribus per
invidiam patris et crimina repetundarum, intercessit
princeps tamquam satis expleta ultione.

---

[1] ⟨ab⟩avia *Sirker*: avia *Med.*, avi *dett.*, aviae *Freinsheim, vulg.*

[1] See VI. 18. Consul at the time of Caligula's assassination,
he had narrowly escaped being despatched by the praetorians
ὡς ἐπ' ἐλευθερίαν τὴν σύγκλητον παρακαλῶν (Jos. *A.J.* XIX.
4, 5). Presumably this show of republicanism gave Suillius
the handle for an accusation which forced him to join the still-
born revolt of Camillus Scribonianus (XII. 52 n.).—For Julia,
see chap. 32; for the elder Poppaea and Asiaticus, XI. 1;
for the Roman knights, Suet. *Claud.* 29 *in CCC amplius equites
R. animadvertit.* Saturninus and Lupus are mentioned, without details, among Claudius' friends and victims, by Seneca
(*Apocol.* 13).

which were ready to hand. By these the venomous indictment which had driven Quintus Pomponius to the necessity of civil war;[1] the hounding to death of Drusus' daughter Julia, and of Poppaea Sabina; the trapping of Valerius Asiaticus, of Lusius Saturninus, and of Cornelius Lupus; finally, the conviction of an army of Roman knights, and the whole tale of Claudius' cruelty,—were laid to the account of Suillius. In defence he urged that none of these acts had been undertaken voluntarily, and that he had merely obeyed the sovereign; until the Caesar cut short his speech by stating that he had definite knowledge from his father's papers that he had compelled no prosecution of any person. Orders from Messalina were now alleged, and the defence began to totter:— " For why had none other been chosen to put his voice at the disposal of that homicidal wanton? Punishment must be measured out to these agents of atrocity, when, after handling the wages of crime, they imputed the crime to others." Hence, after the forfeiture of half his estate—for his son and granddaughter were allowed the other half, and a similar exemption was extended to the property they had derived from their mother's will or their grandmother's—he was banished to the Balearic Isles.[2] Neither with his fate in the balance nor with his condemnation recorded did his spirit break; and it was asserted later that a life of luxury and abundance had made his seclusion not intolerable. When his son Nerullinus was attacked by the accusers, who relied on his father's unpopularity and on charges of extortion, the emperor interposed his veto, on the ground that vengeance was satisfied.

[2] Majorca and Minorca.

XLIV. Per idem tempus Octavius Sagitta plebei
tribunus, Pontiae mulieris nuptae amore vaecors,
ingentibus donis adulterium et mox, ut omitteret
maritum, emercatur, suum matrimonium promittens
ac nuptias eius pactus, Sed ubi mulier vacua fuit,
nectere moras, adversam patris voluntatem causari
repertaque spe ditioris coniugis promissa exuere.
Octavius contra modo conqueri, modo minitari,
famam perditam, pecuniam exhaustam obtestans,
denique salutem, quae sola reliqua esset, arbitrio
eius permittens. Ac postquam spernebatur, noctem
unam ad solacium poscit, qua delenitus modum in
posterum adhiberet. Statuitur nox, et Pontia
consciae ancillae custodiam cubiculi mandat. Ille
uno cum liberto ferrum veste occultum infert. Tum,
ut adsolet in amore et ira, iurgia preces, exprobratio
satisfactio et pars tenebrarum libidini seposita; ex
qua quasi incensus [1] nihil metuentem ferro trans-
verberat et accurrentem ancillam vulnere absterret
cubiculoque prorumpit. Postera die manifesta caedes, haud ambiguus percussor; quippe mansitasse
una convincebatur, sed libertus suum illud facinus
profiteri, se patroni iniurias ultum isse.[2] Commo-
veratque quosdam magnitudine exempli, donec
ancilla ex vulnere refecta verum aperuit. Postu-

---

[1] ex <qua> quasi incensus *Halm (after Bekker and Jac.
Gronovius)* : et quastim census.

[2] isse *Wölfflin :* esse *Med. Compare* IV. 73; VI. 36; XII.
45; XVI. 49.

XLIV. Nearly at the same time, the plebeian tribune Octavius Sagitta, madly in love with a wedded woman called Pontia, purchased by immense gifts first the act of adultery, then her desertion of her husband. He promised marriage on his own part, and had secured a similar pledge on hers. Once free, however, the woman began to procrastinate, to plead the adverse wishes of her father, and, when hopes of a wealthier match presented themselves, to shuffle off her promise. Octavius, on the other side, now remonstrated, now threatened, appealing to the ruin of his reputation, to the exhaustion of his fortune, and finally placing his life, all that he could yet call his own, at her absolute disposal. As he was flouted, he asked for the consolation of one night, to allay his fever and enable him to control himself in future. The night was fixed, and Pontia entrusted the watch over her bedroom to a maid in their confidence. Octavius entered with one freedman, a dagger concealed in his dress. Love and anger now ran their usual course in upbraidings and entreaties, reproach and reparation; and a part of the night was set aside to passion; inflamed by which, as it seemed, he struck her through with his weapon, while she suspected nothing; drove off with a wound the maid who came running up, and broke out of the room. Next day the murder was manifest, and the assassin not in doubt: for that he had been with her was demonstrated. None the less, the freedman asserted that the crime was his own; he had avenged, he said, the injuries of his patron: and so startling was this example of devotion that he had shaken the belief of some, when the maid's recovery from her wound enabled her to disclose the

latusque apud consules a patre interfectae, postquam
tribunatu abierat, sententia patrum et lege de
sicariis condemnatur.

XLV. Non minus insignis eo anno impudicitia mag-
norum rei publicae malorum initium fecit. Erat in
civitate Sabina Poppaea, T. Ollio patre genita, sed
nomen avi materni sumpserat, inlustri memoria
Poppaei Sabini, consulari et triumphali decore
praefulgentis; nam Ollium honoribus nondum
functum amicitia Seiani pervertit. Huic mulieri
cuncta alia fuere praeter honestum animum. Quippe
mater eius, aetatis suae feminas pulchritudine super-
gressa, gloriam pariter et formam dederat; opes
claritudini generis sufficiebant. Sermo comis nec
absurdum ingenium: modestiam praeferre et lascivia
uti; rarus in publicum egressus, idque velata parte
oris, ne satiaret aspectum, vel quia sic decebat.
Famae numquam pepercit, maritos et adulteros non
distinguens; neque adfectui suo aut alieno obnoxia,
unde utilitas ostenderetur, illuc libidinem transfere-
bat. Igitur agentem eam in matrimonio Rufri
Crispini equitis Romani, ex quo filium genuerat,
Otho pellexit iuventa ac luxu et quia flagrantissimus

---

[1] The interest aroused by the case—of which there is an
echo at *Hist.* IV. 44—is shown by the fact that Lucan wrote
specimen speeches for the prosecution and defence (Hosius,
p. 336).

truth. Octavius, after laying down his tribunate, was arraigned before the consuls by the father of the victim, and sentenced by verdict of the senate and under the law of assassination.[1]

XLV. A no less striking instance of immorality proved in this year the beginning of grave public calamities. There was in the capital a certain Poppaea Sabina, daughter of Titus Ollius, though she had taken the name of her maternal grandfather, Poppaeus Sabinus,[2] of distinguished memory, who, with the honours of his consulate and triumphal insignia, outshone her father: for Ollius had fallen a victim to his friendship with Sejanus before holding the major offices. She was a woman possessed of all advantages but a character. For her mother,[3] after eclipsing the beauties of her day, had endowed her alike with her fame and her looks: her wealth was adequate to the distinction of her birth. Her conversation was engaging, her wit not without point; she paraded modesty, and practised wantonness. In public she rarely appeared, and then with her face half-veiled, so as not quite to satiate the beholder,—or, possibly, because it so became her. She was never sparing of her reputation, and drew no distinctions between husbands and adulterers: vulnerable neither to her own nor to alien passion, where material advantage offered, thither she transferred her desires. Thus, whilst living in the wedded state with Rufrius Crispinus,[4] a Roman knight by whom she had had a son, she was seduced by Otho,[5] with his youth, his voluptuousness, and his

[2] IV. 46 n.; VI. sq.   [3] XI. 2 n.
[4] The former praetorian prefect (XI. 1 etc.).
[5] The future emperor: see chap. 12.

in amicitia Neronis habebatur: nec mora quin adulterio matrimonium iungeretur.

XLVI. Otho sive amore incautus laudare formam elegantiamque uxoris apud principem, sive ut accenderet ac, si eadem femina poterentur, id quoque vinculum potentiam ei adiceret. Saepe auditus est consurgens e convivio Caesaris, se quidem [1] ire ad illam, sibi concessam dictitans nobilitatem, pulchritudinem, vota omnium et gaudia felicium. His atque talibus inritamentis non longa cunctatio interponitur. Sed accepto aditu Poppaea primum per blandimenta et artis valescere, imparem cupidini se et forma Neronis captam simulans; mox acri iam principis amore ad superbiam vertens, si ultra unam alteramque noctem attineretur, nuptam esse se dictitans, nec posse matrimonium amittere, devinctam Othoni per genus vitae, quod nemo adaequaret: illum animo et cultu magnificum; ibi se summa fortuna digna visere: at Neronem, paelice ancilla et adsuetudine Actes devinctum, nihil e contubernio servili nisi abiectum et sordidum traxisse. Deicitur familiaritate sueta, post congressu et comitatu Otho, et ad postremum, ne in urbe aemulatus ageret, provinciae Lusitaniae praeficitur; ubi usque ad

---

[1] se quidem *Weissenborn :* seq.

---

[1] Two versions of the affair were in circulation. According to Suetonius, Plutarch, Dio, and, at *Hist.* I. 13, Tacitus himself, the intrigue with Poppaea begins earlier, and the nominal marriage with Otho is a screen for the liaison. The upshot is given in a contemporary epigram :—*Cur Otho mentito sit quaeritis exul honore ?* | *Vxoris moechus coeperat esse suae* (Suet. *Oth.* 3).

[2] From 58 to 68 A.D., when he set the example of joining Galba.

reputed position as the most favoured of Nero's friends: nor was it long before adultery was supplemented by matrimony.[1]

XLVI. Otho, possibly by an amorous indiscretion, began to praise the looks and the graces of his wife in presence of the emperor; or, possibly, his object was to inflame the sovereign's desire, and, by the additional bond of joint ownership in one woman, to reinforce his own influence. His voice was often heard, declaring, as he rose from the Caesar's table, that he at least must be returning to his wife—that to him had fallen that rank and beauty which the world desired and the fortunate enjoyed. In view of these and the like incitements, there was no tedious interval of delay; and Poppaea, admitted to the presence, proceeded to establish her ascendancy; at first, by cajolery and artifice, feigning that she was too weak to resist her passion and had been captured by Nero's beauty; then—as the emperor's love grew fervent—changing to haughtiness, and, if she was detained for more than a second night, insisting that she was a wife and could not renounce her married status, linked as she was to Otho by a mode of life which none could parallel:— " His was true majesty of mind and garb; in him she contemplated the princely manner; while Nero, enchained by his menial paramour and the embraces of an Acte, had derived from that servile cohabitation no tincture of anything but the mean and the shabby." Otho was debarred from his usual intimacy with the sovereign; then from his levées and his suite: finally, to prevent his acting as Nero's rival in Rome, he was appointed to the province of Lusitania; where, till the outbreak of the civil war,[2] he

civilia arma non ex priore infamia, sed integre sancteque egit, procax otii et potestatis temperantior.

XLVII. Hactenus Nero flagitiis et sceleribus velamenta quaesivit. Suspectabat maxime Cornelium Sullam, socors ingenium eius in contrarium trahens callidumque et simulatorem interpretando. Quem metum Graptus ex libertis Caesaris, usu et senecta Tiberio abusque domum principum edoctus, tali mendacio intendit. Pons Mulvius in eo tempore celebris nocturnis inlecebris erat; ventitabatque illuc Nero, quo solutius urbem extra lasciviret. Igitur regredienti per viam Flaminiam compositas insidias fatoque evitatas, quoniam diverso itinere Sallustianos in hortos remeaverit, auctoremque eius doli Sullam ementitur, quia forte redeuntibus ministris principis quidam per iuvenilem licentiam, quae tunc passim exercebatur, inanem metum fecerant. Neque servorum quisquam neque clientium Sullae adgnitus, maximeque despecta et nullius ausi capax natura eius a crimine abhorrebat: perinde tamen, quasi convictus esset, cedere patria et Massiliensium moenibus coerceri iubetur.

XLVIII. Isdem consulibus auditae Puteolanorum

---

[1] Faustus Cornelius Sulla Felix, married to Claudius' daughter Antonia (XII. 2): see XII. 52 and XIV. 57.

[2] Two miles out of Rome on the northern (Flaminian) road.

lived, not in the mode of his notorious past, but uprightly and without reproach, frivolous where his leisure was concerned, more self-controlled as regarded his official powers.

XLVII. Henceforward Nero sought no veil for his debaucheries and crimes. He had a peculiar suspicion of Cornelius Sulla,[1] whose natural slowness of wit he totally misunderstood, reading him as an astute character with a gift for simulation. His fears were deepened by the mendacity of Graptus, a Caesarian freedman, whom experience and age had familiarized with the household of the emperors from Tiberius downward. The Mulvian Bridge[2] at that period was famous for its nocturnal attractions, and Nero was in the habit of frequenting it, so as to allow his extravagances a freer rein outside the city. Graptus accordingly invented the fiction that an ambuscade had been arranged for the prince in the event of his returning by the Flaminian Way; that it had been providentially avoided, as he had come back by the other route to the Gardens of Sallust; and that the author of the plot was Sulla— the foundation of the story being that, as chance would have it, a few rioters, in one of the juvenile escapades then so generally practised, had thrown the emperor's servants, on the road home, into a groundless panic. Neither a slave nor a client of Sulla's had been recognised; and his contemptible nature, incapable of daring in any form, was utterly incompatible with the charge: yet, precisely as though he had been proved guilty, he received orders to leave his country and confine himself within the walls of Massilia.

XLVIII. Under the same consuls, audience was

legationes, quas diversas ordo plebs ad senatum miserant, illi vim multitudinis, hi magistratuum et primi cuiusque avaritiam increpantes. Eaque seditio ad saxa et minas ignium progressa ne caed*em* [1] et arma prolceret, C. Cassius adhibendo remedio delectus. Quia severitatem eius non tolerabant, precante ipso ad Scribonios fratres eo cura transfertur, data cohorte praetoria, cuius terrore et paucorum supplicio rediit oppidanis concordia.

XLIX. Non referrem vulgarissimum [2] senatus consultum, quo civitati Syracusanorum egredi numerum edendis gladiatoribus finitum permittebatur, nisi Paetus Thrasea contra dixisset praebuissetque materiem obtrectatoribus arguendae sententiae. Cur enim, si rem publicam egere libertate senatoria crederet, tam levia consectaretur? Quin de bello aut pace, de vectigalibus et legibus, quibusque aliis *res* Romana contineretur, suaderet dissuaderetve? Licere patribus, quotiens ius dicendae sententiae accepissent, quae vellent expromere relationemque in ea postulare. An solum emendatione dignum, ne Syracusis spectacula largius ederentur: cetera per omnes imperii partes perinde egregia, quam si

---

[1] ne caedem *Nipperdey :* necem.
[2] vulgarissimum *Haase :* vulgatissimum.

---

[1] Pozzuoli.
[2] The town-senate; in Italy and the West, usually consisting of 100 members, necessarily citizens of the place and substantial property-owners.
[3] Scribonius Rufus and Scribonius Proculus. Their death in 67 A.D. was one of the later scandals of Nero's reign (D. Cass. LXIII. 17; cf. *Hist.* IV. 41).
[4] The principal Stoic martyr under Nero, as was his son-in-law, Helvidius Priscus, under Vespasian. A native of Padua, he married a daughter of the famous pair Caecina Paetus and

given to deputations from Puteoli,[1] despatched
separately to the senate by the decurions[2] and the
populace, the former inveighing against the violence
of the mob, the latter against the rapacity of the
magistrates and of the leading citizens in general.
Lest the quarrels, which had reached the point of
stone-throwing and threats of arson, should end by
provoking bloodshed under arms, Gaius Cassius was
chosen to apply the remedy. As the disputants
refused to tolerate his severity, the commission at
his own request was transferred to the brothers
Scribonius;[3] and these were given a praetorian cohort,
the terrors of which, together with a few executions,
restored the town to concord.

XLIX. I should not record a commonplace decree
of the senate which authorized the town of Syracuse
to exceed the numbers prescribed for gladiatorial
exhibitions, had not Thrasea Paetus,[4] by opposing it,
presented his detractors with an opportunity for
censuring his vote. " Why," it was demanded,
" if he believed senatorial freedom a necessity to the
state, did he fasten on such frivolities? Why not
reserve his suasion or dissuasion for the themes of
war or peace, of finance and law, and for the other
matters on which hinged the welfare of Rome?
Every member, each time that he received the privi-
lege of recording his opinion, was free to express
what views he desired and to demand a debate.—
Or was it the one desirable reform, that shows at
Syracuse should not be too liberal? and were all
things else in all departments of the empire as

Arria, and for ten years was the philosopher and friend of his
wife's kinsman Persius. The chief facts of his later life will be
noticed in the following part of the Annals.

non Nero, sed Thrasea regimen eorum teneret?
Quod si summa dissimulatione transmitterentur,
quanto magis inanibus abstinendum? Thrasea
contra, rationem poscentibus amicis, non praesen-
tium ignarum respondebat eius modi consulta corri-
gere, sed patrum honori dare, ut manifestum fieret
magnərum rerum curam non dissimulaturos, qui
animum etiam levissimis adverterent.

L. Eodem anno crebris populi flagitationibus,
inmodestiam publicanorum arguentis, dubitavit Nero,
an cuncta vectigalia omitti iuberet idque pulcherrimum donum generi mortalium daret. Sed impetum
eius, multum prius laudata magnitudine animi,
attinuere senatores,[1] dissolutionem imperii docendo,
si fructus, quibus res publica sustineretur, deminu-
erentur: quippe sublatis portoriis sequens, ut tribu-
torum abolitio expostularetur. Plerasque vectigalium societates a consulibus et tribunis plebei
constitutas acri etiam tum populi Romani libertate;
reliqua mox ita provisa, ut ratio quaestuum et
necessitas erogationum inter se congrueret. Tem-
perandas plane publicanorum cupidines, ne per tot

---

[1] seniores *Lipsius :* senatores.

---

[1] Companies of Roman knights (*vectigalium societates*
below; *societates equitum Romanorum*, IV. 6), farming the indirect taxes, notably the customs and harbour-dues (*portoria*).
The direct taxes (*tributa*) were collected by government officials.

[2] Since Italy, after 167 B.C., was exempt from direct taxation, one result of the gift to the human race would be to throw
upon the provinces the financial burdens of the whole empire.
On the other hand, there would be free trade within the Roman
world. For the *portoria—ad valorem* duties, varying in amount,
upon all exports and imports—were levied not only on the
frontiers of the empire but on those of each province or finan-

entirely admirable as if not Nero's, but Thrasea's, hand were at the helm? But if the highest questions were to be slurred over by ignoring their existence, how much more was it a duty not to touch irrelevances!" Thrasea, on the other side, as his friends pressed for his explanation, answered that it was not ignorance of existing conditions which made him amend decrees of this character, but he was paying members the compliment of making it clear that they would not dissemble their interest in great affairs when they could give attention even to the slightest.

L. In the same year, as a consequence of repeated demands from the public, which complained of the exactions of the revenue-farmers,[1] Nero hesitated whether he ought not to decree the abolition of all indirect taxation and present the reform as the noblest of gifts to the human race.[2] His impulse, however, after much preliminary praise of his magnanimity, was checked by his older advisers, who pointed out that the dissolution of the empire was certain if the revenues on which the state subsisted were to be curtailed :— " For, the moment the duties on imports were removed, the logical sequel would be a demand for the abrogation of the direct taxes. To a large extent, the collecting companies had been set up by consuls and plebeian tribunes while the liberty of the Roman nation was still in all its vigour : later modifications had only been introduced in order that the amount of income and the necessary expenditure should tally. At the same time, a check ought certainly to be placed on the cupidity of the collectors ; otherwise a system which had been endured for

cial group of provinces, while there were in addition a multitude of local tolls to hamper commerce.

annos sine querella tolerata novis acerbitatibus ad invidiam verterent.

LI. Ergo edixit princeps, ut leges cuiusque publici, occultae ad id tempus, proscriberentur; omissas petitiones non ultra annum resumerent; Romae praetor, per provincias qui pro praetore aut consule essent iura adversus publicanos extra ordinem redderent; militibus immunitas servaretur, nisi in iis, quae veno exercerent; aliaque admodum aequa, quae brevi servata, dein frustra habita sunt. Manet tamen abolitio quadragensimae quinquagensimaeque et quae alia exactionibus inlicitis nomina publicani invenerant. Temperata apud transmarinas provincias frumenti subvectio, et ne censibus negotiatorum naves adscriberentur tributumque pro illis penderent, constitutum.

LII. Reos ex provincia Africa, qui proconsulare imperium illic habuerant, Sulpicium Camerinum et Pompeium Silvanum absolvit Caesar, Camerinum adversus privatos et paucos, saevitiae magis quam captarum pecuniarum crimina obicientis. Silvanum magna vis accusatorum circumsteterat poscebatque tempus evocandorum testium: reus ilico defendi postulabat. Valuitque pecuniosa orbitate et senecta, quam ultra vitam eorum produxit, quorum ambitu evaserat.

---

[1] Percentages illegally charged by the companies—on what, is not known

years without a complaint might be brought into ill
odour by new-fashioned harshnesses."

LI. The emperor, therefore, issued an edict that
the regulations with regard to each tax, hitherto
kept secret, should be posted for public inspection.
Claims once allowed to lapse were not to be revived
after the expiry of a year; at Rome, the praetor—in
the provinces, the propraetors or proconsuls—were
to waive the usual order of trial in favour of actions
against collectors; the soldiers were to retain their
immunities except in the case of goods which they
offered for sale: and there were other extremely
fair rulings, which were observed for a time and then
eluded. The annulment, however, of the "fortieth,"
"fiftieth,"[1] and other irregular exactions, for which
the publicans had invented titles, is still in force.
In the provinces over sea, the transport of grain
was made less expensive, and it was laid down that
cargo-boats were not to be included in the assessment
of a merchant's property nor treated as taxable.

LII. Two defendants from the province of Africa,
in which they had held proconsular power, were
acquitted by the Caesar: Sulpicius Camerinus and
Pompeius Silvanus. The opponents of Camerinus
were private persons and not numerous, while the
offences alleged were acts of cruelty rather than of
embezzlement: around Silvanus had gathered a
swarm of accusers, who were demanding time for
the production of their witnesses. The defendant
insisted on presenting his case at once, and carried
his point, thanks to his wealth, his childlessness, and
his advanced age, which he prolonged, however,
beyond the lifetime of the fortune-hunters by whose
intrigues he had escaped.

LIII. Quietae ad id tempus res in Germania fuerant, ingenio ducum, qui pervulgatis triumphi insignibus maius ex eo decus sperabant, si pacem continuavissent. Paulinus Pompeius et L. Vetus ea tempestate exercitui praeerant. Ne tamen segnem militem attinerent, ille inchoatum ante tres et sexaginta annos a Druso aggerem coercendo Rheno absolvit, Vetus Mosellam atque *Ararim* facta inter utrumque fossa conectere parabat, ut copiae per mare, dein Rhodano et Arare subvectae per eam fossam, mox fluvio Mosella in Rhenum, exim Oceanum decurrerent, sublatisque itineris difficultatibus navigabilia inter se Occidentis Septentrionisque litora fierent. Invidit operi Aelius Gracilis Belgicae legatus, deterrendo Veterem, ne legiones alienae provinciae inferret studiaque Galliarum adfectaret, formidolosum id imperatori dictitans, quo plerumque prohibentur conatus honesti.

LIV. Ceterum continuo exercituum otio fama incessit ereptum ius legatis ducendi in hostem. Eoque Frisii iuventutem saltibus aut paludibus, inbellem aetatem per lacus admovere ripae agrosque vacuos et militum usui sepositos insedere, auctore Verrito et Malorige, qui nationem eam regebant, in

---

[1] The date is 55 A.D., and the narrative is spread over three years. Paulinus—probably Seneca's father-in-law—was in command of the Lower Army; L. Antistius Vetus (chap. 11 n.) of the Upper.

[2] On the Gallic side, apparently at the vertex of the delta. It was destroyed later by Civilis (*Hist.* V. 19).

[3] The Saône.

[4] The largest Gallic province; east of the Seine and Saône.

[5] See XI. 19.

[6] Afterwards—between the eighth and thirteenth centuries—merged in the Zuyder Zee.

LIII. Up to this period, quiet had prevailed in Germany, thanks to the temper of our commanders; who, now that triumphal emblems were staled, expected greater distinction from the maintenance of peace. The heads of the army at the time were Pompeius Paulinus and Lucius Vetus.[1] Not to keep the troops inactive, however, the former finished the embankment for checking the inundations of the Rhine,[2] begun sixty-three years earlier by Drusus; while Vetus prepared to connect the Moselle and the Arar[3] by running a canal between the two; so that goods shipped by sea and then up the Rhone and Arar could make their way by the canal, and subsequently by the Moselle, into the Rhine, and in due course into the ocean: a method which would remove the natural difficulties of the route and create a navigable highway between the shores of the West and North. The scheme was nullified by the jealousy of Aelius Gracilis, the governor of Belgica,[4] who discouraged Vetus from introducing his legions into a province outside his competence and so courting popularity in Gaul, " a proceeding," he said, " which would awaken the misgivings of the emperor "—the usual veto upon honourable enterprise.

LIV. However, through the continuous inaction of the armies a rumour took rise that the legates had been divested of authority to lead them against an enemy. The Frisians[5] accordingly moved their population to the Rhine bank; the able-bodied men by way of the forests and swamps, those not of military age by the Lakes.[6] Here they settled in the clearings reserved for the use of the troops, the instigators being Verritus and Malorix, who exercised

quantum Germani regnantur. Iamque fixerant domos, semina arvis intulerant utque patrium solum exercebant, cum Dubius Avitus accepta a Paulino provincia, minitando vim Romanam, nisi abscederent Frisii veteres in locos aut novam sedem a Caesare impetrarent, perpulit Verritum et Malorigem preces suscipere. Profectique Romam dum aliis curis intentum Neronem opperiuntur, inter ea, quae barbaris ostentantur, intravere Pompei theatrum, quo magnitudinem populi viserent. Illic per otium (neque enim ludicris ignari oblectabantur) dum consessum caveae, discrimina ordinum, quis eques, ubi senatus percontantur, advertere quosdam cultu externo in sedibus senatorum; et quinam forent rogitantes, postquam audiverant earum gentium legatis id honoris datum, quae virtute et amicitia Romana praecellerent, nullos mortalium armis aut fide ante Germanos esse exclamant degrediunturque et inter patres considunt. Quod comiter a visentibus exceptum, quasi impetus antiqui et bona aemulatio. Nero civitate Romana ambos donavit, Frisios decedere agris iussit. Atque illis aspernantibus auxiliaris eques repente immissus necessitatem attulit, captis caesisve qui pervicacius restiterant.

---

[1] In the orchestra.

over the tribe such kingship as exists in Germany.
They had already fixed their abodes and sown the
fields, and were tilling the soil as if they had been
born on it, when Dubius Avitus,—who had taken
over the province from Paulinus,—by threatening
them with the Roman arms unless they withdrew to
their old district or obtained the grant of a new site
from the emperor, forced Verritus and Malorix to
undertake the task of presenting the petition. They
left for Rome, where, in the interval of waiting for
Nero, who had other cares to occupy him, they
visited the usual places shown to barbarians, and
among them the theatre of Pompey, where they
were to contemplate the size of the population.
There, to kill time (they had not sufficient knowledge
to be amused by the play), they were putting questions as to the crowd seated in the auditorium—the
distinctions between the orders—which were the
knights?—where was the senate?—when they
noticed a few men in foreign dress on the senatorial
seats.[1] They inquired who they were, and, on
hearing that this was a compliment paid to the
envoys of nations distinguished for their courage and
for friendship to Rome, exclaimed that no people in
the world ranked before Germans in arms or loyalty,
went down, and took their seats among the Fathers.
The action was taken in good part by the onlookers,
as a trait of primitive impetuosity and generous
rivalry. Nero presented both with the Roman
citizenship, and instructed the Frisians to leave the
district. As they ignored the order, compulsion was
applied by the unexpected despatch of a body of
auxiliary horse, which captured or killed the more
obstinate of those who resisted.

LV. Eosdem agros Ampsivarii occupavere, validior gens non modo sua copia, sed adiacentium populorum miseratione, quia pulsi a Chaucis et sedis inopes tutum exilium orabant. Aderatque iis clarus per illas gentis et nobis quoque fidus nomine Boiocalus, vinctum se rebellione Cherusca iussu Arminii referens, mox Tiberio, Germanico ducibus stipendia meruisse, et quinquaginta annorum obsequio id quoque adiungere, quod gentem suam dicioni nostrae subiceret. Quo *tan*tam partem campi iacere, in quam pecora et armenta militum aliquando transmitterentur? Servarent sane receptus gregibus inter hominum famem, modo ne vastitatem et solitudinem mallent quam amicos populos. Chamavorum quondam ea arva, mox Tubantum et post Usiporum fuisse. Sicuti caelum deis, ita terras generi mortalium datas; quaeque vacuae, eas publicas esse. Solem inde suspiciens [1] et cetera sidera vocans quasi coram interrogabat, vellentne contueri inane solum: potius mare superfunderent adversus terrarum ereptores.

LVI. Et commotus his Avitus: patienda meliorum imperia; id dis, quos inplorarent, placitum, ut

---

[1] suspiciens *Heinsius :* despiciens *Med.,* aspiciens *Rhenanus.*

[1] For the approximate position of this and the other tribes mentioned, see the map appended to vol. ii.

[2] The revolt under Arminius, culminating in the destruction of Quintilius Varus with three legions in the forests of Westphalia (9 A.D.).

LV. The same ground was then seized by the Ampsivarii,[1] a more powerful clan, not only in numbers, but in consequence of the pity felt for them by the adjacent tribes, as they had been expelled by the Chauci, and were now a homeless people imploring an unmolested exile. They had also the advocacy of Boiocalus, as he was called, a celebrated personage among those clans, and at the same time loyal to ourselves:—" In the Cheruscan rebellion,"[2] he reminded us, " he had been thrown into chains by order of Arminius; next, he had served under the leadership of Tiberius and Germanicus; and now he was crowning an obedience of fifty years by subjecting his people to our rule. Why should such an extent of clear ground lie waste, merely that on some distant day the flocks and herds of the soldiers could be brought over to it? By all means let them keep reservations for cattle in the midst of starving men, but not to the extent of choosing a desert and a solitude for neighbours in preference to friendly nations! Once on a time those fields had been held by the Chamavi; then by the Tubantes, and later by the Usipi. As heaven had been given to the gods, so had earth to the race of mortal men, and what lacked a tenant was common property." Then, raising his eyes to the sun and invoking the rest of the heavenly host, he demanded, as if face to face with them, " if they wished to look down on an empty earth. Sooner let them flood it with the sea and arrest these ravishers of the land! "

LVI. Avitus, who had been moved by the appeal, replied that all men had to bow to the commands of their betters: it had been decreed by those gods

arbitrĭum penes Romanos maneret, quid darent quid
adimerent, neque alios iudices quam se ipsos pater-
entur. Haec in publicum Ampsivariis respondit,
ipsi Boiocalo ob memoriam amicitiae daturum agros.
Quod ille ut proditionis pretium aspernatus addidit:—
" Deesse nobis terra *ubi* vivam*us*,[1] in qua moriamur,
non potest:" atque ita infensis utrimque animis
discessum. Illi Bructeros, Tencteros, ulteriores etiam
nationes socias bello vocabant: Avitus scripto ad
Curtilium Manciam superioris exercitus legatum, ut
Rhenum transgressus arma a tergo ostenderet, ipse
legiones in agrum Tenc*t*erum induxit, excidium
minitans, ni causam suam dissociarent. Igitur
absistentibus his pari metu exterriti Bructeri; et
ceteris quoque aliena pericula deserentibus [2] sola
Ampsivariorum gens retro ad Usipos et Tubantes
concessit. Quorum terris exacti cum Chattos, dein
Cheruscos petissent, errore longo hospites, egeni,
hostes in alieno quod iuventutis erat caeduntur,
inbellis aetas in praedam divisa est.

LVII. Eadem aestate inter Hermunduros Chattos-
que certatum magno proelio, dum flumen gignendo
sale fecundum et conterminum vi trahunt, super libidinem cuncta armis agendi religione insita, eos max-

[1] terra <ubi> vivamus *Sillig :* terram vivam *Med.,* terra
in vitam *Jac. Gronovius.*

[2] deserentibus *Rhenanus :* defendentibus.

---

[1] Shown by a passage of Phlegon (Περὶ θαυμ. 27) to have
succeeded Antistius Vetus in 56 A.D.

[2] As the Hermunduri were in Thuringia and Franconia, the
Chatti in the Hesse-Nassau district, the river is plausibly
identified with the Werra, still the boundary between Thuringia and Hesse and close to the salt-springs of Salzungen.
Another candidate is the Franconian Saale. Naturally, neither
stream is in itself a salt-spring.

whom they implored that with the Roman people
should rest the decision what to give and what to
take away, and that they should brook no other
judges than themselves." This was his answer to
the Ampsivarii as a people : to Boiocalus he said that
in memory of their friendship he would make him a
grant of land. The offer was indignantly rejected
by the German as the wage of treason :—" We may
lack," he added, " a land to live in, but not one to die
in." They parted, therefore, with bitterness on both
sides. The Ampsivarii invited the Bructeri, the
Tencteri, and still more remote tribes, to join them
in war : Avitus wrote to Curtilius Mancia,[1] the
commander of the upper army, asking him to cross
the Rhine and display his arms in the rear ; he himself led his legions into the territory of the Tencteri,
threatening them with annihilation unless they dis-
sociated their cause from that of the confederates.
They seceded accordingly ; the same threat deterred
the Bructeri ; and as the rest also forsook a dangerous
and alien cause, the Ampsivarian clan, thus left
isolated, fell back to the Usipi and Tubantes. Expelled from their ground, they sought refuge with
the Chatti, then with the Cherusci ; and, after a long
pilgrimage in which they were treated in turn as
guests, as beggars, and as enemies, their younger
men found death on a foreign soil, and those below
fighting age were portioned out as booty.

LVII. In the same summer, a great battle was
waged between the Hermunduri and Chatti, both
attempting to appropriate by force a river which
was at once a rich source for salt and the frontier line
between the tribes.[2] Apart from their passion for
deciding all questions by the sword, they held an

ime locos propinquare caelo precesque mortalium a
deis nusquam propius audiri. Inde indulgentia numinum illo in amne illisque silvis salem provenire, non ut
alias apud gentes eluvie maris arescente unda, sed
super ardentem arborum struem fusa ex contrariis
inter se elementis, igne atque aquis, concretum.
Sed bellum Hermunduris prosperum, Chattis exitio-
sius fuit, quia victores diversam aciem Marti ac
Mercurio sacravere, quo voto equi viri, cuncta [1]
occidioni dantur. Et minae quidem hostiles in ipsos
vertebant. Sed civitas Ubiorum socia nobis malo
inproviso adflicta est. Nam ignes terra editi villas
arva vicos passim corripiebant ferebanturque in ipsa
conditae nuper coloniae moenia. Neque extingui
poterant, non si imbres caderent, non fluvialibus
aquis aut quo alio humore, donec inopia remedii et
ira cladis agrestes quidam eminus saxa iacere, dein
resistentibus flammis propius suggressi ictu fustium
aliisque verberibus ut feras absterrebant: postremo
tegmina corpori derepta iniciunt, quanto magis
profana et usu polluta, tanto magis oppressura
ignis.

[1] cuncta *Becher :* cuncta victa *Med.*, cuncta viva *Danesius.*

---

[1] In reality, of course, by evaporation, if the story—
supported by Pliny—is to be taken seriously.

[2] Tiu and Woden.—The vow of extirpation, a natural consequence of primitive belief, has many analogues, the most
familiar being the Hebraic *ḥérem* on persons and objects hostile
to the theocracy, *e.g.* the anathema on Jericho (*Josh.* vi. 17
sqq.) and on Amalek (1 *Sam.* xv. 3 sqq.). The Gallic practice
is noted by Caesar (*B.G.* VI. 17).

[3] Cologne.

[4] Volcanic action is ruled out by the character of the

ingrained religious belief that this district was peculi-
arly close to heaven and that nowhere did the gods
give more immediate audience to human prayer.
Hence, by the divine favour, salt in that river and in
these forests was not produced, as in other countries,
by allowing water to evaporate in a pool left by the
sea, but by pouring it on a blazing pile of trees,
crystallization taking place through the union of two
opposed elements, water and fire.[1] The struggle,
which went in favour of the Hermunduri, was the
more diastrous to the Chatti in that both sides consecrated, in the event of victory, the adverse host to
Mars and Mercury;[2] a vow implying the extermina-
tion of horses, men, and all objects whatsoever.
The threats of the enemy thus recoiled upon himself.
But the federate Ubian community[3] was visited by
an unlooked-for catastrophe. Fires, breaking from
the ground,[4] fastened on farm-houses, crops, and
villages, in all quarters, and soon were sweeping
towards the very walls of the recently founded[5]
colony. Nothing could extinguish them—neither
falling rain nor running water nor moisture in any
form—until a few rustics, powerless to devise a
remedy and enraged by the havoc, started to throw
stones from a distance. Then, as the flames became
stationary, they went close up and attempted to
scare them away like wild animals by striking them
with clubs and thrashing them with other implements:
finally, they stripped off their clothes and piled them
on the fire, which they were the more likely
to smother as they had been worn and soiled by
common use.

country, and the passage seems to describe with embellish-
ments a heath-fire on a large scale.   [5] In 50 A.D. (XII. 27).

THE ANNALS OF TACITUS

LVIII. Eodem anno Ruminalem arborem in comitio, quae octingentos [1] et triginta [2] ante annos Remi Romulique infantiam texerat, mortuis ramalibus et arescente trunco deminutam prodigii loco habitum est, donec in novos fetus revivesceret.[3]

[1] octingentos] septingentos *Med.*
[2] triginta *Lipsius :* quadraginta.
[3] revivesceret] revivisceret *Nipperdey,* reviresceret *Pichena.*

LVIII. In the same year, the tree in the Comitium, known as the Ruminalis,[1] which eight hundred and thirty years earlier had sheltered the infancy of Remus and Romulus, through the death of its boughs and the withering of its stem, reached a stage of decrepitude which was regarded as a portent, until it renewed its verdure in fresh shoots.

[1] The fig-tree under which the wolf suckled the twins. It migrated spontaneously—*augurante Atto Navio*—from the Lupercal on the Palatine to the Comitium, opposite the senate-house (Plin. *H.N.* XV. 18, 77).

BOOK XIV

LIBER XIV

I. Gaio Vipstano C.[1] Fonteio consulibus diu meditatum scelus non ultra Nero distulit, vestutate imperii coalita audacia et flagrantior in dies amore Poppaeae, quae sibi matrimonium et discidium Octaviae incolumi Agrippina haud sperans crebris criminationibus, aliquando per facetias incusaret principem et pupillum vocaret, qui iussis alienis obnoxius non modo imperii, sed libertatis etiam indigeret. Cur enim differri nuptias suas? Formam scilicet displicere et triumphalis avos, an fecunditatem et verum animum? Timeri ne uxor saltem iniurias patrum, iram populi adversus superbiam avaritiamque matris aperiat. Quod si nurum Agrippina non nisi filio infestam ferre posset, redderetur ipsa Othonis coniugio: ituram quoquo terrarum, ubi audiret potius contumelias imperatoris quam viseret periculis eius inmixta. Haec atque talia lacrimis et arte adulterae penetrantia nemo prohibebat, cupientibus cunctis infringi potentiam matris et credente nullo usque ad caedem eius duratura filii odia.

---

[1] <C.> *Ritter.*

---

[1] Poppaeus Sabinus (XIII. 45).
[2] She had a son by Rufrius Crispinus (XIII. 45).
[3] Lusitania (XIII. 46).

BOOK XIV

I. In the consular year of Gaius Vipstanius and A.V.C. 812 ·· A.D. 59 Gaius Fonteius, Nero postponed no further the long-contemplated crime: for a protracted term of empire had consolidated his boldness, and day by day he burned more hotly with love for Poppaea; who, hopeless of wedlock for herself and divorce for Octavia so long as Agrippina lived, plied the sovereign with frequent reproaches and occasional raillery, styling him " the ward, dependent on alien orders, who was neither the empire's master nor his own. For why was her wedding deferred? Her face, presumably, and her grandsires with their triumphs,[1] did not give satisfaction—or was the trouble her fecundity[2] and truth of heart? No, it was feared that, as a wife at all events, she might disclose the wrongs of the Fathers, the anger of the nation against the pride and greed of his mother! But, if Agrippina could tolerate no daughter-in-law but one inimical to her son, then let her be restored to her married life with Otho: she would go to any corner of earth[3] where she could hear the emperor's ignominy rather than view it and be entangled in his perils." To these and similar attacks, pressed home by tears and adulterous art, no opposition was offered: all men yearned for the breaking of the mother's power; none credited that the hatred of the son would go the full way to murder.

THE ANNALS OF TACITUS

II. Tradit Cluvius ardore retinendae Agrippinam potentiae eo usque provectam, ut medio diei, cum id temporis Nero per vinum et epulas incalesceret, offerret se saepius temulento comptam et incesto paratam. Iamque lasciva oscula et praenuntias flagitii blanditias adnotantibus proximis, Senecam contra muliebres inlecebras subsidium a femina petivisse, inmissamque Acten libertam, quae simul suo periculo et infamia Neronis anxia deferret pervulgatum esse incestum gloriante matre, nec toleraturos milites profani principis imperium. Fabius Rusticus non Agrippinae, sed Neroni cupitum id memorat eiusdemque libertae astu disiectum. Sed quae Cluvius, eadem ceteri quoque auctores prodidere, et fama huc inclinat, seu concepit animo tantum inmanitatis Agrippina, seu credibilior novae libidinis meditatio in ea visa est, quae puellaribus annis stuprum cum Lepido [1] spe dominationis admiserat, pari cupidine usque ad libita Pallantis provoluta et exercita ad omne flagitium patrui nuptiis.

III. Igitur Nero vitare secretos eius congressus, abscedentem in hortos aut Tusculanum vel Antiatem in agrum laudare, quod otium capesseret. Postremo, ubicumque haberetur, praegravem ratus interficere

[1] <M.> Lepido *Nipperdey.*

---

[1] For Cluvius and Fabius Rusticus, see the notes on XIII. 20.

[2] M. Aemilius Lepidus, son of L. Aemilius Paulus and Augustus' granddaughter Julia; a minion of Agrippina's brother Caligula, and married to their sister Drusilla; executed in 39 A.D. as an accomplice in the conspiracy of Lentulus Gaetulicus.

II. It is stated by Cluvius[1] that Agrippina's ardour to keep her influence was carried so far that at midday, an hour at which Nero was beginning to experience the warmth of wine and good cheer, she presented herself on several occasions to her half-tipsy son, coquettishly dressed and prepared for incest. Already lascivious kisses, and endearments that were the harbingers of guilt, had been observed by their intimates, when Seneca sought in a woman the antidote to female blandishments, and brought in the freedwoman Acte, who, alarmed as she was both at her own danger and at Nero's infamy, was to report that the incest was common knowledge, since his mother boasted of it, and that the troops would not submit to the supremacy of a sacrilegious emperor. According to Fabius Rusticus, not Agrippina, but Nero, desired the union, the scheme being wrecked by the astuteness of the same freedwoman. The other authorities, however, give the same version as Cluvius, and to their side tradition leans ; whether the enormity was actually conceived in the brain of Agrippina, or whether the contemplation of such a refinement in lust was merely taken as comparatively credible in a woman who, for the prospect of power, had in her girlish years yielded to the embraces of Marcus Lepidus ;[2] who, for a similar ambition had prostituted herself to the desires of Pallas ; and who had been inured to every turpitude by her marriage with her uncle.

III. Nero, therefore, began to avoid private meetings with her ; when she left for her gardens or the estates at Tusculum and Antium, he commended her intention of resting ; finally, convinced that, wherever she might be kept, she was still an incubus,

constituit, hactenus consultans, veneno an ferro vel
qua alia vi. Placuitque primo venenum. Sed inter
epulas principis si daretur, referri ad casum non
poterat tali iam Britannici exitio; et ministros
temptare arduum videbatur mulieris usu scelerum
adversus insidias intentae; atque ipsa praesumendo
remedia munierat corpus. Ferrum et caedes quonam
modo occultaretur, nemo reperiebat; et ne quis illi
tanto facinori delectus iussa sperneret metuebant.
Obtulit ingenium Anicetus libertus, classi apud
Misenum praefectus et pueritiae Neronis educator ac
mutuis odiis Agrippinae invisus. Ergo navem posse
componi docet, cuius pars ipso in mari per artem
soluta effunderet ignaram: nihil tam capax fortui-
torum quam mare; et si naufragio intercepta sit,
quem adeo iniquum, ut sceleri adsignet, quod venti
et fluctus deliquerint? additurum principem de-
functae templum et aras et cetera ostentandae
pietati.

IV. Placuit sollertia, tempore etiam iuta quando
Quinquatruum festos dies apud Baias frequentabat.
Illuc matrem elicit, ferendas parentium iracundias et
placandum animum dictitans. quo rumorem recon-
ciliationis efficeret acciperetque Agrippina, facili

[1] On March 19–23.
[2] The fashionable Campanian watering-place on the western
side of the Golfo di Pozzuoli (*sinus Baianus*). Its long term
of popularity was ended by malaria, with help from the
Saracens in the ninth century and from Louis XII. in the beginning of the sixteenth.

110

he decided to kill her, debating only whether by
poison, the dagger, or some other form of violence.
The first choice fell on poison. But, if it was to be
given at the imperial table, then the death could not
be referred to chance, since Britannicus had already
met a similar fate. At the same time, it seemed
an arduous task to tamper with the domestics of a
woman whose experience of crime had made her
vigilant for foul play; and, besides, she had herself
fortified her system by taking antidotes in advance.
Cold steel and bloodshed no one could devise a method
of concealing: moreover, there was the risk that the
agent chosen for such an atrocity might spurn his
orders. Mother wit came to the rescue in the person
of Anicetus the freedman, preceptor of Nero's boyish
years, and detested by Agrippina with a vigour which
was reciprocated. Accordingly, he pointed out that
it was possible to construct a ship, part of which
could be artificially detached, well out at sea, and
throw the unsuspecting passenger overboard:—
" Nowhere had accident such scope as on salt water;
and, if the lady should be cut off by shipwreck, who
so captious as to read murder into the delinquency
of wind and wave? The sovereign, naturally, would
assign the deceased a temple and the other displays
of filial piety."

IV. This ingenuity commended itself: the date,
too, was in its favour, as Nero was in the habit of celebrating the festival of Minerva [1] at Baiae. [2] Thither
he proceeded to lure his mother, observing from time
to time that outbreaks of parental anger had to be
tolerated, and that he must show a forgiving spirit;
his aim being to create a rumour of reconciliation,
which Agrippina, with the easy faith of her sex in

feminarum credulitate ad gaudia. Venientem dehinc obvius in litora (nam Antio adventabat) excepit manu et complexu ducitque Baulos. Id villae nomen est, quae promunturium Misenum inter et Baianum lacum flexo mari adluitur. Stabat inter alias navis ornatior, tamquam id quoque honori matris daretur: quippe sueverat triremi et classiariorum remigio vehi. Ac tum invitata ad epulas erat, ut occultando facinori nox adhiberetur. Satis constitit extitisse proditorem, et Agrippinam auditis insidiis, an crederet ambiguam, gestamine sellae Baias pervectam. Ibi blandimentum sublevavit metum: comiter excepta superque ipsum collocata. Iam pluribus sermonibus, modo familiaritate iuvenili Nero et rursus adductus, quasi seria consociaret, tracto in longum convictu, prosequitur abeuntem, artius oculis et pectori haerens, sive explenda simulatione, seu periturae matris supremus aspectus quamvis ferum animum retinebat.

V. Noctem sideribus inlustrem et placido mari quietam quasi convincendum ad scelus di praebuere. Nec multum erat progressa navis, duobus e numero familiarium Agrippinam comitantibus, ex quis Crepereius Gallus haud procul gubernaculis adstabat, Acerronia super pedes cubitantis reclinis paenitentiam filii et reciperatam matris gratiam per

---

[1] The villa—once owned by the orator Hortensius, then by the emperors, and some three centuries later by Symmachus—lay a little south of Baiae.

[2] Apparently the furthest recess of the bay, between Baiae on the west and Puteoli on the east.

[3] Πρὸς τὸ στέρνον προσαγαγὼν καὶ φιλήσας καὶ τὰ ὄμματα καὶ τὰς χεῖρας, D. Cass. LXI. 13.

[4] On the return journey to Bauli.

the agreeable, would probably accept.—In due course, she came. He went down to the beach to meet her (she was arriving from Antium), took her hand, embraced her, and escorted her to Bauli,[1] the name of a villa washed by the waters of a cove between the promontory of Misenum and the lake of Baiae.[2] Here, among others, stood a more handsomely appointed vessel; apparently one attention the more to his mother, as she had been accustomed to use a trireme with a crew of marines. Also, she had been invited to dinner for the occasion, so that night should be available for the concealment of the crime. It is well established that someone had played the informer, and that Agrippina, warned of the plot, hesitated whether to believe or not, but made the journey to Baiae in a litter. There her fears were relieved by the blandishments of a cordial welcome and a seat above the prince himself. At last, conversing freely,—one moment boyishly familiar, the next grave-browed as though making some serious communication,—Nero, after the banquet had been long protracted, escorted her on her way, clinging more closely than usual to her breast and kissing her eyes;[3] possibly as a final touch of hypocrisy, or possibly the last look upon his doomed mother gave pause even to that brutal spirit.

V. A starlit night and the calm of an unruffled sea appeared to have been sent by Heaven to afford proof of guilt. The ship had made no great way,[4] and two of Agrippina's household were in attendance, Crepereius Gallus standing not far from the tiller, while Acerronia, bending over the feet of the recumbent princess, recalled exultantly the penitence of the son and the re-entry of the mother into favour.

gaudium memorabat, cum dato signo ruere tectum
loci multo plumbo grave, pressusque Crepereius et
statim exanimatus est. Agrippina et Acerronia
eminentibus lecti parietibus ac forte validioribus,
quam ut oneri cederent, protectae sunt. Nec dis-
solutio navigii sequebatur, turbatis omnibus et quod
plerique ignari etiam conscios impediebant. Visum
dehinc remigibus unum in latus inclinare atque ita
navem submergere: sed neque ipsis promptus in
rem subitam consensus, et alii contra nitentes dedere
facultatem lenioris in mare iactus. Verum Acerronia,
inprudentia dum se Agrippinam esse utque sub-
veniretur matri principis clamitat, contis, et remis et
quae fors obtulerat navalibus telis conficitur: Agrippina silens eoque minus adgnita (unum tamen vulnus
umero excepit) nando, deinde occursu lenunculorum
Lucrinum in lacum vecta villae suae infertur.

VI. Illic reputans ideo se fallacibus litteris accitam
et honore praecipuo habitam, quodque litus iuxta,
non ventis acta, non saxis impulsa navis summa sui

---

¹ The lake, which virtually ceased to exist with the elevation
of the Monte Nuovo in the sixteenth century, had by Agrippa
and Octavian been converted into a naval base and training
centre for the operations against Sextus Pompeius, the
method being to connect it by a channel with the neighbouring Lake Avernus and to pierce and reinforce the sand
dune separating it from the Gulf of Baiae. The *portus Iulius*
so formed had been useless for years, but the outer passage
was still practicable for craft such as the oyster-fisher's boat
which had picked up Agrippina (Strab. 245).

² This must have been either Bauli or a villa of her own on
the Lucrine. If it was Bauli—the supposition which squares
most easily with the account of her cremation and the subsequent burial in chap. 9,—then the reader is left to infer that,
after landing, she procured a litter to carry her there. On the
other hand, the presence of *suae*, the prefix in *infertur*, the

Suddenly the signal was given: the canopy above them, which had been heavily weighted with lead, dropped, and Crepereius was crushed and killed on the spot. Agrippina and Acerronia were saved by the height of the couch-sides, which, as it happened, were too solid to give way under the impact. Nor did the break-up of the vessel follow: for confusion was universal, and even the men accessory to the plot were impeded by the large numbers of the ignorant. The crew then decided to throw their weight on one side and so capsize the ship; but, even on their own part, agreement came too slowly for a sudden emergency, and a counter-effort by others allowed the victims a gentler fall into the waves. Acerronia, however, incautious enough to raise the cry that she was Agrippina, and to demand aid for the emperor's mother, was despatched with poles, oars, and every nautical weapon that came to hand. Agrippina, silent and so not generally recognised, though she received one wound in the shoulder, swam until she was met by a few fishing-smacks, and so reached the Lucrine lake,[1] whence she was carried into her own villa.[2]

VI. There she reflected on the evident purpose of the treacherous letter of invitation and the exceptional honour with which she had been treated, and on the fact that, hard by the shore, a vessel, driven by no gale and striking no reef, had collapsed at the top

unlikelihood that a half-drowned woman would be able—or, if able, inclined—to make a fairly considerable journey, long after midnight (D. Cass. LXI. 13), past Baiae, and therefore almost under the eyes of her son, to a villa in which the *personnel* consisted of his slaves and freedmen, and to which the ship so narrowly escaped was ostensibly bound, are points which tell forcibly on the other side. See, too, chap. 8 init.

parte veluti terrestre machinamentum concidisset,
observans etiam Acerroniae necem, simul suum
vulnus aspiciens, solum insidiarum remedium esse
sensit,[1] si non intellegerentur; misitque libertum
Agermum,[2] qui nuntiaret filio benignitate deum et
fortuna eius evasisse gravem casum; orare ut quamvis
periculo matris exterritus visendi curam differret;
sibi ad praesens quiete opus. Atque interim securitate simulata medicamina vulneri et fomenta corpori
adhibet; testamentum Acerroniae requiri bonaque
obsignari iubet, id tantum non per simulationem.

VII. At Neroni nuntios patrati facinoris opperienti
adfertur evasisse ictu levi sauciam et hactenus adito
discrimine, ne auctor dubitaretur. Tum pavore
exanimis et iam iamque adfore obtestans vindictae
properam, sive servitia armaret vel militem accenderet, sive ad senatum et populum pervaderet, naufragium et vulnus et interfectos amicos obiciendo:
quod contra subsidium sibi? Nisi quid Burrus et
Seneca; quos statim acciverat, incertum experiens [3]
an et ante gnaros.[4] Igitur longum utriusque
silentium, ne inriti dissuaderent, an eo descensum
credebant, *ut*, nisi praeveniretur Agrippina, pereundum Neroni esset. Post Seneca hactenus

---

[1] <sensit> *Bezzenberger.*

[2] Agermum *Andresen*: Agerinum.

[3] experiens (*before* an) *Wölfflin :* expergens (*before* quos)
Med. The reading is totally uncertain.

[4] gnaros *marg. ed. Gryph. :* ignaros.

like an artificial structure on land. She reviewed
as well the killing of Acerronia, glanced simultaneously at her own wound, and realized that the one
defence against treachery was to leave it undetected.
Accordingly she sent the freedman Agermus to carry
word to her son that, thanks to divine kindness and to
his fortunate star, she had survived a grave accident;
but that, however great his alarm at his mother's
danger, she begged him to defer the attention of
a visit: for the moment, what she needed was rest.
Meanwhile, with affected unconcern, she applied
remedies to her wound and fomentations to her body:
Acerronia's will, she gave instructions was to be
sought, and her effects sealed up,—the sole measure
not referable to dissimulation.

VII. Meanwhile, as Nero was waiting for the
messengers who should announce the doing of the
deed, there came the news that she had escaped
with a wound from a light blow, after running just
sufficient risk to leave no doubt as to its author.
Half-dead with terror, he protested that any moment
she would be here, hot for vengeance. And whether
she armed her slaves or inflamed the troops, or made
her way to the senate and the people, and charged
him with the wreck, her wound, and the slaying of
her friends, what counter-resource was at his own
disposal? Unless there was hope in Seneca and
Burrus! He had summoned them immediately:
whether to test their feeling, or as cognizant already
of the secret, is questionable.—There followed,
then, a long silence on the part of both: either they
were reluctant to dissuade in vain, or they believed
matters to have reached a point at which Agrippina
must be forestalled or Nero perish. After a time,

promptius, *ut* [1] respiceret Burrum ac sciscitaretur, an militi imperanda caedes esset. Ille praetorianos toti Caesarum domui obstrictos memoresque Germanici nihil adversus progeniem eius atrox ausuros respondit: perpetraret Anicetus promissa. Qui nihil cunctatus poscit summam sceleris. Ad eam vocem Nero illo sibi die dari imperium auctoremque tanti muneris libertum profitetur: iret propere duceretque promptissimos ad iussa. Ipse audito venisse missu Agrippinae nuntium Agermum,[2] scaenam ultro criminis parat, gladiumque, dum mandata perfert, abicit inter pedes eius, tum quasi deprehenso vincla inici iubet. ut exitium principis molitam matrem et pudore deprehensi sceleris sponte mortem sumpsisse confingeret.

VIII. Interim vulgato Agrippinae periculo, quasi casu evenisset, ut quisque acceperat, decurrere ad litus. Hi molium objectus, hi proximas scaphas scandere; alii, quantum corpus sinebat, vadere in mare; quidam manus protendere; questibus, votis, clamore diversa rogitantium aut incerta respondentium omnis ora compleri; adfluere ingens multitudo cum luminibus, atque ubi incolumem esse pernotuit, ut ad gratandum sese expedire, donec aspectu armati et minitantis agminis disiecti sunt.

---

[1] <ut> *Doederlein.*
[2] Agermum *Andresen :* Agerinum *Med. And similarly below.*

---

[1] If the villa is on the Lucrine, the *molium obiectus* are evidently the half natural, half artificial barrier—" eight furlongs in length and as broad as a wide carriage-road (Strab. 245)—which separated the lake from the sea." If it is Bauli, the embankments are still explicable by such passages as Hor. *Carm.* II. 18, 19 :—*struis domos Marisque Baiis obstrepentis urges Summovere litora.*

Seneca so far took the lead as to glance at Burrus and inquire if the fatal order should be given to the military. His answer was that the guards, pledged as they were to the Caesarian house as a whole, and attached to the memory of Germanicus, would flinch from drastic measures against his issue: Anicetus must redeem his promise. He, without any hesitation, asked to be given full charge of the crime. The words brought from Nero a declaration that that day presented him with an empire, and that he had a freedman to thank for so great a boon: Anicetus must go with speed and take an escort of men distinguished for implicit obedience to orders. He himself, on hearing that Agermus had come with a message from Agrippina, anticipated it by setting the stage for a charge of treason, threw a sword at his feet while he was doing his errand, then ordered his arrest as an assassin caught in the act; his intention being to concoct a tale that his mother had practised against the imperial life and taken refuge in suicide from the shame of detection.

VIII. In the interval, Agrippina's jeopardy, which was attributed to accident, had become generally known; and there was a rush to the beach, as man after man learned the news. Some swarmed up the sea-wall,[1] some into the nearest fishing-boats: others were wading middle-deep into the surf, a few standing with outstretched arms. The whole shore rang with lamentations and vows and the din of conflicting questions and vague replies. A huge multitude streamed up with lights, and, when the knowledge of her safety spread, set out to offer congratulations; until, at the sight of an armed and threatening column, they were forced to scatter.

Anicetus villam statione circumdat refractaque ianua
obvios servorum abripit, donec ad fores cubiculi
veniret; cui pauci adstabant, ceteris terrore inrumpentium exterritis. Cubiculo modicum lumen
inerat et ancillarum una, magis ac magis anxia
Agrippina, quod nemo a filio ac ne Agermus quidem:
aliam fore laetae rei[1] faciem; nunc solitudinem ac
repentinos strepitus et extremi mali indicia. Abeunte dehinc ancilla "Tu quoque me deseris" pro-
locuta respicit Anicetum, trierarcho Herculeio et
Obarito centurione classiario comitatum: ac, si ad
visendum venisset, refotam nuntiaret, sin facinus
patraturus, nihil se de filio credere; non imperatum
parricidium. Circumsistunt lectum percussores et
prior trierarchus fusti caput eius adflixit. Iam in
mortem centurioni ferrum destringenti protendens
uterum "Ventrem feri" exclamavit multisque vulneribus confecta est.

IX. Haec consensu produntur. Aspexeritne matrem exanimem Nero et formam corporis eius
laudaverit, sunt qui tradiderint, sunt qui abnuant.
Cremata est nocte eadem convivali lecto et exsequiis
vilibus; neque, dum Nero rerum potiebatur, con-
gesta aut clausa humus. Mox domesticorum cura
levem tumulum accepit, viam Miseni propter et
villam Caesaris dictatoris, quae subiectos sinus

---

[1] laetae rei *Bezzenberger :* lataeret.

---

[1] There is more, "on trustworthy authority," in Suetonius
(*Ner.* 34): Dio adds the remark, which is at least in character:—
Οὐκ ᾔδειν ὅτι οὕτω καλὴν μητέρα εἶχον.

Anicetus drew a cordon round the villa, and, breaking down the entrance, dragged off the slaves as they appeared, until he reached the bedroom-door. A few servants were standing by: the rest had fled in terror at the inrush of men. In the chamber was a dim light and a single waiting-maid; and Agrippina's anxiety deepened every instant. Why no one from her son—nor even Agermus? Had matters prospered, they would have worn another aspect. Now, nothing but solitude, hoarse alarms, and the symptoms of irremediable ill! Then the maid rose to go. "Dost thou too forsake me?" she began, and saw Anicetus behind her, accompanied by Herculeius, the trierarch, and Obaritus, a centurion of marines. "If he had come to visit the sick, he might take back word that she felt refreshed. If to do murder, she would believe nothing of her son: matricide was no article of their instructions." The executioners surrounded the couch, and the trierarch began by striking her on the head with a club. The centurion was drawing his sword to make an end, when she proffered her womb to the blow. "Strike here," she exclaimed, and was despatched with repeated wounds.

IX. So far the accounts concur. Whether Nero inspected the corpse of his mother and expressed approval of her figure is a statement which some affirm and some deny.[1] She was cremated the same night, on a dinner-couch, and with the humblest rites; nor, so long as Nero reigned, was the earth piled over the grave or enclosed. Later, by the care of her servants, she received a modest tomb, hard by the road to Misenum and that villa of the dictator Caesar which looks from its dizzy height to the

editissima prospectat. Accenso rogo libertus eius
cognomento Mnester *se* ipse[1] ferro transegit,
incertum caritate in patronam an metu exitii. Hunc
sui finem multos ante annos crediderat Agrippina
contempseratque. Nam consulenti super Nerone
responderunt Chaldaei fore ut imperaret matremque
occideret; atque illa " Occidat " inquit " dum
imperet."

X. Sed a Caesare perfecto demum scelere magni-
tudo eius intellecta est. Reliquo noctis modo per
silentium defixus, saepius pavore exsurgens et mentis
inops lucem opperiebatur tamquam exitium adla-
turam. Atque eum auctore Burro prima centurionum tribunorumque adulatio ad spem firmavit,
prensantium manum gratantiumque, quod discrimen
improvisum et matris facinus evasisset. Amici
dehinc adire templa, et coepto exemplo proxima
Campaniae municipia victimis et legationibus laetitiam testari: ipse diversa simulatione maestus et
quasi incolumitati suae infensus ac morti parentis
inlacrimans. Quia tamen non, ut hominum vultus,
ita locorum facies mutantur, obversabaturque maris
illius et litorum gravis aspectus (et erant qui crederent
sonitum tubae collibus circum editis planctusque
tumulo matris audiri), Neapolim concessit litterasque

---

[1] se ipse *Nipperdey :* ipse *Med.,* ipse se *Ernesti.*

[1] Possibly, but not more than possibly, the promised pre-
diction of Thrasyllus' son (VI. 22 fin.).

[2] Obviously, in spite of Dio (ὑπὸ σαλπίγγων δή τινων,
πολεμικόν τι καὶ θορυβῶδες . . . ἠχουσῶν ἐδειματοῦτο, LXI. 14),
a funeral trumpet (Pers. III. 103 etc.).

bay outspread beneath. As the pyre was kindled, one of her freedmen, by the name of Mnester, ran a sword through his body, whether from love of his mistress or from fear of his own destruction remains unknown. This was that ending to which, years before, Agrippina had given her credence, and her contempt. For to her inquiries as to the destiny of Nero the astrologers answered that he should reign, and slay his mother;[1] and "Let him slay," she had said, "so that he reign."

X. But only with the completion of the crime was its magnitude realized by the Caesar. For the rest of the night, sometimes dumb and motionless, but not rarely starting in terror to his feet with a sort of delirium, he waited for the daylight which he believed would bring his end. Indeed, his first encouragement to hope came from the adulation of the centurions and tribunes, as, at the suggestion of Burrus, they grasped his hand and wished him joy of escaping his unexpected danger and the criminal enterprise of his mother. His friends in their turn visited the temples; and, once the example had been given, the Campanian towns in the neighbourhood attested their joy by victims and deputations. By a contrast in hypocrisy, he himself was mournful, repining apparently at his own preservation and full of tears for the death of a parent. But because the features of a landscape change less obligingly than the looks of men, and because there was always obtruded upon his gaze the grim prospect of that sea and those shores,—and there were some who believed that he could hear a trumpet,[2] calling in the hills that rose around, and lamentations at his mother's grave,— he withdrew to Naples and forwarded to the senate

123

ad senatum misit, quarum summa erat repertum cum ferro percussorem Agermum, ex intimis Agrippinae libertis, et luisse eam poenas [1] conscientia, qua*si* [2] scelus paravisset.

XI. Adiciebat crimina longius repetita, quod consortium imperii iuraturasque in feminae verba praetorias cohortis idemque dedecus senatus et populi speravisset, ac postquam frustra habita [3] sit, infensa militi patribusque et plebi dissuasisset donativum et congiarium periculaque viris inlustribus struxisset. [4] Quanto suo labore perpetratum, ne inrumperet curiam, ne gentibus externis responsa daret. Temporum quoque Claudianorum obliqua insectatione cuncta eius dominationis flagitia in matrem transtulit, publica fortuna exstinctam referens. Namque et naufragium narrabat: quod fortuitum fuisse, quis adeo hebes inveniretur, ut crederet? Aut a muliere naufraga missum cum telo unum, qui cohortes et classes imperatoris perfringeret? Ergo non iam Nero, cuius inmanitas omnium questus anteibat, sed Seneca adverso rumore erat, quod oratione tali confessionem scripsisset.

XII. Miro tamen certamine procerum decernuntur supplicationes apud omnia pulvinaria, utque Quinquatrus, quibus apertae insidiae essent, ludis annuis celebrarentur; aureum Minervae simulacrum in

---

[1] poenas *Nipperdey :* poenam.
[2] quasi *Halm :* qua.
[3] habita *Muretus :* ablata.
[4] struxisset *Ritter :* instruxisset.

a letter, the sum of which was that an assassin with his weapon upon him had been discovered in Agermus, one of the confidential freedman of Agrippina, and that his mistress, conscious of her guilt, had paid the penalty of meditated murder.

XI. He appended a list of charges drawn from the remoter past:—" She had hoped for a partnership in the empire; for the praetorian cohorts to swear allegiance to a woman; for the senate and people to submit to a like ignominy. Then, her ambition foiled, she had turned against the soldiers, the Fathers and the commons; had opposed the donative and the largesse, and had worked for the ruin of eminent citizens. At what cost of labour had he succeeded in preventing her from forcing the door of the senate and delivering her answers to foreign nations! " He made an indirect attack on the Claudian period also, transferring every scandal of the reign to the account of his mother, whose removal he ascribed to the fortunate star of the nation. For even the wreck was narrated: though where was the folly which could believe it accidental, or that a ship-wrecked woman had despatched a solitary man with a weapon to cut his way through the guards and navies of the emperor? The object, therefore, of popular censure was no longer Nero—whose barbarity transcended all protest—but Seneca, who in composing such a plea had penned a confession.

XII. However, with a notable spirit of emulation among the magnates, decrees were drawn up: thanksgivings were to be held at all appropriate shrines; the festival of Minerva, on which the conspiracy had been brought to light, was to be celebrated with annual games; a golden statue of

curia et iuxta principis imago statuerentur; dies
natalis Agrippinae inter nefastos esset. Thrasea
Paetus silentio vel brevi adsensu priores adulationes
transmittere solitus exiit tum senatu, ac sibi causam
periculi fecit, ceteris libertatis initium non praebuit.
Prodigia quoque crebra et inrita intercessere.
Anguem enixa mulier, et alia in concubitu mariti
fulmine exanimata: iam sol repente obscuratus et
tactae de caelo quattuordecim urbis regiones. Quae
adeo sine cura deum eveniebant, ut multos post
annos Nero imperium et scelera continuaverit.
Ceterum quo gravaret invidiam matris eaque demota
auctam lenitatem suam testificaretur, feminas inlustris Iuniam et Calpurniam, praetura functos
Valerium Capitonem et Licinium Gabolum sedibus
patriis reddidit, ab Agrippina olim pulsos. Etiam
Lolliae Paulinae cineres reportari sepulcrumque
exstrui permisit; quosque ipse nuper relegaverat,
Iturium et Calvisium poena exsolvit. Nam Silana
fato functa erat, longinquo ab exilio Tarentum
regressa labante iam Agrippina, cuius inimicitiis con-
ciderat, vel mitigata.

XIII. Tamen [1] cunctari in oppidis Campaniae, quonam modo urbem ingrederetur, an obsequium senatus,
an studia plebis reperiret anxius: contra deterrimus

---

[1] mitigata. Tamen *Halm :* tamen mitigata.

[1] Nov. 6.   [2] See XIII. 41 n.
[3] For Junia, see XII. 4 and 8; for Calpurnia and Lollia
Paulina, XII. 22; for Silana, Iturius, and Calvisius, XIII.
19 sqq. Capito and Gabolus are unknown.

the goddess, with an effigy of the emperor by her
side, was to be erected in the curia, and Agrippina's
birthday [1] included among the inauspicious dates.
Earlier sycophancies Thrasea Paetus had usually
allowed to pass, either in silence or with a curt
assent: this time he walked out of the senate,
creating a source of danger for himself, but im-
planting no germ of independence in his colleagues.
Portents, also, frequent and futile made their appearance: a woman gave birth to a serpent, another
was killed by a thunderbolt in the embraces of her
husband; the sun, again, was suddenly obscured,[2]
and the fourteen regions of the capital were struck
by lightning—events which so little marked the
concern of the gods that Nero continued for years
to come his empire and his crimes. However, to
aggravate the feeling against his mother, and to
furnish evidence that his own mildness had increased
with her removal, he restored to their native soil
two women of high rank, Junia and Calpurnia, along
with the ex-praetors Valerius Capito and Licinius
Gabolus [3]—all of them formerly banished by Agrippina. He sanctioned the return, even, of the ashes
of Lollia Paulina, and the erection of a tomb: Iturius
and Calvisius, whom he had himself relegated some
little while before, he now released from the penalty.
As to Silana, she had died a natural death at Tarentum, to which she had retraced her way, when
Agrippina, by whose enmity she had fallen, was
beginning to totter or to relent.

XIII. And yet he dallied in the towns of Campania,
anxious and doubtful how to make his entry into
Rome. Would he find obedience in the senate?
enthusiasm in the crowd? Against his timidity it

quisque, quorum non alia regia fecundior extitit, invisum Agrippinae nomen et morte eius accensum populi favorem disserunt: iret intrepidus et venerationem sui coram experiretur; simul praegredi exposcunt. Et promptiora quam promiserant inveniunt, obvias tribus, festo cultu senatum, coniugum ac liberorum agmina per sexum et aetatem disposita, exstructos, qua incederet, spectaculorum gradus, quo modo triumphi visuntur. Hinc superbus ac publici servitii victor Capitolium adiit, gratis exsolvit, seque in omnes libidines effudit, quas male coercitas qualiscumque matris reverentia tardaverat.

XIV. Vetus illi cupido erat curriculo quadrigarum insistere, nec minus foedum studium cithara ludicrum in modum canere. Concertare equis [1] regium et antiquis ducibus factitatum memorabat, idque vatum laudibus celebre et deorum honori datum. Enimvero cantus Apollini sacros, talique ornatu adstare non modo Graecis in urbibus, sed Romana apud templa numen praecipuum et praescium. Nec iam sisti poterat, cum Senecae ac Burro visum, ne utraque pervinceret, alterum concedere. Clausumque valle Vaticana spatium, in quo equos regeret, haud promisco spectaculo. Mox ultro vocari populus

---

[1] concertare equis *Halm :* cum celaret (cenaret *M.*[2]) quis.

[1] In his gardens on the east of the Vatican, St. Peter's now occupying part of the site.

was urged by every reprobate—and a court more prolific of reprobates the world has not seen—that the name of Agrippina was abhorred and that her death had won him the applause of the nation. Let him go without a qualm and experience on the spot the veneration felt for his person! At the same time, they demanded leave to precede him. They found, indeed, an alacrity which surpassed their promises: the tribes on the way to meet him; the senate in festal dress; troops of wives and of children disposed according to their sex and years, while along his route rose tiers of seats of the type used for viewing a triumph. Then, flushed with pride, victor over the national servility, he made his way to the Capitol, paid his grateful vows, and abandoned himself to all the vices, till now retarded, though scarcely repressed, by some sort of deference to his mother.

XIV. It was an old desire of his to drive a chariot and team of four, and an equally repulsive ambition to sing to the lyre in the stage manner. "Racing with horses," he used to observe, "was a royal accomplishment, and had been practised by the commanders of antiquity: the sport had been celebrated in the praises of poets and devoted to the worship of Heaven. As to song, it was sacred to Apollo; and it was in the garb appropriate to it that, both in Greek cities and in Roman temples, that great and prescient deity was seen standing." He could no longer be checked, when Seneca and Burrus decided to concede one of his points rather than allow him to carry both; and an enclosure was made in the Vatican valley,[1] where he could manoeuvre his horses without the spectacle being public. Before long, the Roman people received an invitation

Romanus laudibusque extollere, ut est vulgus
cupiens voluptatum et, si eodem princeps trahat,
laetum. Ceterum evulgatus pudor non satietatem,
ut rebantur, sed incitamentum attulit. Ratusque
dedecus molliri, si plures foedasset, nobilium fami-
liarum posteros egestate venalis in scaenam deduxit;
quos fato perfunctos ne nominatim tradam, maioribus
eorum tribuendum puto. Nam et eius flagitium est,
qui pecuniam ob delicta potius dedit, quam ne
delinquerent. Notos quoque equites Romanos operas
arenae promittere subegit donis ingentibus, nisi
quod merces ab eo, qui iubere potest, vim necessitatis
adfert.

XV. Ne tamen adhuc publico theatro dehonestare-
tur, instituit ludos Iuvenalium vocabulo, in quos
passim nomina data. Non nobilitas cuiquam, non
aetas aut acti honores impedimento, quo minus
Graeci Latinive histrionis artem exercerent usque
ad gestus modosque haud virilis. Quin et feminae
inlustres deformia meditari; exstructaque apud
nemus, quod navali stagno circumposuit Augustus,
conventicula et cauponae et posita veno inritamenta
luxui. Dabanturque stipes, quas boni necessitate,
intemperantes gloria consumerent. Inde gliscere
flagitia et infamia, nec ulla moribus olim corruptis
plus libidinum circumdedit quam illa conluvies. Vix

---

[1] To celebrate the first shaving of his beard (D. Cass. LXI.
19 : compare the anecdote, *ib.* 17 and Suet. *Ner.* 34).

[2] *Navalis procli spectaclum populo dedi trans Tiberim in quo
loco nunc nemus est Caesarum,* Mon. Anc. IV. 43.

in form, and began to hymn his praises, as is the way of the crowd, hungry for amusements, and delighted if the sovereign draws in the same direction. However, the publication of his shame brought with it, not the satiety expected, but a stimulus; and, in the belief that he was attenuating his disgrace by polluting others, he brought on the stage those scions of the great houses whom poverty had rendered venal. They have passed away, and I regard it as a debt due to their ancestors not to record them by name. For the disgrace, in part, is his who gave money for the reward of infamy and not for its prevention. Even well-known Roman knights he induced to promise their services in the arena by what might be called enormous bounties, were it not that gratuities from him who is able to command carry with them the compelling quality of necessity.

XV. Reluctant, however, as yet to expose his dishonour on a public stage, he instituted the so-called Juvenile Games,[1] for which a crowd of volunteers enrolled themselves. Neither rank, nor age, nor an official career debarred a man from practising the art of a Greek or Latin mummer, down to attitudes and melodies never meant for the male sex. Even women of distinction studied indecent parts; and in the grove with which Augustus fringed his Naval Lagoon,[2] little trysting-places and drinking-dens sprang up, and every incentive to voluptuousness was exposed for sale. Distributions of coin, too, were made, for the respectable man to expend under compulsion and the prodigal from vainglory. Hence debauchery and scandal throve; nor to our morals, corrupted long before, has anything contributed more of uncleanness than that herd of reprobates.

artibus honestis pudor retinetur, nedum inter certamina vitiorum pudicitia aut modestia aut quicquam probi moris reservaretur. Postremum ipse scaenam incedit, multa cura temptans citharam et praemeditans adsistentibus phonascis.[1] Accesserat cohors militum, centuriones tribunique et maerens Burrus ac laudans. Tuncque primum conscripti sunt equites Romani cognomento Augustianorum,[2] aetate ac robore conspicui, et pars ingenio procaces, alii in spem potentiae. Ii dies ac noctes plausibus personare, formam principis vocemque deum vocabulis appellantes; quasi per virtutem clari honoratique agere.

XVI. Ne tamen ludicrae tantum imperatoris artes notescerent, carminum quoque studium adfectavit, contractis quibus aliqua pangendi facultas necdum insignis erat. Hi cenati[3] considere simul, et adlatos vel ibidem repertos versus connectere atque ipsius verba quoquo modo prolata supplere, quod species ipsa carminum docet, non impetu et instinctu nec ore uno fluens. Etiam sapientiae doctoribus tempus impertiebat post epulas, utque contraria

---

[1] phonascis *Muretus :* facies.

[2] Augustianorum *Nipperdey :* augusttanorum.

[3] erat. hi cenati *Halm (after Muretus and Haase) :* aetatis nati.

---

[1] Some four years later, the corps is said to have included, besides the knights, four thousand sturdy plebeians (soldiers, according to Dio), with fixed salaries for the leaders, a standardized system of applause, and distinctive points of appearance—pomaded hair, ringless left hands, etc. (Suet. *Ner.* 20; D. Cass. LXI. 20).

[2] Examples may be seen in Dio. (LXI. 20).

[3] Suetonius dissents strongly :—*Venere in manus meas pugillares libellique cum quibusdam notissimis versibus, ipsius*

Even in the decent walks of life, purity is hard to
keep: far less could chastity or modesty or any vestige
of integrity survive in that competition of the vices.—
Last of all to tread the stage was the sovereign himself, scrupulously testing his lyre and striking a few
preliminary notes to the trainers at his side. A
cohort of the guards had been added to the audience
—centurions and tribunes; Burrus, also, with his sigh
and his word of praise. Now, too, for the first time
was enrolled the company of Roman knights known as
the Augustiani;[1] conspicuously youthful and robust;
wanton in some cases by nature; in others, through
dreams of power. Days and nights they thundered
applause, bestowed the epithets reserved for deity[2]
upon the imperial form and voice, and lived in a
repute and honour, which might have been earned by
virtue.

XVI. And yet, lest it should be only the histrionic
skill of the emperor which won publicity, he affected
also a zeal for poetry and gathered a group of
associates with some faculty for versification but not
such as to have yet attracted remark. These, after
dining, sat with him, devising a connection for the
lines they had brought from home or invented on the
spot, and eking out the phrases suggested, for better
or worse, by their master; the method being obvious
even from the general cast of the poems,[3] which run
without energy or inspiration and lack unity of style.
Even to the teachers of philosophy he accorded a
little time—but after dinner, and in order to amuse
himself by the wrangling which attended the ex-

*chirographo scriptis; ut facile appareret non translatos, aut
dictante aliquo exceptos, sed plane quasi a cogitante atque
generante exaratos (Ner. 52).*

adseverantium discordia frueretur.[1]   Nec deerant qui ore vultuque tristi inter oblectamenta regia spectari cuperent.

XVII. Sub idem tempus levi initio atrox caedes orta inter colonos Nucerinos Pompeianosque gladiatorio spectaculo, quod Livineius Regulus, quem motum senatu rettuli, edebat.   Quippe oppidana lascivia in vicem incessentes probra, dein saxa, postremo ferrum sumpsere, validiore Pompeianorum plebe, apud quos spectaculum edebatur.   Ergo deportati sunt in urbem multi e Nucerinis trunco per vulnera corpore, ac plerique liberorum aut parentum mortes deflebant. Cuius rei iudicium princeps senatui, senatus consulibus permisit.   Et rursus re ad patres relata, prohibiti publice in decem annos eius modi coetu Pompeiani collegiaque, quae contra leges instituerant, dissoluta ; Livineius et qui alii seditionem conciverant exilio multati sunt.

XVIII. Motus senatu et Pedius Blaesus, accusantibus Cyrenensibus violatum ab eo thesaurum Aesculapii dilectumque militarem pretio et ambitione corruptum.   Idem Cyrenenses reum agebant Acilium Strabonem, praetoria potestate usum et missum disceptatorem a Claudio agrorum, quos regis Apionis quondam avitos et populo Romano cum regno

---

[1] discordia frueretur *Bezzenberger :* discordiae rueretur.

[1] Now Nocera—to the east of Pompeii.

[2] The notice is lost.—Two or three *graffiti* at Pompeii are inspired by this feud.

[3] In conjunction with Crete, Cyrene formed a minor senatorial province.

[4] Ptolemy Apion, a natural son of Ptolemy VII ("Physcon") of Egypt.   By the discovery, seven years ago, of an unexecuted will of Physcon it was shown that Apion's legacy of the Cyrenaica to Rome (96 B.C.) was merely the realization of a project formed by his father.

position of their conflicting dogmas. Nor was there any dearth of gloomy-browed and sad-eyed sages eager to figure among the diversions of majesty.

XVII. About the same date, a trivial incident led to a serious affray between the inhabitants of the colonies of Nuceria[1] and Pompeii, at a gladiatorial show presented by Livineius Regulus, whose removal from the senate has been noticed.[2] During an exchange of raillery, typical of the petulance of country towns, they resorted to abuse, then to stones, and finally to steel; the superiority lying with the populace of Pompeii, where the show was being exhibited. As a result, many of the Nucerians were carried maimed and wounded to the capital, while a very large number mourned the deaths of children or of parents. The trial of the affair was delegated by the emperor to the senate; by the senate to the consuls. On the case being again laid before the members, the Pompeians as a community were debarred from holding any similar assembly for ten years, and the associations which they had formed illegally were dissolved. Livineius and the other fomenters of the outbreak were punished with exile.

XVIII. Pedius Blaesus also was removed from the senate: he was charged by the Cyrenaeans[3] with profaning the treasury of Aesculapius and falsifying the military levy by venality and favouritism. An indictment was brought, again by Cyrene, against Acilius Strabo, who had held praetorian office and been sent by Claudius to adjudicate on the estates, once the patrimony of King Apion,[4] which he had bequeathed along with his kingdom to the Roman

relictos proximus quisque possessor invaserant, diutinaque licentia et iniuria quasi iure et aequo nitebantur. Igitur abiudicatis agris orta adversus iudicem invidia; et senatus ignota sibi esse mandata Claudii et consulendum principem respondit. Nero probata Strabonis sententia, se nihilo minus subvenire sociis et usurpata concedere scripsit.[1]

XIX. Sequuntur virorum inlustrium mortes Domitii Afri et M. Servilii, qui summis honoribus et multa eloquentia viguerant, ille orando causas, Servilius diu foro, mox tradendis rebus Romanis celebris et elegantia vitae, quam clariorem effecit, ut par ingenio, ita morum diversus.

XX. Nerone quartum Cornelio Cosso consulibus quinquennale ludicrum Romae institutum est ad morem Graeci certaminis, varia fama, ut cuncta ferme nova. Quippe erant qui Gnaeum quoque Pompeium incusatum a senioribus ferrent, quod mansuram theatri sedem posuisset. Nam antea subitariis gradibus et scaena in tempus structa ludos edi solitos, vel si vetustiora repetas, stantem populum spectavisse, ne, si consideret theatro dies totos igna-

---

[1] scripsit] rescripsit *Haase.*

[1] IV. 52 n., 66 n.

[2] M. Servilius Nonianus, consul in 35 A.D. He was writing history under Claudius, who attended one of his readings (Plin. *Ep.* I. 13); is coupled by Tacitus with Aufidius Bassus, in contrast to Sisenna and Varro, as a type of modern eloquence (*Dial.* 23; cf. Quint. X. 1, 102); and has been conjectured to be the consular historian who related as an eye-witness an incident at Tiberius' dinner-table (Suet. *Tib.* 61 fin.).

[3] The *Neronia*: see XVI. 4.

[4] Greek games, though not exactly common, had been fairly often presented. The *Neronia*, however, would seem to have been the first instance at Rome of a tripartite contest (Suet. *Ner.* 12), the usual athletes and horses being supplemented by a contest of music (including poetry and rhetoric): a feature

nation. They had been annexed by the neighbouring proprietors, who relied on their long-licensed usurpation as a legal and fair title. Hence, when the adjudication went against them, there was an outbreak of ill-will against the adjudicator; and the senate could only answer that it was ignorant of Claudius' instructions and the emperor would have to be consulted. Nero, while upholding Strabo's verdict, wrote that none the less he supported the provincials and made over to them the property occupied.

XIX. There followed the death of two famous men, Domitius Afer[1] and Marcus Servilius;[2] both of whom had been distinguished as great officials and eloquent orators. Afer's celebrity, however, was due to his practice as an advocate; that of Servilius, primarily to his long activity in the courts, then to his work as a Roman historian, and, again, to a refinement of life made more noticeable by the fact that, while equal in genius to his rival, he was a complete contrast to him in character.

XX. In the consulate of Nero—his fourth term— and of Cornelius Cossus, a quinquennial competition[3] on the stage, in the style of a Greek contest, was introduced at Rome. Like almost all innovations[4] it was variously canvassed. Some insisted that " even Pompey had been censured by his elders for establishing the theatre in a permanent home.[5] Before, the games had usually been exhibited with the help of improvised tiers of benches and a stage thrown up for the occasion; or, to go further into the past, the people stood to watch: seats in the theatre, it was feared, might tempt them to pass whole days in

A.V.O. 813 =
A.D. 60

retained in the better known and longer-lived *agon Capitolinus* of Domitian.

    [5] IV. 7 n.

via continuaret. Spectaculorum quidem antiquitas servaretur, quotiens praetor sederet,[1] nulla cuiquam civium necessitate certandi. Ceterum abolitos paulatim patrios mores funditus everti per accitam lasciviam, ut quod usquam corrumpi et corrumpere queat, in urbe visatur, degeneretque studiis externis iuventus, gymnasia et otia et turpis amores exercendo, principe et senatu auctoribus, qui non modo licentiam vitiis permiserint, sed vim adhibeant, *ut* proceres Romani specie orationum et carminum scaena polluantur. Quid superesse, nisi ut corpora quoque nudent et caestus adsumant easque pugnas pro militia et armis meditentur? An iustitiam auctum iri[2] et decurias equitum egregius[3] iudicandi munus expleturos, si fractos sonos et dulcedinem vocum perite audissent? Noctis quoque dedecori adiectas, ne quod tempus pudori relinquatur, sed coetu promisco, quod perditissimus quisque per diem concupiverit, per tenebras audeat.

XXI. Pluribus ipsa licentia placebat, ac tamen honesta nomina praetendebant. Maiores quoque

[1] praetor sederet] praetores ederent *Lipsius, vulg.*
[2] iustitiam auctum iri *Madvig :* iustitia augurii.
[3] egregius *Madvig :* egregium.

---

[1] Responsibility for the public games had been transferred by Augustus from the aediles to the praetors; but, in the present case, Nero *magistros toti certamini praeposuit consularis sorte, sede praetorum* (Suet. *Ner.* 12)—a passage which, in conjunction with XI. 11 (*sedente Claudio*) and Juv. XI. 192 (*praeda caballorum praetor sedet*) seems a perfectly adequate defence of the manuscript reading as against Lipsius' plausible emendation.

indolence. By all means let the spectacles be retained in their old form, whenever the praetor
presided,[1] and so long as no citizen lay under
any obligation to compete. But the national
morality, which had gradually fallen into oblivion,
was being overthrown from the foundations by this
imported licentiousness; the aim of which was that
every production of every land, capable of either
undergoing or engendering corruption, should be on
view in the capital, and that our youth, under the
influence of foreign tastes, should degenerate into
votaries of the gymnasia, of indolence, and of dis-
honourable amours,—and this at the instigation of
the emperor and senate, who, not content with
conferring immunity upon vice, were applying
compulsion, in order that Roman nobles should
pollute themselves on the stage under pretext of
delivering an oration or a poem.[2] What remained
but to strip to the skin as well, put on the gloves,
and practise that mode of conflict instead of the
profession of arms? Would justice be promoted,
would the equestrian decuries better fulfil their
great judicial functions, if they had lent an expert
ear to emasculated music and dulcet voices? Even
night had been requisitioned for scandal, so that
virtue should not be left with a breathing-space,
but that amid a promiscuous crowd every vilest
profligate might venture in the dark the act for
which he had lusted in the light."

XXI. It was this very prospect of licence which
attracted the majority; and yet their pretexts were
decently phrased:—" Even our ancestors had not

---

[2] Among them was Lucan with a panegyric of Nero (Suet.
vit. Luc. init.).

non abhorruisse spectaculorum oblectamentis pro
fortuna, quae tum erat, eoque a Tuscis accitos
histriones, a Thuriis equorum certamina; et possessa
Achaia Asiaque ludos curatius editos, nec quem-
quam Romae honesto loco ortum ad theatralis artes
degeneravisse, ducentis iam annis a L. Mummii
triumpho, qui primus id genus spectaculi in urbe
praebuerit. Sed et consultum parsimoniae, quod
perpetua sedes theatro locata sit potius, quam im-
menso sumptu singulos per annos consurgeret ac
destrueretur. Nec perinde magistratus rem familiarem exhausturos aut populo efflagitandi Graeca
certamina a magistratibus causam fore, cum eo
sumptu res publica fungatur. Oratorum ac vatum
victorias incitamentum ingeniis adlaturas; nec
cuiquam iudici grave auris studiis honestis et
voluptatibus concessis impertire. Laetitiae magis
quam lasciviae dari paucas totius quinquennii noctes,
quibus tanta luce ignium nihil inlicitum occultari
queat. Sane nullo insigni dehonestamento id spectaculum transiit. Ac ne modica quidem studia plebis
exarsere, quia redditi quamquam scaenae pantomimi
certaminibus sacris prohibebantur. Eloquentiae primas nemo tulit, sed victorem esse Caesarem pro-

---

[1] Liv. VII. 2.   [2] This tradition is not otherwise known.
[3] In 146 and 133 B.C. respectively.   [4] In 145 B.C.
[5] The Neronia were ranked, like the great Greek festivals,

been averse from amusing themselves with spectacles
in keeping with the standard of wealth in their day;
and that was the reason why actors had been imported from Etruria[1] and horse-races from Thurii.[2]
Since the annexation of Achaia and Asia,[3] games had
been exhibited in a more ambitious style; and yet,
at Rome, no one born in a respectable rank of life
had condescended to the stage as a profession, though
it was now two hundred years since the triumph of
Lucius Mummius,[4] who first gave an exhibition of
the kind in the capital. But, more than this, it had
been a measure of economy when the theatre was
housed in a permanent building instead of being
reared and razed, year after year, at enormous
expense. Again, the magistrates would not have
the same drain upon their private resources, nor the
populace the same excuse for demanding contests
in the Greek style from the magistrates, when the
cost was defrayed by the state. The victories of
orators and poets would apply a spur to genius;
nor need it lie heavy on the conscience of any judge,
if he had not turned a deaf ear to reputable arts and
to legitimate pleasures. It was to gaiety, rather than
to wantonness, that a few nights were being given
out of five whole years—nights in which, owing to
the blaze of illuminations, nothing illicit could be
concealed." The display in question, it must be
granted, passed over without any glaring scandal;
and there was no outbreak, even slight, of popular
partisanship, since the pantomimic actors, though
restored to the stage, were debarred from the sacred
contests.[5] The first prize for eloquence was not
awarded, but an announcement was made that the

among the ἱεροὶ ἀγῶνες (ὧν τὰ ἆθλα ἐν στεφάνῳ μονῷ, according
to the definition of Pollux, III. 153).

nuntiatum. Graeci amictus, quis per eos dies plerique incesserant, tum exoleverunt.

XXII. Inter quae et sidus cometes effulsit, de quo vulgi opinio est, tamquam mutationem regnis [1] portendat. Igitur quasi iam depulso Nerone, quisnam deligeretur anquirebant. Et omnium ore Rubellius Plautus celebratur, cui nobilitas per matrem ex Iulia familia. Ipse placita maiorum colebat, habitu severo, casta et secreta domo, quantoque metu occultior, tanto plus famae adeptus. Auxit rumorem pari vanitate orta interpretatio fulguris. Nam quia discumbentis Neronis apud Simbruina stagna *in villa*,[2] cui Sublaqueum nomen est, ictae dapes mensaque disiecta erat, idque finibus Tiburtum acciderat, unde paterna Plauto origo, hunc illum numine deum destinari credebant, fovebantque multi, quibus nova et ancipitia praecolere avida et plerumque fallax ambitio est. Ergo permotus his Nero componit ad Plautum litteras, consuleret quieti urbis seque prava diffamantibus subtraheret: esse illi per Asiam avitos agros, in quibus tuta et inturbida iuventa frueretur. Ita illuc cum coniuge Antistia et paucis familiarium concessit.

---

[1] regnis *Bentley* (*from* Luc. I. 529) : regis.
[2] <in villa> *Bezzenberger*.

---

[1] He had not himself competed for the crown *orationis carminisque Latini*, but it was voluntarily resigned to him by those who had (*honestissimus quisque*, according to Suet. *Ner.* 12). On the other hand, the *citharae corona* fell to him by a regular award of the judges.

[2] XIII. 19 n.

[3] XI. 13 n.

[4] See VI. 27 n.

[5] Antistia Pollitta, daughter of L. Antistius Vetus, whose fate she was to share.

Caesar had proved victorious.[1] The Greek dress, in which a great number of spectators had figured during the festival, immediately went out of vogue.

XXII. Meanwhile, a comet blazed into view—in the opinion of the crowd, an apparition boding change to monarchies. Hence, as though Nero were already dethroned, men began to inquire on whom the next choice should fall; and the name in all mouths was that of Rubellius Plautus,[2] who, on the mother's side, drew his nobility from the Julian house. Personally, he cherished the views of an older generation: his bearing was austere, his domestic life being pure and secluded; and the retirement which his fears led him to seek had only brought him an accession of fame. The rumours gained strength from the interpretation—suggested by equal credulity—which was placed upon a flash of lightning. Because, while Nero dined by the Simbruine lakes[3] in the villa known as the Sublaqueum, the banquet had been struck and the table shivered; and because the accident had occurred on the confines of Tibur, the town from which Plautus derived his origin on the father's side,[4] a belief spread that he was the candidate marked out by the will of deity; and he found numerous supporters in the class of men who nurse the eager and generally delusive ambition to be the earliest parasites of a new and precarious power. Nero, therefore, perturbed by the reports, drew up a letter to Plautus, advising him " to consult the peace of the capital and extricate himself from the scandal-mongers: he had family estates in Asia, where he could enjoy his youth in safety and quiet." To Asia, accordingly, he retired with his wife Antistia[5] and a few of his intimate friends.

Isdem diebus nimia luxus cupido infamiam et periculum Neroni tulit, quia fontem aquae *a Q. Marcio*[1] ad urbem deductae nando incesserat; videbaturque potus sacros et caerimoniam loci corpore loto polluisse. Secutaque anceps valetudo iram deum adfirmavit.

XXIII. At Corbulo post deleta Artaxata utendum recenti terrore ratus ad occupanda Tigranocerta, quibus excisis metum hostium intenderet vel, si pepercisset, clementiae famam adipisceretur, illuc pergit, non infenso exercitu, ne spem veniae auferret, neque tamen remissa cura, gnarus facilem mutatu gentem, ut segnem ad pericula, its infidam ad occasiones. Barbari, pro ingenio quisque, alii preces offerre, quidam deserere vicos et in avia digredi; ac fuere qui se speluncis et carissima secum abderent. Igitur dux Romanus diversis artibus, misericordia adversus supplices, celeritate adversus profugos, inmitis iis, qui latebras insederant, ora et exitus

---

[1] aquae <a Q.> Marcio *Jackson:* aquae margio *Med.,* aquae Marciae *Puteolanus, edd. For the haplography compare for instance, IV.* 61 et quae = et Q.

---

[1] The *aqua Marcia* (the modern *Acqua Pia*), brought to Rome, under commission of the senate, by Q. Marcius Rex in his praetorship. Eulogies of the water as the clearest, coldest and most wholesome in Rome—or the world—are frequent (*e.g.* Stat. *Silv.* I. 5, 25; Plut. *Cor.* 1; Strab. V. 3, 13 fin.; Plin. *H.N.* XXXI. § 24, etc.).—For the tabu upon swimming in certain streams, Lipsius cited Plin. *Ep.* VIII. 8 (the reference is to the Clitumnus):—*Pons terminus sacri profanique: in superiore parte navigare tantum, infra etiam natare concessum.*

About the same date, Nero's passion for extravagance brought him some disrepute and danger: he had entered and swum in the sources of the stream which Quintus Marcius conveyed to Rome;[1] and it was considered that by bathing there he had profaned the sacred waters and the holiness of the site. The divine anger was confirmed by a grave illness which followed.

XXIII. Meanwhile, after razing Artaxata,[2] Corbulo resolved to profit by the first impression of terror in order to seize Tigranocerta, which he could either destroy, and deepen the fears of the enemy, or spare, and earn a reputation for clemency. He marched on the town,[3] then, avoiding offensive operations, so as not to dispel the hope of an amnesty, but at the same time relaxing nothing of his vigilance; for he knew the facile inconstancy of a race which, if slow to confront danger, was quick to embrace an opportunity of treason. The barbarians, according to their moods, either met him with prayers or abandoned their hamlets and dispersed to the wilds: others, again, concealed themselves, together with their most treasured belongings, in caverns. The Roman general, therefore, varied his methods: in the case of the suppliants, he employed pardon; in that of the fugitives, pursuit; to those lurking in covert he was merciless, firing the entrances and

---

[2] The account of Corbulo's operations is resumed from XIII. 41, and opens with the march on Tigranocerta, the date being 59 or 60 A.D. (XIII. 35 n.).

[3] The distance is put at 275 miles as the crow flies: the route can hardly be determined from the data. That the first stage would be from Artaxata to the plain of Bayazid, the last through the pass of Bitlis to Tigranocerta, appears probable: whether the long and difficult march intervening was to the north or south of Lake Van is a matter of conjecture.

specuum sarmentis virgultisque completos igni exurit. Atque illum finis suos praegredientem incursavere Mardi, latrociniis exerciti contraque inrumpentem montibus defensi; quos Corbulo inmissis Hiberis vastavit hostilemque audaciam externo sanguine ultus est.

XXIV. Ipse exercitusque ut nullis ex proelio damnis, ita per inopiam et labores fatiscebant, carne pecudum propulsare famem adacti. Ad hoc penuria aquae, fervida aestas, longinqua itinera sola ducis patientia mitigabantur, eadem pluraque [1] gregario milite tolerantis.[1] Ventum dehinc in locos cultos demessaeque segetes, et ex duobus castellis, in quae confugerant Armenii, alterum impetu captum; qui primam vim depulerant, obsidione coguntur. Unde in regionem Tauraunitium transgressus inprovisum periculum vitavit. Nam haud procul tentorio eius non ignobilis barbarus cum telo repertus ordinem insidiarum seque auctorem et socios per tormenta edidit, convictique et puniti sunt qui specie amicitiae dolum parabant. Nec multo post legati Tigranocerta missi patere moenia adferunt, intentos popularis ad iussa: simul hospitale donum, coronam

---

[1] pluraque *Jacob* . . . tolerantis *Ernesti :* plura quam . . . toleranti.

---

[1] A Kurdish race with the national proclivities—μετανάσται καὶ λῃστρικοί, Strab. 523—and branches in both Persia and Armenia. They were far too widely diffused for their mention to do anything towards solving the problem of Corbulo's march.

[2] The legionary's diet was mainly farinaceous, the cornration—unground—being a bushel a month. For the objection to too much flesh, compare Caes. *B.G.* VII. 17. Barley—*quadrupedum fere cibus,* Plin. *H.N.* XVIII. § 74, ἀλεκτορίδων τροφή, Ath. 214 F—was an equally unpopular alternative (Caes. *B.G.* III. 47, etc.).

exits of their dens, after filling them with lopped branches and bushes. The Mardi,[1] experienced freebooters with a mountain-barrier to secure them against invasion, harassed his march along their frontier: Corbulo threw the Iberians into the country, ravaged it, and chastised the enemy's boldness at the price of purely foreign blood.

XXIV. He himself and his army, though they had sustained no casualties in battle, were yet beginning to feel the strain of short rations and hardship—they had been reduced to keeping starvation at bay by a flesh-diet.[2] Added to this were a shortage of water, a blazing summer, and long marches; the one mitigating circumstance being the patience of the general, who bore the same privations as the common soldier, and even more. In time they reached an agricultural district, cut down the crops, and, out of the two forts in which the Armenians had taken refuge, carried one by storm: the other beat back the first assault and was reduced by blockade. Hence he crossed into the Tauronite district,[3] where he escaped an unexpected danger. A barbarian of some note, who had been found with a weapon not far from Corbulo's tent, disclosed under torture the whole sequence of the plot, his own responsibility for it, and his accomplices. There followed the conviction and punishment of the traitors who, under the cloak of friendship, were designing murder. Nor was it long before envoys from Tigranocerta brought news that the city-gates were open and their countrymen awaiting his orders: at the same time, they handed over a gold crown, presented as a

---

[3] Not identified with any approach to certainty.

auream, tradebant. Accepitque cum honore, nec quicquam urbi detractum, quo promptius obsequium integri retinerent.

XXV. At praesidium Legerda,[1] quod ferox iuventus clauserat, non sine certamine expugnatum est: nam et proelium pro muris ausi erant et pulsi intra munimenta aggeri[2] demum et inrumpentium armis cessere. Quae facilius proveniebant, quia Parthi Hyrcano bello distinebantur. Miserantque Hyrcani ad principem Romanum societatem oratum, attineri se Vologesen pro pignore amicitiae ostentantes. Eos regredientis Corbulo, ne Euphraten transgressi hostium custodiis circumvenirentur, dato praesidio ad litora maris sui[3] deduxit, unde vitatis Parthorum finibus patrias in sedes remeavere.

XXVI. Quin et Tiridaten per Medos extrema Armeniae intrantem, praemisso cum auxiliis Verulano legato atque ipse legionibus citis, abire procul ac spem

---

[1] Legerda *Bezzenberger* : legerat.
[2] aggeri *Boetticher* : aggeris.
[3] sui *Lipsius* : rubri *Med.*, *vulg.* (*a naïve emendation of* ui).

---

[1] Μεταξὺ τοῦ Εὐφράτου καὶ τῶν τοῦ Τίγριδος πηγῶν (Ptol. V. 13, 18–19).
[2] The *mare Hyrcanum*, an alternative name for the Caspian —the only sea which could enter the thoughts of rational men confronted with the problem of reaching Hyrcania from the upper Euphrates. The escort would consist of a nucleus of legionaries with a detachment of Pharasmanes' Iberians, and the route must have been to the north of Armenia. All else is uncertain, except that the traditional *maris rubri*, with the implied excursion into space, commencing at the Persian Gulf and ending felicitously at the south-eastern extremity of the Caspian, must for half a dozen cogent reasons be dismissed as fantastic.

token of welcome. He accepted it with a complimentary speech, and left the city intact, hoping that a population which had lost nothing would retain its loyalty with greater readiness.

XXV. On the other hand, the military post of Legerda,[1] which had been shut against the invader by a body of resolute youths, was carried only with a struggle, as the defenders not merely risked an engagement outside the walls, but, when driven within the ramparts, yielded only to a siege-mound and the arms of a storming-party. These successes were gained with the more ease that the Parthians were fully occupied with the Hyrcanian war. The Hyrcanians, in fact, had sent to the Roman emperor, soliciting an alliance and pointing, as a pledge of friendliness, to their detention of Vologeses. On the return of the deputies, who by crossing the Euphrates might have been intercepted by the enemy's outposts, Corbulo assigned them a guard and escorted them to the shores of their own sea,[2] from which they were able to regain their country, while avoiding Parthian territory.

XXVI.[3] Moreover, as Tiridates was attempting to penetrate the extreme Armenian frontier by way of Media, he sent the legate Verulanus in advance with the auxiliaries, and by his own appearance with

[3] From the description, in chap. 24, of the conditions during the march on Tigranocerta, it is a fair inference that the town could not have been occupied till the autumn. In that case, the remnant of the year cannot accommodate the events crowded into the present chapter—the repulse, for instance, of Tiridates' incursion through Media Atropatene in the far east must have needed the greater part of a summer—and it becomes impossible to acquiesce in Mommsen's ascription of everything in chaps. 23–26 to 60 A.D.

belli amittere [1] subegit; quosque nobis aversos animis [2] cognoverat, caedibus et incendiis perpopulatus possessionem Armeniae usurpabat, cum advenit Tigranes a Nerone ad capessendum imperium delectus, Cappadocum ex nobilitate, regis Archelai nepos,[3] sed quod diu obses apud urbem fuerat, usque ad servilem patientiam demissus. Nec consensu acceptus, durante apud quosdam favore Arsacidarum. At plerique superbiam Parthorum perosi datum a Romanis regem malebant. Additum ei praesidium mille legionarii, tres sociorum cohortes duaeque equitum alae, et quo facilius novum regnum tueretur, pars [4] Armeniae, ut cuique finitima, Pharasmani Polemonique [5] et Aristobulo atque Antiocho parere iussae sunt. Corbulo in Suriam abscessit, morte Ummidii legati vacuam ac sibi permissam.

XXVII. Eodem anno ex inlustribus Asiae urbibus Laodicea tremore terrae prolapsa, nullo *a* nobis remedio, propriis opibus revaluit. At in Italia vetus oppidum Puteoli ius coloniae et cognomentum a Nerone apiscuntur. Veterani Tarentum et Antium adscripti non tamen infrequentiae locorum subvenere, dilapsis pluribus in provincias, in quibus stipendia expleverant; neque coniugiis suscipiendis neque alendis liberis sueti orbas sine posteris domos

[1] amittere] omittere *Agricola*.
[2] aversos animis *Bekker :* ab re (rege *M* [1] *?*) ani nis.
[3] nepos] pronepos *Nipperdey.*
[4] pars] partes *Halm.*
[5] Pharasmani Polemonique *J. F. Gronovius :* pars nipulique.

[1] And, on the father's side, of Herod the Great.
[2] The last king of Pontus. For Aristobulus and Antiochus, see XIII. 7.
[3] See XIII. 22.

the legions after a forced march compelled the prince
to retire to a distance and abandon the thought of
war. After devastating with fire and sword the
districts he had found hostile to ourselves, he remained master of Armenia, when Tigranes, who had
been chosen by Nero to assume the crown, arrived
on the scene—a member of the Cappadocian royal
house and a great-grandson of King Archelaus,[1] but
by his long residence as a hostage in the capital
reduced to a slave-like docility. Nor was his reception unanimous, since in some quarters the popularity of the Arsacidae still persisted: the majority,
however, revolted by Parthian arrogance, preferred
a king assigned by Rome. He was allowed, further,
a garrison of one thousand legionaries, three allied
cohorts, and two squadrons of cavalry; while, to
make his new kingdom more easily tenable, any
district of Armenia adjoining the frontier of Pharasmanes or Polemo,[2] or Aristobulus or Antiochus, was
ordered to obey that prince. Corbulo withdrew to
Syria, deprived of its governor by the death of
Ummidius, and since then left to its own devices.[3]

XXVII. In the same year, Laodicea, one of the
famous Asiatic cities, was laid in ruins by an earthquake, but recovered by its own resources, without
assistance from ourselves. In Italy, the old town of
Puteoli acquired the rights and title of a colony
from Nero. Veterans were drafted into Tarentum
and Antium, but failed to arrest the depopulation
of the districts, the majority slipping away into
the provinces where they had completed their years
of service; while, as they lacked the habit of marrying
wives and rearing families, the homes they left
behind them were childless and without heirs. For

relinquebant.   Non enim, ut olim, universae legiones
deducebantur cum tribunis et centurionibus et sui
cuiusque ordinis militibus, ut consensu et caritate
rem publicam efficerent, sed ignoti inter se, diversis
manipulis,[1] sine rectore, sine adfectibus mutuis,
quasi ex alio genere mortalium repente in unum
collecti, numerus magis quam colonia.

XXVIII. Comitia praetorum   arbitrio   senatus
haberi solita, quod acriore ambitu exarserant, princeps composuit, tris, qui supra numerum petebant,
legioni praeficiendo.   Auxitque patrum honorem
statuendo ut, qui a privatis iudicibus ad senatum
provocavissent, eiusdem pecuniae periculum facerent, cuius si [2] qui imperatorem appellarent; [3] nam
antea vacuum id solutumque poena fuerat.   Fine
anni Vibius Secundus eques Romanus accusantibus
Mauris repetundarum damnatur atque Italia exigitur,
ne graviore poena adficeretur, Vibii Crispi fratris
opibus enisus.

XXIX. Caesennio [4] Paeto et Petronio Turpiliano
consulibus gravis clades in Britannia accepta, in qua

---

¹ <e> manipulis *Nipperdey.*   ² si *Halm:* is.
³ appellarent *Madvig :* appellavere.
⁴ Caesennio *Nipperdey :* cesonio.

---

[1] There were fifteen candidates for twelve vacancies (I.
14 sq.).
[2] A third of the amount at issue in the suit.
[3] Q. Vibius Crispus, born of humble stock (*Dial.* 8), but
famous as an orator and accuser, and high in favour under
the Flavian emperors.   *Pecunia, potentia, ingenio inter claros
magis quam bonos* is the verdict of Tacitus at *Hist.* II. 10;

the days had passed when entire legions—with tribunes, centurions, privates in their proper centuries—were so transplanted as to create, by their unanimity and their comradeship, a little commonwealth. The settlers now were strangers among strangers; men from totally distinct maniples; leaderless; mutually indifferent; suddenly, as if they were anything in the world except soldiers, massed in one place to compose an aggregate rather than a colony.

XXVIII. Since the praetorian elections, regularly left to the discretion of the senate, had been disturbed by an unusually heated struggle for votes, the emperor restored calm by appointing the three candidates over the required number to legionary commands.[1] He also added to the dignity of the Fathers by ruling that litigants appealing from civil tribunals to the senate must risk the same deposit [2] as those who invoked the sovereign: previously, appeal had been unrestricted and immune from penalty.— At the close of the year, the Roman knight, Vibius Secundus, was condemned on a charge of extortion, brought by the Mauretanians, and banished from Italy: that he contrived to escape the infliction of a heavier sentence was due to the resources of his brother Vibius Crispus.[3]

XXIX. In the consulate of Caesennius Paetus [4] and Petronius Turpilianus,[5] a grave reverse was sustained in Britain; where, as I have mentioned,[6] the legate, A.v.c. 814 = A.D. 61

Juvenal, in some admirable lines (IV. 81–93), is much more indulgent.

[4] For his inglorious career in the East, see XV. 6 sqq.

[5] He vacated his office about March, and succeeded Suetonius in Britain (chap. 39).

[6] XII. 40.

neque Aulus *Didius* [1] legatus, ut memoravi, nisi parta
retinuerat, et successor Veranius modicis excursibus
Siluras populatus, quin ultra bellum proferret, morte
prohibitus est, magna, dum vixit, severitatis fama,
supremis testamenti verbis ambitionis manifestus:
quippe multa in Neronem adulatione addidit sub-
iecturum ei provinciam fuisse, si biennio proximo
vixisset. Sed tum Paulinus Suetonius obtinebat
Britannos, scientia militiae et rumore populi, qui
neminem sine aemulo sinit, Corbulonis concertator,
receptaeque Armeniae decus aequare domitis per-
duellibus cupiens. Igitur Monam insulam, incolis
validam et receptaculum perfugarum, adgredi parat,
navesque fabricatur plano alveo adversus breve et
incertum.[2] Sic pedes; equites vado [3] secuti aut
altiores inter undas adnantes equis tramisere.

XXX. Stabat pro litore diversa acies, densa armis
virisque, intercursantibus feminis; in modum Furi-
arum veste ferali, crinibus deiectis faces praefere-
bant; Druidaeque circum, preces diras sublatis ad
caelum manibus fundentes, novitate aspectus percu-

---

[1] Aulus Didius *Jackson*: havitus *Med.*, A. Didius *Lipsius*,
Didius *Nipperdey*. *But* havitus *is clearly a corruption of the*
praenomen *written in full*.
[2] incertum <fretum> *F. Pauly.*
[3] vado *Med.*[1] : vados *Med.*, vada *J. F. Gronovius, vulg.*

---

[1] II. 56, 74; III. 10–19; XII. 5.—He died within a year
(*Agr.* 14) of his arrival in Britain (58 A.D.), and Suetonius had
thus been in command for two full years before his attack on
Anglesey.
[2] A score of years previously, he had quelled a Mauretanian
rising and penetrated a few miles beyond the Atlas range
(Plin. *H.N.* V. 1, 14). Later, he commanded for Otho against
the Vitellians, but was hardly equal to the occasion—*cunctator*

Aulus Didius, had done nothing but retain the ground already won, while his successor Veranius,[1] after harrying the Silurians in a few raids of no great significance, was prevented by death from carrying his arms further. Famous, during life, for uncompromising independence, in the closing words of his testament he revealed the courtier; for amid a mass of flattery to Nero he added that, could he have lived for the next two years, he would have laid the province at his feet. For the present, however, Britain was in the charge of Suetonius Paulinus, in military skill[2] and in popular report—which allows no man to lack his rival—a formidable competitor to Corbulo, and anxious to equal the laurels of the recovery of Armenia by crushing a national enemy. He prepared accordingly to attack the island of Mona,[3] which had a considerable population of its own, while serving as a haven for refugees; and, in view of the shallow and variable channel, constructed a flotilla of boats with flat bottoms. By this method the infantry crossed; the cavalry, who followed, did so by fording or, in deeper water, by swimming at the side of their horses.

XXX. On the beach stood the adverse array, a serried mass of arms and men, with women flitting between the ranks. In the style of Furies, in robes of deathly black and with dishevelled hair, they brandished their torches; while a circle of Druids, lifting their hands to heaven and showering imprecations, struck the troops with such an awe at the

natura et cui cauta potius consilia cum ratione quam prospera ex casu placerent (Hist. II. 25).

[3] Anglesey.—Paulinus' headquarters must have been at Chester (*Deva*).

THE ANNALS OF TACITUS

lere militem, ut quasi haerentibus membris inmobile
corpus vulneribus praeberent. Dein cohortationibus
ducis et se ipsi stimulantes, ne muliebre et fanaticum
agmen pavescerent, inferunt signa sternuntque
obvios et igni suo involvunt. Praesidium posthac
inpositum victis excisique luci saevis superstitionibus
sacri : nam cruore captivo adolere aras et hominum
fibris consulere deos fas habebant. Haec agenti
Suetonio repentina defectio provinciae nuntiatur.

XXXI. Rex Icenorum Prasutagus, longa opulentia
clarus, Caesarem heredem duasque filias scripserat,
tali obsequio ratus regnumque et domum suam
procul iniuria fore. Quod contra vertit, adeo ut
regnum per centuriones, domus per servos velut
capta vastarentur. Iam primum uxor eius Boudicca [1] verberibus adfecta et filiae stupro violatae
sunt : praecipui quique Icenorum,[2] avitis bonis
exuuntur, et propinqui regis inter mancipia habebantur. Qua contumelia et metu graviorum, quando
in formam provinciae cesserant, rapiunt arma, commotis ad rebellationem Trinobantibus et qui alii
nondum servitio fracti resumere libertatem occultis
coniurationibus pepigerant, acerrimo in veteranos
odio. Quippe in coloniam Camulodunum recens

[1] Boudicca *Haase* (*and Med. in chap.* 37) *:* boodicia.
[2] Icenorum *Haase* : Icenorum quasi cunctam regionem
muneri accepissent *Med.—See below.*

---

[1] The subdued part of the island.   [2] XII. 31 n.
[3] Since Haase the accepted orthography, though preserved
by the Mediceus only in chap. 37.   The familiar " Boadicea "
of the Bipontine and Cowper has no warranty.
[4] In Suffolk and Essex, their capital being Colchester
(*Camulodunum*), the old identification with Maldon being now
abandoned.

extraordinary spectacle that, as though their limbs
were paralysed, they exposed their bodies to wounds
without an attempt at movement. Then, reassured
by their general, and inciting each other never to
flinch before a band of females and fanatics, they
charged behind the standards, cut down all who met
them, and enveloped the enemy in his own flames.
The next step was to install a garrison among the
conquered population, and to demolish the groves
consecrated to their savage cults: for they considered it a pious duty to slake the altars with captive
blood and to consult their deities by means of human
entrails.—While he was thus occupied, the sudden
revolt of the province [1] was announced to Suetonius.

XXXI. The Icenian [2] king Prasutagus, celebrated
for his long prosperity, had named the emperor his
heir, together with his two daughters; an act of
deference which he thought would place his kingdom
and household beyond the risk of injury. The
result was contrary—so much so that his kingdom
was pillaged by centurions, his household by slaves;
as though they had been prizes of war. As a
beginning, his wife Boudicca [3] was subjected to the
lash and his daughters violated: all the chief men of
the Icenians were stripped of their family estates,
and the relatives of the king were treated as slaves.
Impelled by this outrage and the dread of worse to
come—for they had now been reduced to the status
of a province—they flew to arms, and incited to
rebellion the Trinobantes [4] and others, who, not yet
broken by servitude, had entered into a secret and
treasonable compact to resume their independence.
The bitterest animosity was felt against the veterans;
who, fresh from their settlement in the colony of

deducti *quasi cunctam regionem muneri accepissent,*[1]
pellebant domibus, exturbabant agris, captivos, servos
appellando, foventibus inpotentiam veteranorum
militibus similitudine vitae et spe eiusdem licentiae.
Ad hoc templum divo Claudio constitutum quasi arx
aeternae dominationis aspiciebatur, delectique sacerdotes specie religionis omnis fortunas effundebant.
Nec arduum videbatur excindere coloniam nullis
munimentis saeptam; quod ducibus nostris parum
provisum erat, dum amoenitati prius quam usui
consulitur.

XXXII. Inter quae nulla palam causa delapsum
Camuloduni simulacrum Victoriae ac retro conversum, quasi cederet hostibus. Et feminae in furorem
turbatae adesse exitium canebant, externosque[2]
fremitus in curia eorum auditos; consonuisse ululati-
bus theatrum visamque speciem in aestuario Tamesae
subversae coloniae: iam Oceanus cruento aspectu,
dilabente aestu humanorum corporum effigies relictae,
ut Britannis ad spem, ita veteranis ad metum trahebantur. Sed quia procul Suetonius aberat, petivere
a Cato Deciano procuratore auxilium. Ille haud
amplius quam ducentos sine iustis armis misit; et
inerat modica militum manus. Tutela templi freti,

---

[1] ⟨quasi . . . accepissent⟩ *Haase.—See above.*
[2] externosque] nocturnosque *Andresen (cl.* Ov. Met. XV.
797). *Bnt see* D. Cass. LXIII. 1 θροῦς νυκτὸς βαρβαρικός.

---

[1] In his lifetime (Sen. *Apocol.* 8).
[2] The title of the colony was Victrix—*colonia victricensis*
(*C.I.L.* XIV. 3955).

Camulodunum, were acting as though they had received a free gift of the entire country, driving the natives from their homes, ejecting them from their lands,—they styled them " captives " and " slaves," —and abetted in their fury by the troops, with their similar mode of life and their hopes of equal indulgence. More than this, the temple raised to the deified Claudius [1] continually met the view, like the citadel of an eternal tyranny; while the priests, chosen for its service, were bound under the pretext of religion to pour out their fortunes like water. Nor did there seem any great difficulty in the demolition of a colony unprotected by fortifications—a point too little regarded by our commanders, whose thoughts had run more on the agreeable than on the useful.

XXXII. Meanwhile, for no apparent reason, the statue of Victory [2] at Camulodunum fell, with its back turned as if in retreat from the enemy. Women, converted into maniacs by excitement, cried that destruction was at hand and that alien cries had been heard in the invaders' senate-house: the theatre had rung with shrieks, and in the estuary of the Thames had been seen a vision of the ruined colony. Again, that the Ocean had appeared blood-red and that the ebbing tide had left behind it what looked to be human corpses, were indications read by the Britons with hope and by the veterans with corresponding alarm. However, as Suetonius was far away, they applied for help to the procurator Catus Decianus. He sent not more than two hundred men, without their proper weapons: in addition, there was a small body of troops in the town. Relying on the protection of the temple, and hampered

et impedientibus qui occulti rebellionis conscii [1]
consilia turbabant, neque fossam aut vallum prae-
duxerunt, neque motis senibus et feminis iuventus
sola restitit : quasi media pace incauti multitudine
barbarorum circumveniuntur. Et cetera quidem
impetu direpta aut incensa sunt : templum, in quo
se miles conglobaverat, biduo obsessum expugna-
tumque. Et victor Britannus Petilio Ceriali, legato
legionis nonae, in subsidium adventanti obvius fudit
legionem, et quod peditum interfecit : Cerialis cum
equitibus evasit in castra et munimentis defensus est.
Qua clade et odiis provinciae, quam avaritia eius [2] in
bellum egerat, trepidus procurator Catus in Galliam
transiit.

XXXIII. At Suetonius mira constantia medios
inter hostis Londinium perrexit, cognomento quidem

---

[1] [eonscii] *Ernesti (cf.* VI. 36).
[2] avaritia eius *Ritter :* avaritiae.

---

[1] A near relative and trusted lieutenant of Vespasian (*Hist.*
III. 59, etc.); suppressed Civilis' rising (*Hist.* IV. 68 sqq.);
active and successful as legatus of Britain in 71–74 A.D. (*Agr.*
8, 17)   It is in his mouth that Tacitus puts the most famous
of his speeches—the apologia for Roman dominion of *Hist.*
IV. 73 sq.
[2] The legion (*nona Hispana*) was probably stationed at
Lincoln (*Lindum*), and Cerialis—*contemnendis quam cavendis
hostibus melior* (*Hist.* IV. 71)—marched at once by the Ermine
Street for Colchester. Where the Britons encountered him is
uncertain : Wormingford, near Colchester, comes into consideration :
[3] He had revoked and was reclaiming the grants made by
Claudius to the leading tribesmen and formally confirmed by
the Senate (D. Cass. LXII. 2 init., LX. 23 fin.).
[4] The starting point was doubtless Chester. The objective,
it is presumed, was Colchester; the road followed, the Watling

also by covert adherents of the rebellion who inter-
fered with their plans, they neither secured their
position by fosse or rampart nor took steps, by
removing the women and the aged, to leave only
able-bodied men in the place. They were as care-
lessly guarded as if the world was at peace, when
they were enveloped by a great barbarian host.
All else was pillaged or fired in the first onrush:
only the temple, in which the troops had massed
themselves, stood a two days' siege, and was then
carried by storm. Turning to meet Petilius Cerialis,[1]
commander of the ninth legion, who was arriving to
the rescue,[2] the victorious Britons routed the legion
and slaughtered the infantry to a man: Cerialis with
the cavalry escaped to the camp, and found shelter
behind its fortifications. Unnerved by the disaster
and the hatred of the province which his rapacity
had goaded into war,[3] the procurator Catus crossed
to Gaul.

XXXIII. Suetonius, on the other hand, with
remarkable firmness, marched straight through the
midst of the enemy upon London;[4] which, though

Street, which led through London. The probable course of
events seems to have been roughly this:—Suetonius hurried
ahead with his light troops, while the fourteenth legion and
part of the twentieth followed by forced marches: the second
had been summoned to join him, probably at Wroxeter
(*Viroconium*), but its commander Poenius Postumus refused
to leave his own front defenceless against the Silures of S.
Wales. At London, the situation was found to be desperate,
with the rebels in overwhelming force and the ninth legion
virtually exterminated. Suetonius, therefore, fell back along
the Watling Street until he met the legionaries, was forced
to an engagement "somewhere in the Midlands," and
only survived through being allowed to choose his own
ground.

coloniae non insigne, sed copia negotiatorum et
commeatuum maxime celebre. Ibi ambiguus, an
illam sedem bello deligeret, circumspecta infrequentia militis, satisque magnis documentis temeritatem Petilii coercitam, unius oppidi damno servare
universa statuit. Neque fletu et lacrimis auxilium
eius orantium flexus est, quin daret profectionis
signum et comitantis in partem agminis acciperet:
si quos inbellis sexus aut fessa aetas vel loci dulcedo
attinuerat, ab hoste oppressi sunt. Eadem clades
municipio Verulamio fuit, quia barbari omissis
castellis praesidiisque militarium,[1] quod uberrimum
spolianti et defendentibus intutum, laeti praeda et
laborum segnes petebant. Ad septuaginta milia
civium et sociorum iis quae memoravi locis cecidisse
constitit. Neque enim capere aut venundare aliudve
quod belli commercium, sed caedes patibula ignes
cruces, tamquam reddituri supplicium at[2] praerepta
interim ultione, festinabant.

XXXIV. Iam Suetonio quarta decuma legio cum
vexillariis vicensimanis et *e* proximis auxiliares,
decem ferme milia armatorum erant, cum omittere
cunctationem et congredi acie parat. Deligitque
locum artis faucibus et a tergo silva clausum, satis

---

[1] militarium] militaribus *Pichena*, militare horreum *Madvig*.
[2] at *Med.?:* ac *vulg.*

---

[1] Adjoining St. Albans.
[2] The estimate is probably valueless.
[3] There are atrocious details, whatever their worth, in Dio
(LXII. 7 fin.).

not distinguished by the title of colony, was none the
less a busy centre, chiefly through its crowd of
merchants and stores. Once there, he felt some
doubt whether to choose it as a base of operations;
but, on considering the fewness of his troops and the
sufficiently severe lesson which had been read to the
rashness of Petilius, he determined to save the country as a whole at the cost of one town. The laments
and tears of the inhabitants, as they implored his
protection, found him inflexible: he gave the signal
for departure, and embodied in the column those
capable of accompanying the march: all who had
been detained by the disabilities of sex, by the
lassitude of age, or by local attachment, fell into the
hands of the enemy. A similar catastrophe was
reserved for the municipality of Verulamium;[1] as
the natives, with their delight in plunder and their
distaste for exertion, left the forts and garrison-posts
on one side, and made for the point which offered the
richest material for the pillager and was unsafe for
a defending force. It is established that close upon
seventy thousand[2] Roman citizens and allies fell
in the places mentioned. For the enemy neither
took captive nor sold into captivity; there was none
of the other commerce of war; he was hasty with
slaughter and the gibbet, with arson and the cross,[3]
as though his day of reckoning must come, but only
after he had snatched his revenge in the interval.

XXXIV. Suetonius had already the fourteenth
legion, with a detachment of the twentieth and
auxiliaries from the nearest stations, altogether
some ten thousand armed men, when he prepared
to abandon delay and contest a pitched battle. He
chose a position approached by a narrow defile and

cognito nihil hostium nisi in fronte et apertam planitiem esse, sine metu insidiarum. Igitur legionarius frequens ordinibus, levis circum armatura, conglobatus pro cornibus eques adstitit. At Britannorum copiae passim per catervas et turmas exsultabant, quanta non. alias multitudo, et animo adeo feroci,[1] ut coniuges quoque testis victoriae secum traherent plaustrisque inponerent, quae super extremum ambitum campi posuerant.

XXXV. Boudicca curru filias prae se vehens, ut quamque nationem accesserat, solitum quidem Britannis feminarum ductu bellare testabatur, sed tunc non ut tantis maioribus ortam regnum et opes, verum ut unam e vulgo libertatem amissam, confectum verberibus corpus, contrectatam filiarum pudicitiam ulcisci. Eo provectas Romanorum cupidines, ut non corpora, ne senectam quidem aut virginitatem inpollutam relinquant. Adesse tamen deos iustae vindictae: cecidisse legionem, quae proelium ausa sit; ceteros castris occultari aut fugam circumspicere. Ne strepitum quidem et clamorem tot milium, nedum impetus et manus perlaturos: si copias armatorum, si causas belli secum expenderent, vincendum illa acie vel cadendum esse. Id mulieri destinatum: viverent viri et servirent.

---

[1] feroci *Doederlein :* fero.

secured in the rear by a wood, first satisfying himself that there was no trace of an enemy except in his front, and that the plain there was devoid of cover and allowed no suspicion of an ambuscade. The legionaries were posted in serried ranks, the light-armed troops on either side, and the cavalry massed on the extreme wings. The British forces, on the other hand, disposed in bands of foot and horse were moving jubilantly in every direction. They were in unprecedented numbers, and confidence ran so high that they brought even their wives to witness the victory and installed them in waggons, which they had stationed just over the extreme fringe of the plain.

XXXV. Boudicca, mounted in a chariot with her daughters before her, rode up to clan after clan and delivered her protest:—" It was customary, she knew, with Britons to fight under female captaincy; but now she was avenging, not, as a queen of glorious ancestry, her ravished realm and power, but, as a woman of the people, her liberty lost, her body tortured by the lash, the tarnished honour of her daughters. Roman cupidity had progressed so far that not their very persons, not age itself, nor maidenhood, were left unpolluted. Yet Heaven was on the side of their just revenge: one legion, which ventured battle, had perished; the rest were skulking in their camps, or looking around them for a way of escape. They would never face even the din and roar of those many thousands, far less their onslaught and their swords!—If they considered in their own hearts the forces under arms and the motives of the war, on that field they must conquer or fall. Such was the settled purpose of a woman—the men might live and be slaves! "

XXXVI. Ne Suetonius quidem in tanto discrimine silebat. Quamquam confideret virtuti, tamen exhortationes et preces miscebat, ut spernerent sonores barbarorum et inanes minas : plus illic feminarum quam iuventutis aspici. Inbellis inermis cessuros statim, ubi ferrum virtutemque vincentium totiens fusi adgnovissent. Etiam in multis legionibus paucos, qui proelia profligarent : gloriaeque eorum accessurum, quod modica manus universi exercitus famam adipiscerentur. Conferti tantum et pilis emissis, post umbonibus et gladiis stragem caedemque continuarent, praedae inmemores : parta victoria cuncta ipsis cessura. Is ardor verba ducis sequebatur, ita se ad intorquenda pila expedierat vetus miles et multa proeliorum experientia, ut certus eventus Suetonius daret pugnae signum.

XXXVII Ac primum legio gradu inmota et angustias loci pro munimento retinens, postquam *in* propius suggressos [1] hostis certo iactu tela exhauserat, velut cuneo erupit. Idem auxiliarium impetus ; et eques protentis hastis perfringit quod obvium et validum erat. Ceteri terga praebuere, difficili effugio, quia circumiecta vehicula saepserant abitus. Et

[1] <in> propius suggressos *Doederlein :* propius suggressus.

166

XXXVI. Even Suetonius, in this critical moment, broke silence. In spite of his reliance on the courage of the men, he still blended exhortation and entreaty: " They must treat with contempt the noise and empty menaces of the barbarians: in the ranks opposite, more women than soldiers met the eye. Unwarlike and unarmed, they would break immediately, when, taught by so many defeats, they recognized once more the steel and the valour of their conquerors. Even in a number of legions, it was but a few men who decided the fate of battles; and it would be an additional glory that they, a handful of troops, were gathering the laurels of an entire army. Only, keeping their order close, and, when their javelins were discharged, employing shield-boss and sword, let them steadily pile up the dead and forget the thought of plunder: once the victory was gained, all would be their own." Such was the ardour following the general's words—with such alacrity had his veteran troops, with their long experience of battle, prepared themselves in a moment to hurl the pilum—that Suetonius, without a doubt of the issue, gave the signal to engage.

XXXVII. At first, the legionaries stood motionless, keeping to the defile as a natural protection: then, when the closer advance of the enemy had enabled them to exhaust their missiles with certitude of aim, they dashed forward in a wedge-like formation. The auxiliaries charged in the same style; and the cavalry, with lances extended, broke a way through any parties of resolute men whom they encountered. The remainder took to flight, though escape was difficult, as the cordon of waggons had blocked the outlets. The troops gave no quarter

miles ne mulierum quidem neci temperabat, confixaque telis etiam iumenta corporum cumulum auxerant. Clara et antiquis victoriis par ea die laus parta: quippe sunt qui paulo minus quam octoginta milia Britannorum cecidisse tradant, militum quadringentis ferme interfectis nec multo amplius vulneratis. Boudicca vitam veneno finivit. Et Poenius Postumus, praefectus castrorum secundae legionis, cognitis quartadecumanorum vicensimanorumque prosperis rebus, quia pari gloria legionem suam fraudaverat abnueratque contra ritum militiae iussa ducis, se ipse [1] gladio transegit.

XXXVIII. Contractus deinde omnis exercitus sub pellibus habitus est ad reliqua belli perpetranda. Auxitque copias Caesar missis ex Germania duobus legionariorum milibus, octo auxiliarium cohortibus ac mille equitibus, quorum adventu nonani legionario milite suppleti sunt. Cohortes alaeque novis hibernaculis locatae, quodque nationum ambiguum aut adversum fuerat, igni atque ferro vastatum.[2] Sed nihil aeque quam fames adfligebat serendis frugibus incuriosos, et omni aetate ad bellum versa, dum nostros commeatus sibi destinant . . .[3] gentesque praeferoces tardius ad pacem inclinabant, quia Iulius Classicianus, successor Cato missus et Suetonio discors, bonum

[1] ipse *A. Ruperti :* ipsum.
[2] vastatum *Ernesti :* vastatur.
[3] . . . *Nipperdey.*

---

[1] The figures for both sides are equally incredible.

even to the women : the baggage animals themselves
had been speared and added to the pile of bodies.
The glory won in the course of the day was remarkable, and equal to that of our older victories : for, by
some accounts, little less than eighty thousand
Britons fell, at a cost of some four hundred Romans
killed [1] and a not much greater number of wounded.
Boudicca ended her days by poison ; while Poenius
Postumus, camp-prefect of the second legion,
informed of the exploits of the men of the fourteenth
and twentieth, and conscious that he had cheated
his own corps of a share in the honours and had
violated the rules of the service by ignoring the
orders of his commander, ran his sword through his
body.

XXXVIII. The whole army was now concentrated
and kept under canvas, with a view to finishing what
was left of the campaign.   Its strength was increased
by the Caesar, who sent over from Germany two
thousand legionaries, eight cohorts of auxiliaries,
and a thousand cavalry.   Their advent allowed the
gaps in the ninth legion to be filled with regular
troops ; the allied foot and horse were stationed in
new winter quarters ; and the tribes which had
shown themselves dubious or disaffected were
harried with fire and sword.   Nothing, however,
pressed so hard as famine on an enemy who, careless
about the sowing of his crops, had diverted all ages
of the population to military purposes, while marking
out our supplies for his own property. ⟨Still, hatred
of Rome was persistent⟩ ; and the fierce-tempered
clans inclined the more slowly to peace because
Julius Classicianus, who had been sent in succession
to Catus and was not on good terms with Suetonius,

publicum privatis simultatibus impediebat disperse-
ratque novum legatum opperiendum esse, sine
hostili ira et superbia victoris clementer deditis
consulturum. Simul in urbem mandabat, nullum
proeliorum finem exspectarent, nisi succederetur
Suetonio, cuius adversa pravitati ipsius, prospera ad
fortunam referebat.

XXXIX. Igitur ad spectandum Britanniae statum
missus est e libertis Polyclitus, magna Neronis spe
posse auctoritate eius non modo inter legatum pro-
curatoremque concordiam gigni, sed et rebellis
barbarum animos pace conponi. Nec defuit Polyclitus, quo minus ingenti agmine Italiae Galliaeque
gravis, postquam Oceanum transmiserat, militibus
quoque nostris terribilis incederet. Sed hostibus
inrisui fuit, apud quos flagrante etiam tum libertate
nondum cognita libertinorum potentia erat; mira-
banturque, quod dux et exercitus tanti belli confector
servitiis oboedirent. Cuncta tamen ad imperatorem
in mollius relata; detentusque rebus gerundis
Suetonius, quod post*ea* [1] paucas naves in litore
remigiumque in iis amiserat, tamquam durante bello
tradere exercitum Petronio Turpiliano, qui iam
consulatu abierat, iubetur. Is non inritato hoste

---

[1] postea *Halm :* post.

---

[1] See *Hist.* I. 37; II. 95.

was hampering the public welfare by his private animosities, and had circulated a report that it would be well to wait for a new legate; who, lacking the bitterness of an enemy and the arrogance of a conqueror, would show consideration to those who surrendered. At the same time, he reported to Rome that no cessation of fighting need be expected until the supersession of Suetonius, the failures of whom he referred to his own perversity, his successes to the kindness of fortune.

XXXIX. Accordingly Polyclitus,[1] one of the freedmen, was sent to inspect the state of Britain, Nero cherishing high hopes that, through his influence, not only might a reconciliation be effected between the legate and the procurator, but the rebellious temper of the natives be brought to acquiesce in peace. Polyclitus, in fact, whose immense train had been an incubus to Italy and Gaul, did not fail, when once he had crossed the seas, to render his march a terror even to Roman soldiers. To the enemy, on the other hand, he was a subject of derision: with them, the fire of freedom was not yet quenched; they had still to make acquaintance with the power of freedmen; and they wondered that a general and an army who had accounted for such a war should obey a troop of slaves. None the less, everything was reported to the emperor in a more favourable light. Suetonius was retained at the head of affairs; but, when later on he lost a few ships on the beach, and the crews with them, he was ordered, under pretence that the war was still in being, to transfer his army to Petronius Turpilianus, who by now had laid down his consulate. The new-comer abstained from provoking the enemy, was not challenged himself,

171

neque lacessitus honestum pacis nomen segni otio imposuit.

XL. Eodem anno Romae insignia scelera, alterum senatoris, servili alterum audacia, admissa sunt. Domitius Balbus erat praetorius, simul longa senecta, simul orbitate et pecunia insidiis obnoxius. Ei propinquus Valerius Fabianus, capessendis honoribus destinatus, subdidit testamentum ascitis Vinicio Rufino et Terentio Lentino equitibus Romanis. Illi Antonium Primum et Asinium Marcellum socia- verant. Antonius audacia promptus, Marcellus Asinio Pollione proavo clarus neque morum spernen- dus habebatur, nisi quod paupertatem praecipuum malorum credebat. Igitur Fabianus tabulas sociis [1] quos memoravi et aliis minus inlustribus obsignat. Quod apud patres convictum, et Fabianus Antonius- que cum Rufino et Terentio lege Cornelia damnantur. Marcellum memoria maiorum et preces Caesaris poenae magis quam infamiae exemere.

XLI. Perculit is dies Pompeium quoque Aelianum iuvenem quaestorium, tamquam flagitiorum Fabiani gnarum, eique Italia et Hispania, in qua ortus erat, interdictum est. Pari ignominia Valerius Ponticus

[1] sociis *Nipperdey* : iis.

---

[1] The true reason for the supersession of Suetonius was the harshness of his punitive measures (*Agr.* 16) : the sneer at the conciliatory policy of Petronius seems totally unjustified.

[2] M. Antonius Primus, of Toulouse : a name writ large in the *Histories* (II. 86; III.-IV. passim). Restored to the senate— *inter alia belli mala*—in 68 A.D., he received the command of the seventh legion from Galba; was believed to have offered his services to Otho; then bent the whole of his unscrupulous energies to the task of seating Vespasian on the throne.

and conferred on this spiritless inaction the honourable name of peace.[1]

XL. In the same year, two remarkable crimes, one due to a senator, one to the audacity of a slave, were perpetrated at Rome. There was an ex-praetor, Domitius Balbus, who, alike by his great age and by his childlessness and wealth, was exposed to conspiracy. Valerius Fabianus, a relative of his, who was destined for the official career, drew up a false will in his name, in concert with the Roman knights, Vinicius Rufinus and Terentius Lentinus. These, again, had taken Antonius Primus [2] and Asinius Marcellus into the confederacy. Antonius was a ready and daring spirit: Marcellus had the distinction of being the great-grandson of Asinius Pollio, and passed for a man of tolerable character, except for the fact that he regarded poverty as the supreme evil. Fabianus, then, sealed the document, attested by the accomplices I have mentioned and by some others of less note. The fraud was brought home to them in the senate, and Fabianus and Antonius, with Rufinus and Terentius, were sentenced under the Cornelian Law.[3] Marcellus was redeemed from punishment rather than from infamy by the memory of his ancestors and the intercession of the Caesar.

XLI. The same day brought also the fall of a youthful ex-quaestor, Pompeius Aelianus, charged with complicity in the villainies of Fabianus: he was outlawed from Italy and also from Spain, the country of his origin. The same humiliation was inflicted on Valerius Ponticus, because, to save the accused

---

[3] Of Sulla (81 B.C.). It was directed against the various forms of fraudulence in connection with wills.

adficitur, quod reos, ne apud praefectum urbis arguerentur, ad praetorem detulisset, interim specie legum, mox praevaricando ultionem elusurus. Additur senatus consulto, qui talem operam emptitasset vendidissetve, perinde poena teneretur ac publico iudicio calumniae condemnatus.

XLII. Haud multo post praefectum urbis Pedanium Secundum servus ipsius interfecit, seu negata libertate, cui pretium pepigerat, sive amore exoleti incensus et dominum aemulum non tolerans. Ceterum cum vetere ex more familiam omnem, quae sub eodem tecto mansitaverat, ad supplicium agi oporteret, consursu plebis, quae tot innoxios protegebat, usque ad seditionem ventum est senatusque *obsessus*,[1] in quo ipso erant studia nimiam severitatem aspernantium, pluribus nihil mutandum censentibus. Ex quis C. Cassius sententiae loco in hunc modum disseruit:

XLIII. " Saepe numero, patres conscripti, in hoc ordine interfui, cum contra instituta et leges maiorum nova senatus decreta postularentur; neque sum adversatus, non quia dubitarem, super omnibus negotiis melius atque rectius olim provisum et quae

---

[1] <obsessus> Jacob.

[1] For the office, see VI. 10 n. What was the exact scope of the prefect's jurisdiction at this period is not clear, but evidently it was more summary than that of the praetor.

[2] That condemning Ponticus—known later as the *senatus consultum Turpilianum*, after this years' *consul ordinarius*.

[3] Calumniari *est falsa crimina intendere*, praevaricari *vera crimina abscondere*, tergiversari *in universum ab accusatione desistere* (Marcianus in *Dig.* XLVIII. 16). The penalty for the first was, in criminal cases, relegation, exile, or loss of rank, according to circumstances.

[4] Compare XIII. 32 and, for the republican period, Cic. *Ad fam.* IV. 12.   [5] The jurist (XII. 11 n.).

from prosecution before the city prefect,[1] he had
entered the case for trial by the praetor, with the
intention of defeating justice for the moment by a
legal subterfuge, and in the long run by collusion.
A clause was added to the senatorial decree,[2] pro-
viding that any person buying or selling this form of
connivance was to be liable to the same penalty as
if convicted of calumny [3] in a criminal trial.

XLII. Shortly afterwards, the city prefect, Pedanius Secundus, was murdered by one of his own
slaves; either because he had been refused emancipation after Pedanius had agreed to the price, or
because he had contracted a passion for a catamite,
and declined to tolerate the rivalry of his owner.
Be that as it may, when the whole of the domestics
who had been resident under the same roof ought,
in accordance with the old custom,[4] to have been led
to execution, the rapid assembly of the populace,
bent on protecting so many innocent lives, brought
matters to the point of sedition, and the senate
house was besieged. Even within its walls there was
a party which protested against excessive harshness,
though most members held that no change was
advisable. Gaius Cassius,[5] one of the majority, when
his turn to speak arrived, argued in the following
strain:—

XLIII. " I have frequently, Conscript Fathers,
made one of this body, when demands were being
presented for new senatorial decrees in contravention
of the principles and the legislation of our fathers.
And from me there came no opposition—not because
I doubted that, whatever the issue, the provision
made for it in the past was the better conceived and
the more correct, and that, where revision took

converterentur *in* deterius mutari, sed ne nimio
amore antiqui moris studium meum extollere viderer.
Simul quidquid hoc in nobis auctoritatis est, crebris
contradictionibus destruendum non existimabam, ut
maneret integrum, si quando res publica consiliis
eguisset. Quod hodie venit,[1] consulari viro domi
suae interfecto per insidias serviles, quas nemo
prohibuit aut prodidit quamvis nondum concusso
senatus consulto, quod supplicium toti familiae mini-
tabatur. Decernite hercule inpunitatem: ut [2] quem
dignitas sua defendat,[2] cum praefecto urbis non
profuerit ? [3] quem numerus servorum tueatur,[4] cum
Pedanium Secundum quadringenti non protexerint ?
cui familia opem ferat, quae ne in metu quidem
pericula nostra advertit ? An, ut quidam fingere
non erubescunt, iniurias suas ultus est interfector,
quia de paterna pecunia transegerat aut avitum
mancipium detrahebatur ? Pronuntiemus ultro dominum iure caesum videri.

XLIV. Libet argumenta conquirere in eo, quod
sapientioribus deliberatum est ? Sed et si nunc
primum statuendum haberemus, creditisne servum
interficiendi domini animum sumpsisse, ut non vox

---

[1] venit] evenit *G.*
[2] ut . . . defendat *Med.*: at . . . defendet *Puteolanus*
(*Halm, Fisher*).
[3] cum . . . profuerit *Puteolanus :* cui . . . profuit *Med.*
praefecto *Andresen :* praefectus *Med.*, praefectura *Puteolanus.*
[4] tueatur *Nipperdey :* tuebitur.

---

[1] See XIII. 32.
[2] The sarcasm is, of course, levelled at the motives suggested
at the outset of chap. 42. A slave, needless to say, had neither
rights nor wrongs.
[3] The standing formula for a verdict of justifiable homicide,

place, the alteration was for the worse; but because
I had no wish to seem to be exalting my own branch
of study by an overstrained affection for ancient
usage. At the same time, I considered that what
little influence I may possess ought not to be frittered
away in perpetual expressions of dissent: I preferred it to remain intact for an hour when the state
had need of advice. And that hour is come to-day,
when an ex-consul has been done to death in his own
home by the treason of a slave—treason which none
hindered or revealed, though as yet no attacks had
shaken the senatorial decree[1] which threatened the
entire household with execution. By all means
vote impunity! But whom shall his rank defend,
when rank has not availed the prefect of Rome?
Whom shall the number of his slaves protect, when
four hundred could not shield Pedanius Secundus?
Who shall find help in his domestics, when even
fear for themselves cannot make them note our
dangers? Or—as some can feign without a blush
—did the killer avenge his personal wrongs because
the contract touched his patrimony, or because he
was losing a slave from his family establishment?[2]
Let us go the full way and pronounce the owner
justly slain![3]

XLIV. " Is it your pleasure to muster arguments
upon a point which has been considered by wiser
minds than ours? But even if we had now for the
first time to frame a decision, do you believe that a
slave took the resolution of killing his master without

and therefore, in the eyes of Cassius, a crowning absurdity in
such a case : compare Sen. *N.Q.* I. 16, *hunc divitem avarum
. . . divus Augustus indignum vindicta iudicavit, cum a servis
occisus esset, et tantum non pronuntiavit iure caesum videri.*

minax excideret, nihil per temeritatem prolo-
queretur? Sane consilium occultavit, telum inter
ignaros paravit: num excubias transire, cubiculi
fores recludere, lumen inferre, caedem patrare *poterat*[1] omnibus nesciis? Multa sceleris indicia prae-
veniunt: servi si prodant, possumus singuli inter
plures, tuti inter anxios, postremo si pereundum sit,
non inulti inter nocentis agere.[2] Suspecta maioribus nostris fuerunt ingenia servorum, etiam cum
in agris aut domibus isdem nascerentur caritatemque
dominorum statim acciperent. Postquam vero nationes in familiis habemus, quibus diversi ritus,
externa sacra aut nulla sunt, conluviem istam non
nisi metu coercueris. At quidam insontes peribunt.
Nam et ex fuso exercitu cum decumus quisque fusti
feritur, etiam strenui sortiuntur. Habet aliquid ex
iniquo omne magnum exemplum, quod contra
singulos utilitate publica rependitur."

XLV. Sententiae Cassii ut nemo unus contra ire
ausus est, ita dissonae voces respondebant numerum
aut aetatem aut sexum ac plurimorum indubiam
innocentiam miserantium: praevaluit tamen pars,
quae supplicium decernebat. Sed obtemperari non
poterat, conglobata multitudine et saxa ac faces
minante. Tum Caesar populum edicto increpuit

---

[1] <poterat> *Halm.*
[2] *The sentence is obviously illogical, but there is no plausible emendation.*

---

[1] An allusion to the practice of decimation: see III. 21 n.

an ominous phrase escaping him, without one word
uttered in rashness? Assume, however, that he
kept his counsel, that he procured his weapon in an
unsuspecting household. Could he pass the watch,
carry in his light, and perpetrate his murder without
the knowledge of a soul? A crime has many ante-
cedent symptoms. So long as our slaves disclose
them, we may live solitary amid their numbers,
secure amid their anxieties, and finally—if die we
must—certain of our vengeance amid the guilty
crowd. To our ancestors the temper of their slaves
was always suspect, even when they were born on
the same estate or under the same roof, and drew
in affection for their owners with their earliest
breath. But now that our households comprise
nations—with customs the reverse of our own, with
foreign cults or with none, you will never coerce such
a medley of humanity except by terror.—' But some
innocent lives will be lost!'—Even so; for when
every tenth man of the routed army drops beneath
the club,[1] the lot falls on the brave as well. All
great examples carry with them something of injustice—injustice compensated, as against individual
suffering, by the advantage of the community."

XLV. While no one member ventured to contro-
vert the opinion of Cassius, he was answered by a
din of voices, expressing pity for the numbers, the
age, or the sex of the victims, and for the undoubted
innocence of the majority. In spite of all, the party
advocating execution prevailed; but the decision
could not be complied with, as a dense crowd
gathered and threatened to resort to stones and
firebrands. The Caesar then reprimanded the
populace by edict, and lined the whole length of

atque omne iter, quo damnati ad poenam ducebantur, militaribus praesidiis saepsit. Censuerat
Cingonius Varro ut liberti quoque, qui sub eodem
tecto fuissent, Italia deportarentur. Id a principe
prohibitum est, ne mos antiquus, quem misericordia
non minuerat, per saevitiam intenderetur.

XLVI. Damnatus isdem consulibus Tarquitius Priscus repetundarum Bithynis interrogantibus, magno
patrum gaudio, qui accusatum ab eo Statilium Taurum
pro consule ipsius meminerant. Census per Gallias
a Q. Volusio et Sextio Africano Trebellioque Maximo
acti sunt, aemulis inter se per nobilitatem Volusio
atque Africano: Trebellium dum uterque dedignatur,
supra tulere.

XLVII. Eo anno mortem obiit Memmius Regulus,
auctoritate constantia fama, in quantum prae-
umbrante imperatoris fastigio datur, clarus, adeo
ut Nero aeger valetudine, et adulantibus circum, qui
finem imperio adesse dicebant, si quid fato pateretur,
responderit habere subsidium rem publicam. Ro-
gantibus dehinc, in quo potissimum, addiderat in
Memmio Regulo. Vixit tamen post haec Regulus,
quiete defensus et quia nova generis claritudine
neque invidiosis opibus erat. Gymnasium eo anno
dedicatum a Nerone praebitumque oleum equiti ac
senatui Graeca facilitate.

---

[1] *Hist.* I. 6, 37; Plut. *Galb.* 14 sq.
[2] The incident was mentioned at XII. 59.   [3] I. 31 n.
[4] By ignoring him as a competitor they left him free to
rise. He failed completely, however, as governor of Britain
in succession to Turpilianus: see *Hist.* I. 60; II. 65;
Agr. 16.   [5] V. 11 n.
[6] Built for the *Neronia*, in the Campus Martius, adjoining
the Thermae Neronianae.—The oil, of course, was applied to
the body before taking part in an athletic contest. In Athens,
it would have been gratuitously supplied by the γυμνασίαρχοι
as part of their duties.

road, by which the condemned were being marched
to punishment, with detachments of soldiers. Cingonius Varro [1] had moved that even the freedmen,
who had been present under the same roof, should
be deported from Italy. The measure was vetoed
by the emperor, lest gratuitous cruelty should
aggravate a primitive custom which mercy had
failed to temper.

XLVI. Under the same consulate, Tarquitius
Priscus was found guilty of extortion, at the suit of
the Bithynians, much to the joy of the senate, which
remembered his accusation of Statilius Taurus,[2] his
own proconsul. In the Gallic provinces, an assessment [3] was held by Quintus Volusius, Sextius Africanus, and Trebellius Maximus. Between Volusius
and Africanus there subsisted a rivalry due to their
rank : for Trebellius they entertained a common
contempt, which enabled him to surpass them both.[4]

XLVII. The year saw the end of Memmius
Regulus,[5] whose authority, firmness, and character
had earned him the maximum of glory possible in
the shadows cast by imperial greatness. So true
was this that Nero, indisposed and surrounded by
sycophants predicting the dissolution of the empire,
should he go the way of fate, answered that the
nation had a resource. To the further inquiry,
where that resource was specially to be found, he
subjoined : " In Memmius Regulus." Yet Regulus
survived : he was shielded by his quietude of life ;
he sprang from a recently ennobled family ; and his
modest fortune aroused no envy.—In the course of
the year, Nero consecrated a gymnasium,[6] oil being
supplied to the equestrian and senatorial orders—a
Greek form of liberality.

THE ANNALS OF TACITUS

XLVIII. P. Mario L. Afinio[1] consulibus Antistius
praetor, quem in tribunatu plebis licenter egisse
memoravi, probrosa adversus principem carmina
factitavit vulgavitque celebri convivio, dum apud
Ostorium Scapulam epulatur. Exim a Cossutiano
Capitone, qui nuper senatorium ordinem precibus
Tigellini soceri sui receperat, maiestatis delatus est.
Tum primum revocata ea lex, credebaturque haud
perinde exitium Antistio quam imperatori gloriam
quaeri, ut condemnatum[2] a senatu intercessione
tribunicia morti eximeret.[3] Et cum Ostorius nihil
audivisse pro testimonio dixisset, adversis testibus
creditum; censuitque Iunius Marullus consul designatus adimendam reo praeturam necandumque
more maiorum. Ceteris inde adsentientibus, Paetus
Thrasea, multo cum honore Caesaris et acerrime
increpito Antistio, non quidquid nocens reus pati
mereretur, id egregio sub principe et nulla necessitate
obstricto senatui statuendum disseruit: carnificem
et laqueum pridem abolita, et esse poenas legibus
constitutas, quibus sine iudicum saevitia et temporum

---

[1] Afinio *Borghesi :* asinio.
[2] condemnatum *Ritter :* condemnatus.
[3] eximeret] eximeretur *G.*

---

[1] See XIII. 28.
[2] The courageous son of the former governor of Britain
(XII. 31). For his subsequent destruction by Antistius,
see XVI. 14 sq.
[3] XI. 6 n.
[4] The infamous favourite of Nero. The authority for the
vicissitudes of his early days is a well informed scholium on
Juv. I. 155. The salient facts of his public career may be
gleaned from the rest of the Annals : for his suicide under Otho,
and a highly coloured character-sketch, see *Hist.* I. 72.
[5] See I. 73 etc. The law had been abolished in name by
Caligula (D. Cass. LIX. 4); in effect, by Claudius (LX. 3).

XLVIII. In the consulate of Publius Marius and A.V.C. 815 =
A.D. 62
Lucius Afinius, the praetor Antistius, whose licence
of conduct in his plebeian tribuneship I have already
mentioned,[1] composed a number of scandalous verses
on the sovereign, and gave them to the public at
the crowded table of Ostorius Scapula,[2] with whom
he was dining.   He was thereupon accused of treason
by Cossutianus Capito,[3] who, by the intercession of
his father-in-law Tigellinus,[4] had lately recovered his
senatorial rank.   This was the first revival of the
statute;[5] and it was believed that the object sought
was not so much the destruction of Antistius as the
glorification of the emperor, whose tribunician veto
was to snatch him from death when already condemned by the senate.   Although Ostorius had
stated in evidence that he had heard nothing, the
witnesses on the other side were credited; and the
consul designate, Junius Marullus, moved for the
accused to be stripped of his praetorship and executed
in the primitive manner.[6]   The other members were
expressing assent, when Thrasea Paetus, after a large
encomium upon the Caesar and a most vigorous
attack on Antistius, took up the argument:—" It did
not follow that the full penalty which a guilty
prisoner deserved to undergo was the one that ought
to be decided upon, under an excellent emperor
and by a senate not fettered by any sort of compulsion.   The executioner and the noose were forgotten things;[7] and there were punishments established by various laws under which it was possible to
inflict a sentence branding neither the judges with

[6] IV. 30 n.

[7] Garotting was, in theory, the regular method of execution
(cf. III. 50; V. 9): in practice, it was replaced by suicide of the
condemned person.

infamia supplicia decernerentur. Quin in insula publicatis bonis, quo longius sontem vitam traxisset, eo privatim miseriorem et publicae clementiae maximum exemplum futurum.

XLIX. Libertas Thraseae servitium aliorum rupit, et postquam discessionem consul permiserat, pedibus in sententiam eius iere, paucis exceptis, in quibus adulatione promptissimus fuit A. Vitellius, optimum quemque iurgio lacessens et respondenti reticens, ut pavida ingenia solent. At consules perficere decretum senatus non ausi, de consensu scripsere Caesari. Ille inter pudorem et iram cunctatus. postremo rescripsit :—Nulla iniuria provocatum Antistium gravissimas in principem contumelias dixisse ; earum ultionem a patribus postulatam, et pro magnitudine delicti poenam statui par fuisse. Ceterum se, qui severitatem decernentium impediturus fuerit, moderationem non prohibere : statuerent ut vellent, datam et absolvendi licentiam. His atque talibus recitatis et offensione manifesta, non ideo aut consules mutavere relationem aut Thrasea decessit sententia ceterive quae probaverant deseruere, pars, ne principem obiecisse invidiae viderentur, plures

---

[1] The future emperor.

brutality nor the age with infamy. In fact, on an island, with his property confiscated, the longer he dragged out his criminal existence, the deeper would be his personal misery, and he would also furnish a noble example of public clemency."

XLIX. The independence of Thrasea broke through the servility of others, and, on the consul authorizing a division, he was followed in the voting by all but a few dissentients—the most active sycophant in their number being Aulus Vitellius,[1] who levelled his abuse at all men of decency, and, as is the wont of cowardly natures, lapsed into silence when the reply came. The consuls, however, not venturing to complete the senatorial decree in form, wrote to the emperor and stated the opinion of the meeting. He, after some vacillation between shame and anger, finally wrote back that "Antistius, unprovoked by any injury, had given utterance to the most intolerable insults upon the sovereign. For those insults retribution had been demanded from the Fathers; and it would have been reasonable to fix a penalty proportioned to the gravity of the offence. Still, as he had proposed to check undue severity in their sentence, he would not interfere with their moderation; they must decide as they pleased—they had been given liberty even to acquit." These observations, and their like, were read aloud, and the imperial displeasure was evident. The consuls, however, did not change the motion on that account; Thrasea did not waive his proposal; nor did the remaining members desert the cause they had approved; one section, lest it should seem to have placed the emperor in an invidious position; a majority, because there was safety in their numbers;

numero tuti, Thrasea sueta firmitudine animi et ne gloria intercideret.

L. Haud dispari crimine Fabricius Veiento conflictatus est, quod multa et probrosa in patres et sacerdotes composuisset iis libris, quibus nomen codicillorum dederat. Adiciebat Tullius Geminus accusator venditata ab eo munera principis et adipiscendorum honorum ius. Quae causa Neroni fuit suscipiendi iudicii, convictumque Veientonem Italia depulit et libros exuri iussit, conquisitos lectitatosque, donec cum periculo parabantur : mox licentia habendi oblivionem attulit.

LI. Sed gravescentibus in dies publicis malis subsidia minuebantur, concessitque vita Burrus, incertum valetudine an veneno. Valetudo ex eo coniectabatur, quod in se tumescentibus paulatim faucibus et impedito meatu spiritum finiebat. Plures iussu Neronis, quasi remedium adhiberetur, inlitum palatum eius noxio medicamine adseverabant, et Burrum intellecto scelere, cum ad visendum eum princeps venisset, aspectum eius aversatum sciscitanti hactenus respondisse :—" Ego me bene habeo." Civitati grande desiderium eius mansit per memoriam virtutis et successorum alterius segnem innocentiam,

---

[1] A prominent informer under Domitian (*grande et conspicuum nostro quoque tempore monstrum*, Juv. IV. 115), and a favourite even with Nerva (Plin. *Ep.* IV. 22).

[2] His libels were embodied in an imaginary will. For as candour, under the empire, was safest when posthumous, this was a favourite vehicle for attacks upon the great : cf. Luc. *Nigr.* 30, προστιθεὶς ὅτι μίαν φωνὴν Ῥωμαίων παῖδες ἀληθῆ παρ' ὅλον τὸν βίον προΐενται, τὴν ἐν ταῖς διαθήκαις λέγων. See the cases of Fulcinius Trio and Petronius (VI. 38; XVI. 19).

Thrasea, through his usual firmness of temper, and a desire not to let slip the credit he had earned.

L. Fabricius Veiento [1] succumbed to the not dissimilar charge of composing a series of libels on the senate and priests in the books to which he had given the title of his *Will*.[2] The accuser, Tullius Geminus, also maintained that he had consistently sold the imperial bounty and the right to official promotion. This last count decided Nero to take the case into his own hands. He convicted Veiento, relegated him from Italy, and ordered his books to be burned. These, while they were only to be procured at a risk were anxiously sought and widely read: oblivion came when it was permissible to own them.

LI. But, while the evils of the state were growing daily more serious, the resources of the state were dwindling, and Burrus took his leave of life; whether by sickness or by poison may be doubted. Sickness was conjectured from the fact that he ceased to breathe as the result of a gradual swelling of the interior of the throat, and the consequent obstruction of the windpipe. It was more generally asserted that, by Nero's instructions, his palate was smeared with a poisonous drug, ostensibly as a remedial measure, and that Burrus, who had penetrated the crime, on receiving a visit from the emperor, averted his eyes from him, and answered his inquiries with the bare words: "*I* am well."[3] He was regretted deeply and permanently by a country mindful of his virtue, and of his successors—one of them tamely

---

[3] Gronovius cited the anecdote related by Seneca (*Ep.* 24) of Pompey's father-in-law :—*Cum teneri navem suam vidisset ab hostibus, ferro se transverberavit et quaerentibus ubi imperator esset, 'Imperator,' inquit, 'se bene habet.'*

alterius flagrantissima flagitia.[1] Quippe Caesar duos
praetoriis cohortibus imposuerat, Faenium Rufum
ex vulgi favore, quia rem frumentariam sine quaestu
tractabat, Sofonium Tigellinum, veterem inpudicitiam
atque infamiam in eo secutus. Atque illi pro
cognitis moribus fuere, validior Tigellinus in animo
principis et intimis libidinibus adsumptus, prospera
populi et militum fama Rufus, quod apud Neronem
adversum experiebatur.

LII. Mors Burri infregit Senecae potentiam, quia
nec bonis artibus idem virium erat altero velut duce
amoto, et Nero ad deteriores inclinabat. Hi variis
criminationibus Senecam adoriuntur, tamquam in-
gentis et privatum modum evectas opes adhuc
augeret, quodque studia civium in se verteret,
hortorum quoque amoenitate et villarum magnificentia quasi principem supergrederetur. Obicie-
bant etiam eloquentiae laudem uni sibi adsciscere et
carmina crebrius factitare, postquam Neroni amor
eorum venisset. Nam oblectamentis principis palam
iniquum detrectare vim eius equos regentis, inludere
voces,[2] quotiens caneret. Quem ad finem nihil in re
publica clarum fore, quod non ab illo reperiri cre-
datur? Certe finitam Neronis pueritiam et robur

---

[1] flagitia *Orelli :* flagitia . adulteria.
[2] voces] vocem *Muratus.*

---

[1] XIII. 22.

innocent, the other flagrantly criminal. For the Caesar had appointed two commanders to the praetorian cohorts: Faenius Rufus, commended by the favour of the crowd, as he superintended the provisioning of the capital[1] without profit to himself; and Sofonius Tigellinus, in whose case the attractions were the licentiousness of his past and his infamy. Neither belied his known habits: Tigellinus took the firmer hold over the mind of the prince and was made free of his most intimate debauches; Rufus enjoyed an excellent character with the people and the troops, and laboured under that disadvantage in his relations with Nero.

LII. The death of Burrus shook the position of Seneca: for not only had the cause of decency lost in power by the removal of one of its two champions, but Nero was inclining to worse counsellors. These brought a variety of charges to the assault on Seneca, " who was still augmenting that enormous wealth which had transcended the limits of a private fortune; who was perverting the affection of his countrymen to himself; who even in the charm of his pleasure-grounds and the splendour of his villas appeared bent on surpassing the sovereign. The honours of eloquence," so the count proceeded, " he arrogated to himself alone; and he was writing verse more frequently, now that Nero had developed an affection for the art. For of the emperor's amusements in general he was an openly captious critic, disparaging his powers when he drove his horses and deriding his notes when he sang! How long was nothing to be counted brilliant in Rome, unless it was believed the invention of Seneca? Beyond a doubt, Nero's boyhood was finished, and the full vigour of youth

iuventae adesse: exueret magistrum, satis amplis doctoribus instructus maioribus suis.

LIII. At Seneca criminantium non ignarus, prodentibus iis, quibus aliqua honesti cura, et familiaritatem eius magis aspernante Caesare, tempus sermoni orat et accepto ita incipit: " Quartus decumus annus est, Caesar, ex quo spei tuae admotus sum, octavus, ut imperium obtines: medio temporis tantum honorum atque opum in me cumulasti, ut nihil felicitati meae desit nisi moderatio eius. Utar magnis exemplis, nec meae fortunae, sed tuae. Abavus tuus Augustus M. Agrippae Mytilenense secretum, C. Maecenati urbe in ipsa velut peregrinum otium permisit; quorum alter bellorum socius, alter Romae pluribus laboribus iactatus ampla quidem, sed pro ingentibus meritis, praemia acceperant. Ego quid aliud munificentiae *tuae* adhibere potui quam studia, ut sic dixerim, in umbra educata, et quibus claritudo venit, quod iuventae tuae rudimentis adfuisse videor, grande huius rei pretium. At tu gratiam inmensam, innumeram pecuniam circumdedisti, adeo ut plerumque intra me ipse volvam: egone, equestri et

---

[1] *Desideravit enim* (Augustus) *nonnunquam* . . . *et M. Agrippae patientiam et Maecenatis taciturnitatem, cum ille ex levi rigoris suspicione, et quod Marcellus sibi anteferretur, Mytilenas se, relictis omnibus, contulisset* (23 B.C.); *hic secretum de comperta Murenae coniuratione* (23 or 22 B.C.) *uxori Terentiae* (sister of Murena) *prodidisset* (Suet. *Aug.* 66).

had arrived: let him discharge his pedagogue—
he had a sufficiently distinguished staff of teachers
in his own ancestors."

LIII. Seneca was aware of his maligners: they
were revealed from the quarters where there was
some little regard for honour, and the Caesar's
avoidance of his intimacy was becoming marked.
He therefore asked to have a time fixed for an interview; it was granted, and he began as follows:—
"It is the fourteenth year, Caesar, since I was
associated with your hopeful youth, the eighth that
you have held the empire: in the time between,
you have heaped upon me so much of honour and of
wealth that all that is lacking to complete my
happiness is discretion in its use. I shall appeal
to great precedents, and I shall draw them not from
my rank but from yours. Augustus, the grandfather
of your grandfather, conceded to Marcus Agrippa
the privacy of Mytilene, and to Gaius Maecenas,
within the capital itself, something tantamount
to retirement abroad.[1] One had been the partner
of his wars, the other had been harassed by more
numerous labours at Rome, and each had received
his reward—a magnificent reward, it is true, but
proportioned to immense deserts. For myself,
what incentive to your generosity have I been able
to apply except some bookish acquirements, cultivated, I might say, in the shadows of the cloister?
Acquirements to which fame has come because I am
thought to have lent a helping hand in your own
first youthful efforts—a wage that overpays the
service! But *you* have invested me with measureless
influence, with countless riches; so that often I put
the question to myself:—' Is it I, born in the station

provinciali loco ortus, proceribus civitatis adnumeror?
Inter nobiles et longa decora praeferentes novitas
mea enituit? Ubi est animus ille modicis contentus?
Talis hortos exstruit et per haec suburbana incedit et
tantis agrorum spatiis, tam lato faenore exuberat?
una defensio occurrit, quod muneribus tuis obniti
non debui.

LIV. Sed uterque mensuram inplevimus, et *tu*
quantum princeps tribuere amico posset, et ego
quantum amicus a principe accipere: cetera invidiam
augent. Quae quidem, ut omnia mortalia, infra
tuam magnitudinem iacet, sed mihi incumbit, mihi
subveniendum est. Quo modo in militia aut via
fessus adminiculum orarem, ita in hoc itinere vitae
senex et levissimis quoque curis inpar, cum opes
meas ultra sustinere non possim, praesidium peto.
Iube rem [1] per [2] procuratores tuos administrari, ın
tuam fortunam recipi. Nec me in paupertatem ipse
detrudam, sed traditis quorum fulgore praestringor,
quod temporis hortorum aut villarum curae seponitur,
in animum revocabo. Superest tibi robur et tot per
annos visum *summi* [3] fastigii regimen: possumus
seniores amici quietem reposcere.[4] Hoc quoque in
tuam gloriam cedet, eos ad summa vexisse,[5] qui et
modica tolerarent."

LV. Ad quae Nero sic ferme respondit: " Quod
meditatae orationi tuae statim occurram, id primum

[1] iube rem *Baiter* (iube rem meam *Doederlein*): iubere
Med.[1], iuvere *Med.?*
[2] per] *Added by Med.*[2]
[3] <summi> *Halm. No emendation is entirely satisfactory.*
[4] reposcere *Halm:* respondere.
[5] vexisse] evexisse *Heinsius.*

---

[1] The family came from Cordova.

of a simple knight and a provincial,[1] who am numbered
with the magnates of the realm? Among these
nobles, wearing their long-descended glories, has my
novel name swum into ken? Where is that spirit
which found contentment in mediocrity? Building
these terraced gardens?—Pacing these suburban
mansions?—Luxuriating in these broad acres, these
world-wide investments?'—A single defence sug-
gests itself—that I had not the right to obstruct
your bounty.

LIV. " But we have both filled up the measure:
you, of what a prince may give to his friend; and I,
of what a friend may take from his prince. All
beyond breeds envy! True, envy, like everything
mortal, lies far beneath your greatness; but by me
the burden is felt—to me a relief is necessary. As I
should pray for support in warfare, or when wearied
by the road, so in this journey of life, an old man and
unequal to the lightest of cares, I ask for succour:
for I can bear my riches no further. Order my
estates to be administered by your procurators,
to be embodied in your fortune. Not that by my
own action I shall reduce myself to poverty: rather,
I shall resign the glitter of wealth which dazzles me,
and recall to the service of the mind those hours
which are now set apart to the care of my gardens
or my villas. You have vigour to spare; you have
watched for years the methods by which supreme
power is wielded: we, your older friends, may demand our rest. This, too, shall redound to your
glory—that you raised to the highest places men who
could also accept the lowly."

LV. Nero's reply, in effect, was this:—" If I am
able to meet your studied eloquence with an im-

tui muneris habeo, qui me non tantum praevisa, sed subita expedire docuisti. Abavus meus Augustus Agrippae et Maecenati usurpare otium post labores concessit, sed in ea ipse aetate, cuius auctoritas tueretur quidquid illud et qualecumque tribuisset; ac tamen neutrum datis a se praemiis exuit. Bello et periculis meruerant; in iis enim iuventa Augusti versata est. Nec mihi tela et manus tuae defuissent in armis agenti: sed quod praesens condicio poscebat, ratione consilio praeceptis pueritiam, dein iuventam meam fovisti. Et tua quidem erga me munera, dum vita suppetet, aeterna erunt: quae a me habes, horti et faenus et villae, casibus obnoxia sunt. Ac licet multa videantur, plerique haudquaquam artibus tuis pares plura tenuerunt. Pudet referre libertinos, qui ditiores spectantur. Unde etiam mihi rubori est, quod praecipuus caritate nondum omnis fortuna antecellis; *nisi forte aut te Vitellio ter consuli aut me Claudio postponis, et quantum Volusio longa parsimonia quaesivit, tantum in te mea liberalitas explere non potest.*[1]

LVI. Verum et tibi valida aetas rebusque et fructui rerum sufficiens, et nos prima imperii spatia ingredimur. Quin, si qua in parte lubricum adule-

---

[1] ⟨nisi forte . . . non potest⟩ *Spengel, Nipperdey. In the Mediceus the words follow* ingredimur *below. Haase preferred to place them after* tenuerunt *above.*

---

[1] XI. 2 n., etc.   [2] XIII. 30 fin.

mediate answer, that is the first part of my debt to you, who have taught me how to express my thought not merely after premeditation but on the spur of the moment. Augustus, the grandfather of my grandfather, allowed Agrippa and Maecenas to rest after their labours, but had himself reached an age, the authority of which could justify whatever boon, and of whatever character, he had bestowed upon them. And even so he stripped neither of the rewards conferred by himself. It was in battle and jeopardy they had earned them, for such were the scenes in which the youth of Augustus moved; and, had my own days been spent in arms, your weapons and your hand would not have failed me; but you did what the actual case demanded, and fostered first my boyhood, then my youth, with reason, advice, and precept. And your gifts to me will be imperishable, so long as life may last; but mine to you—gardens, capital, and villas—are vulnerable to accident. They may appear many; but numbers of men, not comparable to you in character have held more. Shame forbids me to mention the freedmen who flaunt a wealth greater than yours! And hence I even blush that you, who have the first place in my love, do not as yet excel all in fortune. Or is it, by chance, the case that you deem either Seneca lower than Vitellius,[1] who held his three consulates, or Nero lower than Claudius, and that the wealth which years of parsimony won for Volusius[2] is incapable of being attained by my own generosity to you?

LVI. "On the contrary, not only is yours a vigorous age, adequate to affairs and to their rewards, but I myself am but entering the first stages of my sovereignty. Why not recall the uncertain steps of

scentiae nostrae declinat, revocas ornatumque robur
subsidio inpensius regis? Non tua moderatio, si
reddideris pecuniam, nec quies, si reliqueris principem, sed mea avaritia, meae crudelitatis metus in
ore omnium versabitur. Quod si maxime conti-
nentia tua laudetur, non tamen sapienti viro decorum
fuerit, unde amico infamiam paret, inde gloriam sibi
recipere." His adicit complexum et oscula, factus
natura et consuetudine exercitus velare odium fallacibus blanditiis. Seneca, qui finis omnium cum
dominante sermonum, gratis agit: sed instituta
prioris potentiae commutat, prohibet coetus salutantium, vitat comitantis, rarus per urbem, quasi
valetudine infensa aut sapientiae studiis domi
adtineretur.

LVII. Perculso Seneca promptum fuit Rufum Faenium inminuere Agrippinae amicitiam in eo crimi-
nantibus. Validiorque in dies Tigellinus et malas
artis, quibus solis pollebat, gratiores ratus, si principem societate scelerum obstringeret, metus eius
rimatur; conpertoque Plautum et Sullam maxime
timeri, Plautum in Asiam, Sullam in Galliam Narbonensem nuper amotos, nobilitatem eorum et
propinquos huic Orientis, illi Germaniae exercitus
commemorat. Non se, ut Burrum, diversas spes,
sed solam incolumitatem Neronis spectare; cui

---

[1] A reminiscence of Sen. *De ira*, II. 33 (for the famous *odisse
quem laeseris* of *Agr.* 42 is from the same source) :—*Notissima
vox eius qui in cultu regum consenuerat : cum illum quidam
interrogaret quomodo rarissimam rem in aula consecutus esset,
senectutem, 'Iniurias,' inquit, 'accipiendo et gratias agendo.'*

my youth, if here and there they slip, and even more zealously guide and support the manhood which owes its pride to you. Not your moderation, if you give back your riches; not your retirement, if you abandon your prince; but *my* avarice, and the terrors of *my* cruelty, will be upon all men's lips. And, however much your abnegation may be praised, it will still be unworthy of a sage to derive credit from an act which sullies the fair fame of a friend." He followed his words with an embrace and kisses— nature had fashioned him and use had trained him to veil his hatred under insidious caresses. Seneca— such is the end of all dialogues with an autocrat— expressed his gratitude:[1] but he changed the established routine of his former power, banished the crowds from his antechambers, shunned his attendants, and appeared in the city with a rareness ascribed to his detention at home by adverse health or philosophic studies.

LVII. With Seneca brought low, it was a simple matter to undermine Faenius Rufus, the charge in his case being friendship with Agrippina. Tigellinus, too, growing stronger with every day, and convinced that the mischievous arts, which were his one source of power, would be all the more acceptable, could he bind the emperor to himself by a partnership in crime, probed his fears, and, discovering the main objects of his alarm to be Plautus and Sulla—both lately removed, the former to Asia, the latter to Narbonese Gaul—began to draw attention to their distinguished lineage and their nearness, respectively, to the armies of the East and of Germany. " Unlike Burrus," he said, " he had not in view two irreconcilable hopes, but purely the safety of Nero. In the capital, where

caveri utcumque ab urbanis insidiis praesenti opera : [1]
longinquos motus quonam modo comprimi posse ?
Erectas Gallias ad nomen dictatorium, nec minus
suspensos Asiae populos claritudine avi Drusi.
Sullam inopem, unde praecipuam audaciam, et simulatorem segnitiae, dum temeritati locum reperiret.
Plautum magnis opibus ne fingere quidem cupidinem
otii, sed veterum Romanorum imitamenta praeferre,
adsumpta etiam Stoicorum adrogantia sectaque,
quae turbidos et negotiorum adpetentis faciat.
Nec ultra mora. Sulla sexto die pervectis Massiliam
percussoribus ante metum et rumorem interficitur,
cum epulandi causa discumberet. Relatum [2] caput
eius inlusit Nero tamquam praematura canitie
deforme.

LVIII. Plauto parari necem non perinde occultum
fuit, quia pluribus salus eius curabatur, et spatium
itineris ac maris tempusque interiectum moverat
famam ; vulgoque fingebant petitum ab eo Corbulonem, magnis tum exercitibus praesidentem et, clari
atque insontes *si* [3] interficerentur, praecipuum ad pericula. Quin et Asiam favore iuvenis arma cepisse, nec
milites ad scelus missos aut numero validos aut
animo promptos, postquam iussa efficere nequiverint,
ad spes novas transisse. Vana haec more famae

---

[1] praesenti opera *Lipsius* : praesentiora.
[2] relatum (*Fisher*) : prelatum *Med.* ("*linea per* p *ducta* "),
perlatum *Agricola, vulg.*
[3] <si> *Bezzenberger*.

---

[1] Plautus (XIII. 19 n.) was a son of Drusus' daughter
Julia ; Sulla (XII. 52 n.), a descendant of the dictator.
[2] Throughout the period from Nero to Domitian, Roman
stoicism was, on the whole, definitely hostile to the empire.
Other prominent members of the school to perish in this reign
were Seneca, Lucan, Barea Soranus, and Thrasea Paetus.

he could work on the spot, the imperial security was more or less provided for; but how were outbreaks at a distance to be stifled? Gaul was alert at the sound of the Dictator's name; and equally the peoples of Asia were unbalanced by the glory of such a grandsire as Drusus.[1] Sulla was indigent, therefore greatly daring, and wore the mask of lethargy only till he could find an occasion for temerity. Plautus, with his great fortune, did not even affect a desire for peace, but, not content to parade his mimicries of the ancient Romans, had taken upon himself the Stoic arrogance and the mantle of a sect which inculcated sedition and an appetite for politics." [2] There was no further delay. On the sixth day follow-ing, the slayers had made the crossing to Massilia, and Sulla, who had taken his place at the dinner-table, was despatched before a whisper of alarm had reached him. The head was carried back to Rome, where the premature grey hairs disfiguring it provoked the merriment of Nero.

LVIII. That the murder of Plautus was being arranged was a secret less excellently kept; for the number of persons interested in his safety was larger; while the length of the journey by land and sea, and the interval of time, had set report at work. It was a general story that he had made his way to Corbulo, then at the head of large armies, and should there be a killing of the famous and the innocent, especially exposed to danger. More than this, Asia had taken arms in sympathy with the youth, and the soldiers sent on the criminal errand, not too strong in numbers and not too enthusiastic at heart, after proving unable to carry out their orders, had passed over to the cause of revolution. These figments, in the

credentium otio augebantur; ceterum libertus
Plauti celeritate ventorum praevenit centurionem et
mandata L. Antistii soceri attulit :—Effugeret segnem
mortem, dum suffugium esset [1] : magni nominis
miseratione reperturum bonos, consociaturum au-
daces : nullum interim subsidium aspernandum.
Si sexaginta milites (tot enim adveniebant) propu-
lisset, dum refertur nuntius Neroni, dum manus alia
permeat, multa secutura, quae adusque bellum
evalescerent. Denique aut salutem tali consilio
quaeri, aut nihil gravius audenti quam ignavo
patiendum esse.

LIX. Sed Plautum ea non movere sive nullam
opem providebat inermis atque exul, seu taedio am-
biguae spei, an amore coniugis et liberorum, quibus
placabiliorem fore principem rebatur nulla sollicitudine turbatum. Sunt qui alios a socero nuntios venisse
ferant, tamquam nihil atrox immineret; doctoresque
sapientiae, Coeranum Graeci, Musonium Tusci
generis, constantiam opperiendae mortis pro incerta
et trepida vita suasisse. Repertus est certe per
medium diei nudus exercitando corpori. Talem eum
centurio trucidavit coram Pelagone spadone, quem

---

[1] dum . . . esset *Andresen* : otium . . . et.

---

[1] XIII. 11; XVI. 10.
[2] Only known otherwise from a couple of words in the elder
Pliny's *index auctorum* to his second book.
[3] C. Musonius Rufus, one of the great names of Stoicism;
born at Vulsinii in Etruria of an equestrian family; teacher of
Epictetus while he was still a slave (*Diss.* I. 9, 29); banished to
Gyara as privy to the Pisonian conspiracy (XV. 71; Philostr.
V.A. VII. 16): returned after the death of Nero (*Hist.* III. 81;
IV. 10, 40); specially exempted in the banishment of philo-

manner of all rumours, were amplified by indolent
credulity; in reality, a freedman of Plautus, with the
help of quick winds, outstripped the centurion, and
carried his patron instructions from his father-in-law,
Lucius Antistius:[1]—" He was to escape a coward's
death, while a refuge was still open. Compassion
for his great name would win him the support of the
good, the alliance of the bold; in the meantime, no
resource should be disdained. If he repelled sixty
soldiers " (the number arriving), " then in the
interval—while the news was travelling back to
Nero—while another force was moving to the scene
—there would be a train of events which might
develop into war. In fine, either he saved his life
by this course or hardihood would cost him no dearer
than timidity."

LIX. All this, however, left Plautus unmoved.
Either, exiled and unarmed, he foresaw no help;
or he had wearied of hope and its incertitudes; or
possibly the cause was affection for his wife and children, to whom he supposed the emperor would prove
more placable if no alarms had disturbed his equani-
mity. There are those who state that fresh couriers
had arrived from his father-in-law with news that
no drastic measures were pending, while his teachers
of philosophy—Coeranus[2] and Musonius,[3] Greek and
Tuscan respectively by origin—had advised him to
have the courage to await death, in preference to
an uncertain and harassed life. At all events,
he was found in the early afternoon, stripped for
bodily exercise. In that condition he was cut down
by the centurion, under the eyes of the eunuch

sophers under Vespasian (D. Cass. LXVI. 13). Extensive
fragments of his works survive, principally in Stobaeus.

THE ANNALS OF TACITUS

Nero centurioni et manipulo, quasi satellitibus ministrum regium, praeposuerat. Caput interfecti relatum; cuius aspectu (ipsa principis verba referam) " Cur," inquit, " Nero . . .? [1] " et posito metu nuptias Poppaeae ob eius modi terrores dilatas maturare parat Octaviamque coniugem amoliri, quamvis modeste ageret, nomine patris et studiis populi gravem. Sed ad senatum litteras misit de caede Sullae Plautique haud confessus, verum utriusque turbidum ingenium esse, et sibi incolumitatem rei publicae magna cura haberi. Decretae eo nomine supplicationes, utque Sulla et Plautus senatu moverentur, gravioribus iam [2] ludibriis quam malis.

LX. Igitur accepto patrum consulto, postquam cuncta scelerum suorum pro egregiis accipi videt, exturbat Octaviam, sterilem dictitans; exim Poppaeae coniungitur. Ea diu paelex et adulteri Neronis, mox mariti potens, quendam ex ministris Octaviae impulit servilem ei amorem obicere. Destinaturque reus cognomento Eucaerus, natione Alexandrinus, canere tibiis perdoctus.[3] Actae ob id de ancillis quaestiones, et vi tormentorum victis quibusdam, ut falsa adnuerent, plures perstitere

---

[1] . . . *Walther. Halm supplied:*—⟨hominem nasutum timuisti ?⟩.

[2] iam *Freinsheim : tam Med.*, tamen *G.*

[3] tibiis perdoctus *Jackson :* per tybias doctus *Med.*, tibiis doctus *G. vulg.*

---

[1] Halm's supplement is suggested by Dio (LXII. 14):— " Οὐκ ᾔδειν, ἔφη, ὅτι μεγάλην ῥῖνα εἶχεν," ὥσπερ φεισάμενος ἂν αὐτοῦ εἰ τοῦτο προηπίστατο.

[2] They had the reputation of being περὶ αὐλοὺς μουσικώτατοι (Ath. 176 F. init.).

Pelago, placed by Nero in charge of the centurion and his detachment like a king's minion over his satellites. The head of the victim was carried back to Rome; and at sight of it the prince exclaimed (I shall give the imperial words exactly):—" Nero, ⟨why did you fear a man with such a nose?⟩ " [1] And laying aside his anxieties, he prepared to accelerate the marriage with Poppaea—till then postponed through suchlike terrors—and also to remove his wife Octavia; who, unassuming as her behaviour might be, was intolerable as the daughter of her father and the favourite of the people. Yet he sent a letter to the Senate, not confessing the execution of Sulla and Plautus, but observing that both were turbulent spirits and that he was watching with extreme care over the safety of the commonwealth. On that ground, a national thanksgiving was voted, together with the expulsion of Sulla and Plautus from the senate—an insulting mockery now more deadly than the evils inflicted on them.

LX. On the reception, therefore, of the senatorial decree, since it was evident that his crimes each and all passed muster as eminent virtues, he ejected Octavia on the pretext of sterility, then consummated his union with Poppaea. Long the paramour of Nero, and dominating him first as an adulterer, then as a husband, she incited one of the domestics of Octavia to accuse her of a love affair with a slave: the part of defendant was assigned to a person named Eucaerus; a native of Alexandria,[2] and an expert performer on the flute. Her waiting-maids, in pursuance of the scheme, were examined under torture; and, although a few were forced by their agony into making groundless admissions, the

sanctitatem dominae tueri; ex quibus una instanti
Tigellino castiora esse muliebria Octaviae respondit
quam os eius. Movetur tamen primo civilis discidii
specie domumque Burri, praedia Plauti, infausta dona
accipit: mox in Campaniam pulsa est addita militari
custodia. Inde crebri questus nec occulti per
vulgum, cui minor sapientia *et* ex mediocritate fortunae pauciora pericula sunt. His . . .[1] tamquam [2]
Nero paenitentia flagitii, coniugem revocarit [2]
Octaviam.

LXI. Exim laeti Capitolium scandunt deosque
tandem venerantur. Effigies Poppaeae proruunt,
Octaviae imagines gestant umeris, spargunt floribus
foroque ac templis statuunt. Itur etiam in principis
laudes strepitu [3] venerantium. Iamque et Palatium
multitudine et clamoribus complebant, cum emissi
militum globi verberibus et intento ferro turbatos
disiecere. Mutataque quae per seditionem verte-
rant, et Poppaeae honos repositus est. Quae semper
odio, tum et metu atrox, ne aut vulgi acrior vis
ingrueret aut Nero inclinatione populi mutaretur,
provoluta genibus eius, non eo loci res suas agi,[4]
ut de matrimonio certet, quamquam id sibi vita
potius, sed vitam ipsam in extremum adductam a

---

[1] . . . *Nipperdey.*
[2] tamquam . . . revocarit *Nipperdey* : quamquam . . .
revocavit.
[3] strepitu *Andresen* : repetitum.
[4] agi] ait *Bezzenberger.*

greater number steadfastly maintained the honour
of their mistress, one of them retorting under pressure
from Tigellinus that Octavia's body was chaster
than his own mouth. She was removed, however,
first under colour of a civil divorce, and received—
two ominous gifts—the mansion of Burrus and the
estates of Plautus. A little later, she was banished
to Campania and put under military supervision.
The measure led to general and undisguised protests
from the common people, endowed with less discretion than their superiors, and—thanks to their
humble station—faced by fewer perils. ⟨Then came
a rumour⟩ that Nero had repented of his outrage
and recalled Octavia to his side.

LXI. At once exulting crowds scaled the Capitol,
and Heaven at last found itself blessed. They
hurled down the effigies of Poppaea, they carried
the statues of Octavia shoulder-high, strewed them
with flowers, upraised them in the forum and the
temples. Even the emperor's praises were essayed
with vociferous loyalty. Already they were filling
the Palace itself with their numbers and their cheers,
when bands of soldiers emerged and scattered them
in disorder with whipcuts and levelled weapons.
All the changes effected by the outbreak were
rectified, and the honours of Poppaea were reinstated. She herself, always cruel in her hatreds,
and now rendered more so by her fear that either
the violence of the multitude might break out in a
fiercer storm or Nero follow the trend of popular
feeling, threw herself at his knees:— " Her affairs,"
she said, " were not in a position in which she could
fight for her marriage, though it was dearer to her
than life: that life itself had been brought to the

clientelis et servitiis Octaviae, quae plebis sibi
nomen indiderint, ea in pace ausi, quae vix bello
evenirent. Arma illa adversus principem sumpta;
ducem tantum defuisse, qui motis rebus facile
reperiretur, omitteret modo Campaniam et in urbem
ipsa [1] pergeret, ad cuius nutum absentis tumultus
cierentur. Quod alioquin suum delictum? Quam
cuiusquam offensionem? An quia veram progeniem
penatibus Caesarum datura sit? Malle populum
Romanum tibicinis Aegyptii subolem imperatorio
fastigio induci? Denique, si id rebus conducat,
libens quam coactus acciret dominam, vel consuleret
securitati. Iusta ultione et modicis remediis primos
motus consedisse: at si desperent uxorem Neronis
fore Octaviam, illi maritum daturos.

LXII. Varius sermo et ad metum atque iram
accommodatus terruit simul audientem et accendit.
Sed parum valebat suspicio in servo et quaestionibus
ancillarum elusa erat. Ergo confessionem alicuius
quaeri placet, cui rerum quoque novarum crimen
adfingeretur. Et visus idoneus maternae necis
patrator Anicetus, classi apud Misenum, ut memoravi,
praefectus, levi post admissum scelus gratia, dein

---

[1] ipsa *Boetticher* : ipsam.

---

[1] Chap. 3.

verge of destruction by those retainers and slaves of
Octavia who had conferred on themselves the name of
the people and dared in peace what would scarcely
happen in war. Those arms had been lifted against
the sovereign; only a leader had been lacking, and,
once the movement had begun, a leader was easily
come by,—the one thing necessary was an excursion
from Campania, a personal visit to the capital by
her whose distant nod evoked the storm! And
apart from this, what was Poppaea's transgression?
In what had she offended anyone? Or was the
reason that she was on the point of giving an authentic heir to the hearth of the Caesars? Did the
Roman nation prefer the progeny of an Egyptian
flute-player to be introduced to the imperial throne?
—In brief, if policy so demanded, then as an act of
grace, but not of compulsion, let him send for the
lady who owned him—or else take thought for his
security! A deserved castigation and lenient remedies had allayed the first commotion; but let the
mob once lose hope of seeing Octavia Nero's wife
and they would soon provide her with a husband!"

LXII. Her varied arguments, with their calculated
appeal to fear and to anger, at once terrified and
incensed the listener. But suspicion resting on a
slave had little force; and it had been nullified by
the examinations of the waiting-women. It was
therefore decided to procure a confession from some
person to whom there could also be imputed a
false charge of contemplated revolution. Anicetus,
perpetrator of the matricide, was thought suitable.
Prefect, as I have mentioned,[1] of the squadron at
Misenum, he had, after the commission of his
murder, experienced some trivial favour, afterwards

graviore odio, quia malorum facinorum ministri
quasi exprobrantes aspiciuntur. Igitur accitum
eum Caesar operae prioris admonet : solum incolumitati principis adversus insidiantem matrem sub-
venisse ; locum haud minoris gratiae instare, si
coniugem infensam depelleret. Nec manu aut telo
opus : fateretur Octaviae adulterium. Occulta
quidem ad praesens, sed magna ei praemia et secessus
amoenos promittit, vel, si negavisset, necem intentat.
Ille insita vaecordia et facilitate priorum flagitiorum,
plura etiam quam iussum erat fingit fateturque apud
amicos, quos velut consilio adhibuerat princeps.
Tum in Sardiniam pellitur, ubi non inops exilium
toleravit et fato obiit.

LXIII. At Nero praefectum in spem sociandae
classis corruptum, et incusatae paulo ante sterilitatis
oblitus, abactos partus conscientia libidinum, eaque
sibi conperta edicto memorat insulaque Pandateria
Octaviam claudit. Non alia exul visentium oculos
maiore misericordia adfecit. Meminerant adhuc
quidam Agrippinae a Tiberio, recentior Iuliae memoria obversabatur a Claudio pulsae : sed illis robur
aetatis adfuerat ; laeta aliqua viderant et praesentem saevitiam melioris olim fortunae recordatione

---

[1] Selected, it is to be feared, as a notoriously unhealthy
island (cf. II. 85 fin.).

[2] I. 53 n.

[3] The wife of Germanicus. Book V. breaks short just before
her banishment to Pandateria (29 A.D.).

[4] Julia Livilla, youngest child of Germanicus and Agrippina,
born in 18 A.D.; exiled by her brother Caligula in 37 A.D.;
recalled by Claudius at the outset of his reign, then, at the
instigation of Messalina, banished again on a charge of adultery
with Seneca, and shortly afterwards put to death (D. Cass.
LX. 4, 8).

[5] The words are applicable only to Agrippina.

replaced by a more serious dislike, since the instruments of crime are counted a visible reproach. He was summoned accordingly, and the Caesar reminded him of his earlier service:— " Singly he had ensured the emperor's safety in opposition to a treacherous mother. The opportunity for a not less grateful action was at hand, if he could remove a malignant wife. Not even force or cold steel was necessary: he had simply to admit adultery with Octavia." He promised him a reward, secret, it might be, at the outset, but large; also, a pleasant place of retirement: should he refuse he held out the threat of death. Anicetus, with inbred perversity and an ease communicated by former crimes, invented and confessed more than had been ordered, in the presence of the friends convened by the emperor to play the part of a privy council. He was then banished to Sardinia,[1] where he supported a not impecunious exile, and died by a natural death.

LXIII. Nero, for his part, announced by edict that Octavia had seduced the prefect in the hope of gaining the co-operation of his squadron; that, conscious of her infidelities, she had procured abortion,—he failed to remember his recent charge of sterility!—and that these were facts ascertained by himself. He then confined her in the island of Pandateria.[2] No woman in exile ever presented a more pitiful spectacle to the eye of the beholder. There were yet some who recollected the banishment of Agrippina[3] by Tiberius; the more recent memory of Julia's[4] expulsion by Claudius still dwelt in the minds of men. But to these the maturity of life had come;[5] they had seen some little happiness, and could soften the cruelty of the present by recalling

adlevabant. Huic primum nuptiarum dies loco funeris fuit, deductae in domum, in qua nihil nisi luctuosum haberet, erepto per venenum patre et statim fratre; tum ancilla domina validior et Poppaea non nisi in perniciem uxoris nupta, postremo crimen omni exitio gravius.

LXIV. Ac puella vicesimo [1] aetatis anno inter centuriones et milites, praesagio malorum iam vitae exempta, nondum tamen morte adquiescebat. Paucis dehinc interiectis diebus mori iubetur, cum iam viduam se et tantum sororem testaretur communisque Germanicos et postremo Agrippinae nomen cieret, qua incolumi infelix quidem matrimonium, sed sine exitio pertulisset. Restringitur vinclis venaeque eius per omnis artus exsolvuntur; et quia pressus pavore sanguis tardius labebatur, praefervidi balnei vapore enecatur. Additurque atrocior saevitia, quod caput amputatum latumque in urbem Poppaea vidit. Dona ob haec templis decreta quem [2] ad finem memorabimus? Quicumque casus temporum illorum nobis vel aliis auctoribus noscent, praesumptum habeant, quotiens fugas et caedes iussit princeps, totiens gratis deis actas, quaeque rerum secundarum olim, tum publicae cladis insignia

---

[1] vicesimo] duo et vicesimo *Nipperdey*, quinto et v. *Ritter*.
[2] decreta quem *Doederlein* : decretaque.

---

[1] As a matter of fact, she was older than Britannicus; who was born on Feb. 13, 41 A.D.
[2] Through the adoption of Nero by Claudius.
[3] The surname was conferred by the senate on Tiberius' brother Drusus and his descendants. His grandson Claudius was father of Octavia; his granddaughter Agrippina, mother of Nero.

the brighter fortunes of the past. To Octavia, first of all, her day of marriage had been tantamount to a day of burial, entering as she did a house where mourning alone awaited her—where her father was snatched away by poison, to be followed at once by her brother. Then had come the maid, more potent than her mistress, and Poppaea turning bride only to destroy a wife; last of all, an accusation more bitter than any doom.

LXIV. And so this girl, in the twentieth year of her age,[1] surrounded by centurions and soldiers, cut off already from life by foreknowledge of her fate, still lacked the peace of death. There followed an interval of a few days; then she was ordered to die— though she protested she was husbandless now, a sister[2] and nothing more, evoking the Germanici[3] whose blood they shared, and, in the last resort, the name of Agrippina, in whose lifetime she had supported a wifehood, unhappy enough but still not fatal. She was tied fast with cords, and the veins were opened in each limb: then, as the blood, arrested by terror, ebbed too slowly, she was suffocated in the vapour of a bath heated to an extreme temperature. As a further and more hideous cruelty, the head was amputated and carried to Rome, where it was viewed by Poppaea. For all these things offerings were decreed to the temples —how often must those words be said? Let all who make their acquaintance with the history of that period in my narrative or that of others take so much for granted: as often as the emperor ordered an exile or a murder, so often was a thanksgiving addressed to Heaven; and what formerly betokened prosperity was now a symbol of public

fuisse. Neque tamen silebimus, si quod senatus consultum adulatione novum aut patientia postremum fuit.

LXV. Eodem anno libertorum potissimos veneno interfecisse creditus est, Doryphorum quasi adversatum nuptiis Poppaeae, Pallantem, quod inmensam pecuniam longa senecta detineret. Romanus [1] secretis criminationibus incusaverat Senecam ut C. Pisonis socium, sed validius a Seneca eodem crimine perculsus est. Unde Pisoni timor et orta insidiarum in Neronem magna moles et inprospera.

[1] Romanus] . . . Romanus *Ritter.*

calamity. Nevertheless, where a senatorial decree achieved a novelty in adulation or a last word in self-abasement, I shall not pass it by in silence.

LXV. In the same year, he was credited with the poisoning of two of his principal freedmen: Doryphorus,[1] as an opponent of the marriage with Poppaea; Pallas, because he kept his vast riches to himself by a too protracted old age.—Romanus [2] had attacked Seneca, in private informations, as the associate of Gnaeus Piso, but was himself more surely struck down by Seneca on the same charge. The result was the alarm of Piso and the birth of an elaborate and luckless conspiracy against Nero.

[1] *Libertus a libellis* in succession to Callistus.
[2] Possibly another Caesarian freedman, unless there is a gap in the text.

BOOK XV

LIBER XV

I. Interea rex Parthorum Vologeses cognitis Corbulonis rebus regemque alienigenam Tigranen Armeniae impositum, simul fratre Tiridate pulso spretum Arsacidarum fastigium ire ultum volens, magnitudine rursum Romana et continui foederis reverentia diversas ad curas trahebatur, cunctator ingenio et defectione Hyrcanorum, gentis validae, multisque ex eo bellis inligatus. Atque illum ambiguum novus insuper nuntius contumeliae exstimulat: quippe egressus Armenia Tigranes Adiabenos, conterminam nationem, latius ac diutius quam per latrocinia vastaverat, idque primores gentium aegre tolerabant: eo contemptionis descensum, ut ne duce quidem Romano incursarentur, sed temeritate obsidis tot per annos inter mancipia habiti. Accendebat dolorem eorum Monobazus, quem penes Adiabenum regimen, quod praesidium aut unde peteret rogitans. Iam de Armenia concessum, proxima trahi; et nisi defendant Parthi, levius servitium apud Romanos deditis quam captis esse.

---

[1] The narrative reverts to the end of XIV. 26. The events recorded in the first seventeen chapters of this book, though given under the one annalistic year 62 A.D., extend from 61 to 63 A.D.

[2] It had existed without a formal rupture since 20 B.C., the year of the restitution of the standards captured from Crassus at Carrhae (53 B.C.).

BOOK XV

I. MEANWHILE,[1] the Parthian king Vologeses—apprized of Corbulo's feats and the elevation of the alien Tigranes to the throne of Armenia, and anxious furthermore to take steps to avenge the slur cast upon the majesty of the Arsacian line by the expulsion of his brother Tiridates—was drawn, on the other hand, to different lines of thought by considerations of Roman power and by respect for a long-standing treaty.[2] For he was by nature prone to temporize, and he was hampered by a revolt of the powerful Hyrcanian tribe and by the numerous campaigns which it involved. He was still in doubt, when news of a fresh indignity stung him into action: for Tigranes, emerging from Armenia, had ravaged the bordering country of Adiabene too widely and too long for a plundering foray, and the grandees of the nations were becoming restive; complaining that they had sunk to a point of humiliation where they could be harried, not even by a Roman general, but by the temerity of a hostage whom for years the enemy had counted among his chattels. Their resentment was inflamed by Monobazus, the ruling prince of Adiabene:—" What protection," he kept demanding, " was he to seek? or from what quarter? Armenia had already been ceded; the adjacent country was following; and, if Parthia refused protection, then the Roman yoke pressed more lightly upon a surrendered than upon a conquered nation!" Tiri-

Tiridates quoque regni profugus per silentium aut modice querendo gravior erat:—Non enim ignavia magna imperia contineri; virorum armorumque faciendum certamen; id in summa fortuna aequius quod validius, et sua retinere privatae domus, de alienis certare regiam laudem esse.

II. Igitur commotus his Vologeses concilium vocat et proximum sibi Tiridaten constituit atque ita orditur:—" Hunc ego eodem mecum patre genitum, cum mihi per aetatem summo nomine concessisset, in possessionem Armeniae deduxi, qui tertius potentiae gradus habetur: nam Medos Pacorus ante ceperat. Videbarque contra vetera fratrum odia et certamina familiae nostrae penatis rite composuisse. Prohibent Romani et pacem numquam ipsis prospere lacessitam nunc quoque in exitium suum abrumpunt. Non ibo infitias: aequitate quam sanguine, causa quam armis retinere parta maioribus malueram. Si cunctatione deliqui, virtute corrigam. Vestra quidem vis et gloria *in* integro est, addita modestiae fama, quae neque summis mortalium spernenda est et a dis aestimatur." Simul diademate caput Tiridatis evinxit, promptam equitum manum, quae regem ex more sectatur, Monaesi nobili viro tradidit, adiectis Adiabenorum auxiliis mandavitque Tigranen Armenia exturba*ndum* [1] dum

---

[1] exturbandum *Becher :* exturba *Med.*, exturbare *Ernesti, vulg.*

---

[1] His remaining brother, to whom had been assigned the Arsacian appanage of Media Atropatene (between Armenia and Media proper).

dates too, dethroned and exiled, carried a weight
increased by his silence or his restrained protests :—
" Great empires were not conserved by inaction—
they needed the conflict of men and arms. With
princes might was the only right. To retain its own
possessions was the virtue of a private family : in
contending for those of others lay the glory of a king."

II. Vologeses, accordingly, moved by all this,
convened a council, installed Tiridates next to
himself, and opened thus :— " This prince, the issue
of the same father as myself, having renounced to
me the supreme title upon grounds of age, I placed
him in possession of Armenia, the recognized third
degree of power; for Media had already fallen to
Pacorus.¹ And it seemed to me that, in contrast
with the old brotherly hatreds and jealousies, I had
by fair means brought order to our domestic hearth.
The Romans forbid; and the peace, which they have
never themselves challenged with success, they are
now again breaking to their destruction. I shall
not deny it : equity and not bloodshed, reason and
not arms, were the means by which I should have
preferred to retain the acquisitions of my fathers.
If I have erred by hesitancy, I shall make amends by
valour. In any event, *your* power and fame are
intact; and you have added to them that character
for moderation which is not to be scorned by the most
exalted of mankind and is taken into account by
Heaven."—Therewith he bound the diadem on the
brows of Tiridates. A body of cavalry, regularly
in attendance on the king, was at hand : he transferred it to a noble named Monaeses, adding a
number of Adiabenian auxiliaries, and commissioned
him to eject Tigranes from Armenia; while he

ipse positis adversus Hyrcanos discordiis viris intimas molemque belli ciet, provinciis Romanis minitans.

III. Quae ubi Corbuloni certis nuntiis audita sunt, legiones duas cum Verulano Severo et Vettio Bolano subsidium Tigrani mittit, occulto praecepto, compositius cuncta quam festinantius agerent: quippe bellum habere quam gerere malebat. Scripseratque Caesari proprio duce opus esse, qui Armeniam defenderet: Suriam ingruente Vologese acriore in discrimine esse. Atque interim reliquas legiones pro ripa Euphratis locat, tumultuariam provincialium manum armat, hostilis ingressus praesidiis intercipit. Et quia egena aquarum regio est, castella fontibus inposita; quosdam rivos congestu harenae abdidit.

IV. Ea dum a Corbulone tuendae Suriae parantur, acto raptim agmine Monaeses, ut famam sui praeiret, non ideo nescium aut incautum Tigranen offendit. Occupaverat Tigranocertam, urbem copia defensorum et magnitudine moenium validam. Ad hoc Nicephorius amnis haud spernenda latitudine partem murorum ambit, et ducta ingens fossa, qua fluvio diffidebatur. Inerantque milites et provisi ante

---

[1] XIV. 26.

[2] Appointed *legatus* of Britain by Vitellius, and afterwards proconsul of Asia. Statius, whose *Protrepticon ad Crispinum* (*Silv.* V. 2) is addressed to his son, does what must be ample justice to his services in Armenia (*l.l.* 31–50).

[3] The identification of the Nicephorius depends on that of the site of Tigranocerta. If the town is placed, with Sachau and others, at Tell Ermen to the south of Mt. Masius (*et-Tûr*), which agrees with the data furnished by Tacitus and Strabo (522, 747), though not with those of Pliny (*H.N.* VI. 27, 129; *ib.* 9, 26), the stream is the Zergan, which falls into the Khabûr, a tributary of the Euphrates. If, on the other hand, Tigranocerta is taken, as by Egli, to have occupied the position of

himself laid aside his quarrel with Hyrcania and called up his internal forces, with the full machinery of war, as a threat to the Roman provinces.

III. So soon as Corbulo had the news by sure messengers, he sent two legions under Verulanus Severus[1] and Vettius Bolanus[2] to reinforce Tigranes; with private instructions, however, that all their actions were to be circumspect rather than rapid; for in truth, he was more desirous to have war upon his hands than to wage it. Also he had written to Nero that a separate commander was required for the defence of Armenia: Syria, he observed, stood in the graver danger, if Vologeses attacked. In the interval, he stationed his remaining legion on the Euphrates bank, armed an improvised force of provincials, and closed the hostile avenues of approach by garrison-posts. Further, as the region is deficient in water, forts were thrown up to command the springs: a few brooks he buried under piles of sand.

IV. While Corbulo was thus preparing for the defence of Syria, Monaeses, who had marched at full speed in order to outstrip the rumour of his coming, failed none the less to catch Tigranes unawares or off his guard. He had occupied Tigranocerta, a town formidable by the number of its defenders and the scale of its fortifications. In addition, a part of the walls is encircled by the Nicephorius,[3] a river of respectable width; and a huge fosse had been drawn at points where the stream was not to be relied upon. Within lay Roman troops, and supplies to which attention had been

Sert, north of Mt. Masius and south-west of Lake Van, it stood on the Bitlis-su.

commeatus, quorum subvectu pauci avidius progressi et repentinis hostibus circumventi ira magis quam metu ceteros accenderant. Sed Partho ad exsequendas obsidiones nulla comminus audacia : raris sagittis neque clausos exterret et semet frustratur. Adiabeni cum promovere scalas et machinamenta inciperent, facile detrusi, mox erumpentibus nostris caeduntur.

V. Corbulo tamen, quamvis secundis rebus suis, moderandum fortunae ratus misit ad Vologesen, qui expostularent vim provinciae inlatam : socium amicumque regem, cohortis Romanas circumsideri. Omitteret potius obsidionem, aut se quoque in agro hostili castra positurum. Casperius centurio in eam legationem delectus apud oppidum Nisibin, septem et triginta milibus passuum a Tigranocerta distantem, adiit regem et mandata ferociter edidit. Vologesi vetus et penitus infixum erat arma Romana vitandi, nec praesentia prospere fluebant. Inritum obsidium, tutus manu et copiis Tigranes, fugati qui expugnationem sumpserant, missae in Armeniam legiones, et aliae pro Suria paratae ultro inrumpere ; sibi inbecillum equitem pabuli inopia : nam exorta vis locustarum ambederat quidquid herbidum aut frondosum. Igitur metu abstruso mitiora obtendens, missurum ad

---

[1] By crossing the Euphrates and invading Mesopotamia.

[2] In north-eastern Mesopotamia. The town—ἦν οἱ μὲν βάρβαροι Νίσιβιν [Syr. N'tsībhīn], οἱ δ' Ἕλληνες 'Αντιόχειαν Μυγδονικὴν προσηγόρευον (Plut. Luc. 32)—was of high strategic importance from the time of Lucullus to that of John Zimisces, but is now reduced to a couple of hundred mud huts.

[3] This is said to determine the month as June or July.

given beforehand: that, in bringing them up, a few men had advanced too eagerly and been cut off by the sudden appearance of the enemy, had excited more anger than alarm in the remainder. But the Parthian lacks the boldness at close quarters demanded for the prosecution of a siege: he resorts to occasional flights of arrows, which both fail to terrify the garrison and delude himself. The Adiaberi, on beginning to push forward their ladders and machines, were easily thrown back, then cut to pieces by a sally of our men.

V. Corbulo, however, favourably though matters were turning, decided not to press fortune too hard, and forwarded a protest to Vologeses:—" Violence had been offered to his province: siege was being laid to an allied and friendly monarch and to Roman cohorts. It would be better to raise the blockade, or he also would pitch his camp in hostile territory." [1] The centurion Casperius, who had been selected for the mission, approached the king at Nisibis,[2] a town thirty-seven miles distant from Tigranocerta, and delivered his message with spirit. With Vologeses it was an old and deep-seated principle to avoid the Roman arms; nor at the moment was the current of events too smooth. The siege had been fruitless; Tigranes was safe with his garrison and supplies; the force which had undertaken to storm the position had been routed; legions had been sent into Armenia, and more stood ready on the Syrian frontier to take the offensive by an invasion. His own cavalry, he reflected, was incapacitated by lack of fodder; for a swarm of locusts [3] had made its appearance and destroyed every trace of grass or foliage. Hence, while keeping his fears in the background, he adopted

imperatorem Romanum legatos super petenda
Armenia et firmanda pace respondet. Monaesen
omittere Tigranocertam iubet, ipse retro concedit.

VI. Haec plures ut formidine regis et Corbulonis
minis patrata ac magnifica extollebant: alii occulte
pepigisse interpretabantur, ut omisso utrimque bello
et abeunte Vologese Tigranes quoque Armenia
abscederet. Cur enim exercitum Romanum a
Tigranocertis deductum? Cur deserta per otium
quae bello defenderant? An melius hibernavisse
in extrema Cappadocia, raptim erectis tuguriis, quam
in sede regni modo retenti? Dilata prorsus arma,
ut Vologeses cum alio quam cum Corbulone certaret,
Corbulo meritae tot per annos gloriae non ultra periculum faceret. Nam, ut rettuli, proprium ducem
tuendae Armeniae poposcerat, et adventare Caesennius Paetus audiebatur. Iamque aderat, copiis
ita divisis, ut quarta et duodecuma legiones addita
quinta, quae recens e Moesis excita erat, simul
Pontica et Galatarum Cappadocumque auxilia Paeto
oboedirent, tertia et sexta et decuma legiones
priorque Suriae miles apud Corbulonem manerent;
cetera ex rerum usu sociarent partirenturve. Sed

---

[1] The arrangement with Vologeses had been reached late
in the year, and the winter is that of 61-62 A.D.: the comments
are those of the spring or summer of 62 A.D.

[2] The consul of 60 A.D. (XIV. 29). Corbulo's request for
a special commander, *qui Armeniam defenderet* was mentioned
in chap. 3.

a milder tone, and replied that he would send ambassadors to the Roman emperor to discuss his application for Armenia and the establishment of peace on a firm footing. Monaeses he ordered to abandon Tigranocerta, while he himself began his retirement.

VI. By the majority of men these results were acclaimed as a triumph due to the fears of the king and to Corbulo's threats. Others found the explanation in a private compact stipulating that, if hostilities were suspended on both sides and Vologeses withdrew, Tigranes would also make his exit from Armenia. " For why," it was asked, " should the Roman army have been withdrawn from Tigranocerta? Why abandon in peace what they had defended in war? Was it an advantage to have wintered [1] upon the verge of Cappadocia in hastily erected hovels rather than in the capital of a kingdom which they had but lately saved? The fact was, the clash had been deferred, so that Vologeses might be pitted against another antagonist than Corbulo, and Corbulo risk no further the laurels earned in the course of so many years!" For, as I have related, he had demanded a separate general for the defence of Armenia, and it was heard that Caesennius Paetus [2] was at hand. Before long he was on the spot, the forces being so divided that the fourth and twelfth legions, reinforced by the fifth, which had recently been called up from Moesia, and the auxiliaries of Pontus, Galatia, and Cappadocia, were placed at the orders of Paetus; the third, sixth, and tenth legions, and the old troops in Syria, remaining with Corbulo, while the rest were to be employed in conjunction or separately as the course of events should require. However, not only was

neque Corbulo aemuli patiens, et Paetus, cui satis
ad gloriam erat, si proximus haberetur, despiciebat
gesta, nihil caedis aut praedae, usurpatas nomine
tenus urbium expugnationes dictitans : se tributa
ac leges et pro umbra regis Romanum ius victis
impositurum.

VII. Sub idem tempus legati Vologesis, quos ad
principem missos memoravi, revertere inriti bel-
lumque propalam sumptum a Parthis. Nec Paetus
detrectavit, sed duabus legionibus, quarum quartam
Funisulanus Vettonianus eo in tempore, duodecumam
Calavius Sabinus regebant, Armeniam intrat tristi
omine. Nam in transgressu Euphratis, quem ponte
tramittebant, nulla palam causa turbatus equus, qui
consularia insignia gestabat, retro evasit. Hostiaque,
quae muniebantur, hibernaculis adsistens semifacta
opera fuga perrupit seque vallo extulit. Et pila
militum arsere, magis insigni prodigio, quia Parthus
hostis missilibus telis decertat.

VIII. Ceterum Paetus spretis ominibus, necdum
satis firmatis hibernaculis, nullo rei frumentariae
provisu, rapit exercitum trans montem Taurum
reciperandis, ut ferebat, Tigranocertis vastandisque
regionibus, quas Corbulo integras omisisset. Et
capta quaedam castella, gloriaeque et praedae

---

[1] A couple of inscriptions show that he had an extraordinarily
distinguished career under the Flavians : Calavius Sabinus is
unknown.

[2] He crosses from Cappadocia into Armenia, probably at
Melitene (*Malatia*) and in the autumn, then marches south,
across the Taurus range, in the direction of Tigranocerta.

[3] It was being prepared in advance for the coming winter
(62–63 A.D.).

Corbulo impatient of rivals, but Paetus, for whom it might have been glory enough to rank second to such a leader, treated his achievements with high disdain. "Bloodshed and booty," he kept repeating, "there had been none; to speak of the storming of cities was nothing but a form of words: it remained for himself to impose on the conquered tributes, laws, and Roman jurisdiction in place of a phantom king."

VII. Almost at the same time, the deputies of Vologeses, whose mission to the emperor I have already noticed, returned without result, and Parthia embarked upon undisguised war. Paetus did not evade the challenge, but with two legions—the fourth, at that time commanded by Funisulanus Vettonianus,[1] and the twelfth, under Calavius Sabinus —entered Armenia under sinister auspices. For at the passage of the Euphrates,[2] which the troops were crossing by a bridge, the horse carrying the consular insignia took fright for no obvious reason and escaped to the rear. A victim standing by in the winter camp,[3] while it was being fortified, broke away, dashed through the half-completed works, and made its way out of the entrenchments. Fire, too, played on the javelins of the troops—a prodigy the more striking that the Parthian is an enemy whose battles are decided by missiles.

VIII. Paetus, however, ignoring the portents, with his winter quarters still inadequately protected, and no provision made for his supply of grain, hurried the army across the Taurus range, with the avowed intention of recovering Tigranocerta and devastating the districts which Corbulo had left untouched. He took, in fact, a few fortified places, and gained a certain amount of glory and plunder, had he but accepted

nonnihil partum, si aut gloriam cum modo aut praedam cum cura habuisset. Longinquis itineribus percursando quae obtineri nequibant, corrupto qui captus erat commeatu et instante iam hieme, reduxit exercitum conposuitque ad Caesarem litteras quasi confecto bello, verbis magnificis, rerum vacuas.

IX. Interim Corbulo numquam neglectam Euphratis ripam crebrioribus praesidiis insedit: et ne ponti iniciendo impedimentum hostiles turmae adferrent (iam enim subiectis campis magna specie volitabant), navis magnitudine praestantis et conexas trabibus ac turribus auctas agit per amnem catapultisque et balistis proturbat barbaros, in quos saxa et hastae longius permeabant, quam ut contrario sagittarum iactu adaequarentur. Dein pons continuatus collesque adversi per socias cohortis, post legionum castris occupantur, tanta celeritate et ostentatione virium, ut Parthi omisso paratu invadendae Suriae spem omnem in Armeniam verterent, ubi Paetus imminentium nescius quintam legionem procul in Ponto habebat, reliquas promiscis militum commeatibus infirmaverat, donec adventare Vologesen magno et infenso agmine auditum.

---

[1] His position was doubtless at Zeugma, the usual point of passage, and his *têtes de pont* had the effect of keeping open the door for a Roman invasion of Mesopotamia, while closing it against a Parthian attempt on Syria. Vologeses, therefore, whose base was probably at Nisibis, changed his objective, turned north, and marched into Armenia to try conclusions with Caesennius Paetus in the short interval before winter arrived in earnest.

his glory with moderation or kept his plunder with vigilance. But, while he was overrunning in protracted marches districts impossible of retention, the grain he had captured was ruined, and winter began to threaten: he therefore led back the army, and, to give the impression that the war was now closed, indited a letter to the Caesar, as grandiloquently phrased as it was void of content.

IX. In the meantime, Corbulo occupied the bank of the Euphrates,[1] which he had never neglected, with a still closer line of posts; while, to ensure that the task of laying a pontoon should not be impeded by the mounted squadrons of the enemy—already an imposing spectacle, as they manoeuvred in the adjacent plains—he threw across the stream a number of large-sized vessels connected with planking and surmounted by turrets, and, using his catapults and ballistae, forced back the barbarians, the stones and spears being effective at a range with which the counter-discharge of arrows was unable to compete. The bridge was now completed, and the hills in front were occupied, first by the allied cohorts, then by a legionary camp, with a speed and a display of strength which induced the Parthians to drop their preparations for invading Syria and to stake their whole hopes upon Armenia; where Paetus, unconscious of the impending storm, was keeping the fifth legion sequestered in Pontus, and had weakened the rest[2] by indiscriminate grants of furlough, till news came that Vologeses was on the march with a formidable and threatening array.

[2] The fourth and twelfth, which are shown by the next sentence to have been quartered separately.

X. Accitur legio duodecuma, et unde famam aucti
exercitus speraverat, prodita infrequentia, qua tamen
retineri castra et eludi Parthus tractu belli poterat,
si Paeto aut in suis aut in alienis consiliis constantia
fuisset: verum ubi a viris militaribus adversus
urguentis casus firmatus erat, rursus, ne alienae
sententiae indigens videretur, in diversa ac deteriora
transibat. Et tunc relictis hibernis non fossam
neque vallum sibi, sed corpora et arma in hostem
data clamitans, duxit legiones quasi proelio certaturus.
Deinde amisso centurione et paucis militibus, quos
visendis hostium copiis praemiserat, trepidus re-
meavit. Et quia minus acriter Vologeses institerat,
vana rursus fiducia tria milia delecti peditis proximo
Tauri iugo imposuit, quo transitum regis arcerent;
alaris quoque Pannonios, robur equitatus, in parte
campi locat. Coniunx ac filius castello, cui Arsamosata nomen est, abditi, data in praesidium cohorte
ac disperso milite, qui in uno habitus vagum hostem
promptius sustentavisset. Aegre compulsum ferunt,
ut instantem Corbuloni fateretur. Nec a Corbulone
properatum, quo gliscentibus periculis etiam subsidii

---

[1] To join Paetus and the fourth legion at "Rhandeia"—
The name is preserved by Dio (LXII. 21)—on the north bank
of the "Arsanias," which may safely be taken as the Murâd-su.
The exact site of the camp is naturally doubtful: probably
it lay a little east of Kharput.

X. The twelfth legion was called to the scene,[1] and the measure by which he had hoped to advertise the increase in his forces revealed their inadequacy. Even so, he might still have held the camp and foiled the Parthian by a strategy of delay, had he possessed the strength of mind to stand either by his own decisions or by the decisions of another. As it was, no sooner had the professional soldiers given him courage to face an urgent crisis than he changed front, and, reluctant to seem dependent on outside advice, passed over to the opposite and more disadvantageous course. So now, leaving his winter quarters and clamouring that not moat or rampart but men and arms were the means assigned him for dealing with a foe, he led on his legions as if to contest a pitched field; then, after the loss of one centurion and a few soldiers whom he had sent ahead to inspect the enemy's force, he retraced his steps in trepidation. And as Vologeses had pressed the pursuit less keenly than he might, his inane self-confidence returned, and he posted three thousand picked infantry on the neighbouring heights of the Taurus, where they were to bar the passage of the king: the Pannonian squadrons, also, composing the flower of his cavalry, were stationed in a part of the plain. His wife and son found concealment in a fortress known as Arsamosata, to which he allowed a cohort by way of garrison; thus dispersing a force which, if concentrated, might have coped more effectively with its shifting adversary. Only with a struggle, it is said, could he be brought to admit the hostile pressure to Corbulo. Nor was there any haste on the part of Corbulo himself, who hoped that, if the dangers came to a head, the glory

laus augeretur. Expediri tamen itineri singula milia ex tribus legionibus et alarios octingentos, parem numerum e cohortibus iussit.

XI. At Vologeses, quamvis obsessa a Paeto itinera hinc peditatu inde equite accepisset, nihil mutato consilio, sed vi ac minis alaris exterruit, legionarios obtrivit, uno tantum centurione Tarquitio Crescente turrim, in qua praesidium agitabat, defendere auso factaque saepius eruptione et caesis, qui barbarorum propius suggrediebantur, donec ignium iactu circumveniretur. Peditum si quis integer longinqua et avia, vulnerati castra repetivere, virtutem regis, saevitiam et copias gentium, cuncta metu extollentes, facili credulitate eorum, qui eadem pavebant. Ne dux quidem obniti adversis, sed cuncta militiae munia deseruerat, missis iterum ad Corbulonem precibus, veniret propere, signa et aquilas et nomen reliquum infelicis exercitus tueretur: se fidem interim, donec vita subpeditet, retenturos.

XII. Ille interritus et parte copiarum apud Suriam relicta, ut munimenta Euphrati inposita retinerentur, qua proximum et commeatibus non egenum, regionem Commagenam, exim Cappadociam inde Armenios petivit. Comitabantur exercitum

---

[1] II. 42 n.

of a rescue would also be heightened. Still, he ordered a thousand men from each of the three legions, with eight hundred auxiliary horse, and a body of similar strength from the cohorts, to prepare themselves for the road.

XI. Vologeses, on the other hand, though he had information that Paetus had beset the routes with infantry here and cavalry there, made no change in his plan, but by force and threats struck panic into the mounted squadrons and crushed the legionaries; of whom a solitary centurion, Tarquitius Crescens, had courage to defend the tower which he was garrisoning, repeating his sorties and cutting down the barbarians who ventured too close up, until he succumbed to showers of firebrands. The few infantrymen unhurt took their way to the distant wilds: the wounded made back for the camp, exalting in their fear the prowess of the king, the fierceness and numbers of the tribes, in one word everything, and finding easy belief among listeners agitated by the same alarms. Even the commander offered no resistance to adversity, but had abdicated all his military functions after sending a second petition to Corbulo:—" He must come quickly and save the eagles and standards, and the name which was all that was left of an unhappy army; they, meanwhile, would preserve their loyalty while life held out."

XII. Corbulo, undismayed, left part of his forces in Syria to hold the forts erected on the Euphrates, and made his way by the shortest route not destitute of supplies to the district of Commagene,[1] then to Cappadocia, and from Cappadocia to Armenia. Over and above the usual appurtenances of war, the

praeter alia sueta bello magna vis camelorum onusta frumenti, ut simul hostem famemque depelleret. Primum e perculsis Paccium primi pili centurionem obvium habuit, dein plerosque militum; quos diversas fugae causas obtendentis redire ad signa et clementiam Paeti experiri monebat: se nisi victoribus immitem esse. Simul suas legiones adire, hortari, priorum admonere, novam gloriam ostendere. Non vicos aut oppida Armeniorum, sed castra Romana duasque in iis legiones pretium laboris peti. Si singulis manipularibus praecipua servati civis corona imperatoria manu tribueretur, quod illud et quantum decus, ubi par eorum numerus aspiceretur,[1] qui adtulissent salutem et qui accepissent! His atque talibus in commune alacres (et erant quos pericula fratrum aut propinquorum propriis stimulis incenderent) continuum diu noctuque iter properabant.

XIII. Eoque intentius Vologeses premere obsessos, modo vallum legionum, modo castellum, quo inbellis aetas defendebatur, adpugnare, propius incedens quam mos Parthis, si ea temeritate hostem in proelium eliceret. At illi vix contuberniis extrahi,[2] nec aliud quam munimenta propugnabant, pars iussu ducis, et alii propria ignavia aut

---

[1] aspiceretur *Lipsius*: apisceretur *Med. But it may be doubted whether the emendation is adequate.*

[2] extrahi *Nipperdey*: extracti.

---

[1] Paccius Orfitus (XIII. 36), now reduced to his old rank.

[2] The " civic " crown (III. 21 n.).

army was accompanied by a large train of camels loaded with corn, so that he had means of defence as well against hunger as the enemy. The first of the beaten army whom he met was the leading centurion Paccius,[1] soon followed by a crowd of private soldiers, whose contradictory excuses for their flight he answered by advising them to return to their standards and test the mercy of Paetus :— "For his own part, he was implacable, except to conquerors." At the same time, he went up to his own legionaries, encouraged them, reminded them of their past, and pointed to fresh glory :—"Their goal was not Armenian villages or towns, but a Roman camp and in it two legions as the reward of their labour. If the glorious wreath[2] which commemorated the saving of a Roman life was conferred on the individual soldier by the hand of his emperor, how inestimable the meed of honour, when the rescued were seen to be in equal numbers with the rescuers!" Animated with a common alacrity by this appeal and others similar, the troops—some of whom, with brothers or relatives in danger, had incentives of their own to fire them—marched day and night at their best speed without a break.

XIII. With all the more vigour did Vologeses press the besieged, at one time threatening the legionary encampment, at another the fort which sheltered the non-combatants; venturing closer in than is usual with the Parthians, on the chance of luring the enemy to an engagement by his rashness. His opponents, however, could with difficulty be drawn from their quarters and confined themselves to defending the fortifications; some by command of the general, others from cowardice or a desire to

Corbulonem opperientes, ac vis *si*[1] ingrueret, provisis exemplis Caudinae Numanti*naeque cladis*;[2] neque eandem vim Samnitibus, Italico populo, ac Parthis,[3] Romani imperii aemulis. Validam quoque et laudatam antiquitatem, quotiens fortuna contra daret, saluti consuluisse. Qua desperatione exercitus dux subactus primas tamen litteras ad Vologesen non supplices, sed in modum querentis composuit, quod pro Armeniis semper Romanae dicionis aut subiectis regi, quem imperator delegisset, hostilia faceret: pacem ex aequo utilem; ne praesentia tantum spectaret. Ipsum adversus duas legiones totis regni viribus advenisse : at Romanis orbem terrarum reliquum, quo bellum iuvarent.

XIV. Ad ea Vologeses nihil pro causa, sed opperiendos sibi fratres Pacorum ac Tiridaten rescripsit; illum locum tempusque consilio destinatum, quid de Armenia cernerent; adiecisse deos dignum Arsacidarum, simul ut de legionibus Romanis statuerent. Missi posthac[4] Paeto nuntii et regis conloquium petitum, qui Vasacen praefectum equitatus ire iussit. Tum Paetus Lucullos, Pompeios et si qua Caes*ares* optinendae donandaeve Armeniae egerant, Vasaces imaginem retinendi largiendive penes nos, vim penes Parthos memorat. Et multum in vicem

---

[1] <si> *Walther.*

[2] Caudinae Numanti⟨naeque cladis⟩; neque eandem *Haase* : caudi nenum antineque eandem.

[3] ac Parthis *Halm :* aut paenis.   [4] posthac <a> *Haase.*

---

[1] In 321 B.C. the Roman army was passed under the Samnite yoke at Caudium : in 137 B.C. the consul C. Hostilius Mancinus was disgracefully defeated by the Celtiberians of Numantia (at the confluence of the Duero and the Tera). In both cases, the terms of capitulation were repudiated at Rome.

wait for Corbulo, coupled with the reflection that, if the attack were pressed home, there were the precedents of the Caudine and Numantine disasters.[1] " Nor, indeed," they argued, " had the Samnites, a tribe of provincial Italy, the strength of the Parthians who rivalled imperial Rome. Even the stout and lauded ancients, whenever fortune registered an adverse verdict, had taken thought for their lives! " Beaten though he was by the despondency in the ranks, the general's first letter to Vologeses was couched less in the terms of a petition than of a protest against his armed action on behalf of the Armenians, always under Roman suzerainty or subject to a king selected by the emperor. " Peace was an interest of both parties alike: the king must not look solely to the present—*he* had come up against a couple of legions with the full forces of his realm. Rome had the world in reserve, with which to support the war."

XIV. Vologeses wrote an evasive reply, to the effect that he must wait for his brothers, Pacorus and Tiridates:— " This was the date and place they had arranged for considering what was to be their decision with regard to Armenia: Heaven had added a task worthy of the Arsacian house—that of settling at the same time the fate of Roman legions." Messengers were then sent by Paetus, asking for an interview with the king, who ordered his cavalry-commander Vasaces to go. At the meeting, Paetus recalled the names of Lucullus and Pompey, and the various acts by which the Caesars had kept or given away the crown of Armenia; Vasaces, the fact that only a phantom power of retention or disposal rested with us—the reality was with Parthia. After

disceptato, Monobazus Adiabenus in diem posterum testis iis quae pepigissent adhibetur. Placuitque liberari obsidio legiones et decedere omnem militem finibus Armeniorum castellaque et commeatus Parthis tradi, quibus perpetratis copia Vologesi fieret mittendi ad Neronem legatos.

XV. Interim flumini Arsaniae (is castra prae-fluebat) pontem imposuit, specie sibi illud iter expedientis, sed Parthi quasi documentum victoriae iusserant; namque iis usui fuit, nostri per diversum iere. Addidit rumor sub iugum missas legiones et alia ex rebus infaustis, quorum simulacrum ab Armeniis usurpatum est. Namque et munimenta ingressi sunt, antequam agmen Romanum excederet, et circumstetere vias, captiva olim mancipia aut iumenta adgnoscentes abstrahentesque : raptae etiam vestes, retenta arma, pavido milite et concedente, ne qua proelii causa existeret. Vologeses armis et corporibus caesorum aggeratis, quo cladem nostram testaretur, visu fugientium legionum abstinuit : fama moderationis quaerebatur, postquam superbiam expleverat. Flumen Arsaniam elephanto insidens, proximus quisque regem vi equorum perrupere, quia

much parleying on both sides, Monobazus of Adiabene was called in for the following day as witness to
the arrangement concluded. The agreement was
that the blockade of the legions should be raised, the
whole of the troops withdrawn from Armenian
territory, and the forts and supplies handed over to
the Parthians. When all this had been consummated, Vologeses was to be accorded leave to send
an embassy to Nero.

XV. In the interval, Paetus threw a bridge over
the river Arsanias (which ran hard past the camp),
ostensibly to prepare himself a line of retreat in
that direction, though the work had, in fact, been
ordered by the Parthians as evidence of their victory:
for it was they who utilized it—our men leaving by
the opposite route. Rumour added that the legions
had been passed under the yoke; and other particu-
lars were given, harmonizing well enough with our
unfortunate position, and indeed paralleled by the
behaviour of the Armenians. For not only did they
enter the fortifications before the Roman column
left, but they lined the roads, identifying and
dragging off slaves or sumpter-animals which had
been captured long before: even clothing was
snatched and weapons detained, our terrified
troops offering no resistance, lest some pretext for
hostilities should emerge. Vologeses, after piling
up the arms and corpses of the slain to serve as
evidence of our disaster, abstained from viewing the
flight of the legions: he was laying up a character
for moderation, now that his arrogance had been
satisfied. Mounted on an elephant, he charged
through the stream of the Arsanias, while his immediate attendants followed with an effort on horse-

rumor incesserat pontem cessurum oneri dolo fabricantium: sed qui ingredi ausi sunt, validum et fidum intellexere.

XVI. Ceterum obsessis adeo suppeditavisse rem frumentariam constitit, ut horreis ignem inicerent, contraque prodiderit Corbulo Parthos inopes copiarum et pabulo attrito relicturos oppugnationem, neque se plus tridui itinere afuisse. Adicit iure iurando Paeti cautum apud signa, adstantibus iis, quos testificando rex misisset, neminem Romanum Armeniam ingressurum, donec referrentur litterae Neronis, an paci adnueret. Quae ut augendae infamiae composita, sic reliqua non in obscuro habentur, una die quadraginta milium spatium emensum esse Paetum, desertis passim sauciis, neque minus deformem illam fugientium trepidationem, quam si terga in acie vertissent. Corbulo cum suis copiis apud ripam Euphratis obvius non eam speciem insignium et armorum praetulit, ut diversitatem exprobraret. Maesti manipuli ac vicem commilitonum miserantes ne lacrimis quidem temperare: vix prae fletu usurpata consalutatio. Decesserat certamen virtutis et ambitio gloriae, felicium hominum adfectus: sola misericordia valebat, et apud minores magis.

---

[1] In his memoirs, to which, in spite of the caveat below, it is probable that the portraits of Paetus and Corbulo owe rather too much of their light and shade.

[2] The regulation day's march in summer was twenty miles, or, in exceptional cases, twenty-four; after which, *quidquid addideris iam cursus est, cuius spatium non potest definiri* (Veget. I. 9).

back; for a rumour had gained currency that the bridge, by a ruse of the constructors, would succumb beneath its burden. Those, however, who ventured upon it found it substantial and trustworthy.

XVI. For the rest, it is established that the beleaguered forces were so well supplied with corn that they set fire to their granaries; while, on the other hand, Corbulo has put it on record[1] that the Parthians were on the point of raising the siege through the scarcity of supplies and the dwindling of their forage, and that he himself was not more than three days' march distant. He adds that a sworn guarantee was given by Paetus, in face of the standards and in presence of witnesses deputed by the king, that not a Roman would enter Armenia until Nero's despatch came to hand intimating whether he assented to the peace. This version was doubtless composed to darken the disgrace, but to the rest of the tale no obscurity attaches:— that in one day Paetus covered a distance of forty miles,[2] abandoning his wounded everywhere; and that the panic-stricken rush of fugitives was not less ugly than if they had turned their backs on a field of battle. Corbulo, who met them with his own force on the bank of the Euphrates, made no such display of ensigns and arms as to turn the contrast into a reproach: the rank and file, gloomy and affected by the lot of their brother-soldiers, could not so much as restrain their tears; the military salute could hardly be exchanged for weeping. All rivalry in valour and all competition for glory, emotions confined to the fortunate, had taken their leave: pity alone held sway—more particularly among the inferior ranks.

XVII. Ducum inter se brevis sermo secutus est, hoc conquerente [1] inritum laborem, potuisse bellum fuga Parthorum finiri : ille integra utrique cuncta respondit : converterent aquilas et iuncti invaderent Armeniam abscessu Vologesis infirmatam. Non ea imperatoris habere mandata Corbulo : periculo legionum commotum e provincia egressum ; quando in incerto habeantur Parthorum conatus, Suriam repetiturum : sic quoque optimam fortunam orandam, ut pedes confectus spatiis itinerum alacrem et facilitate camporum praevenientem equitem adsequeretur. Exim Paetus per Cappadociam hibernavit : at Vologesis ad Corbulonem missi nuntii, detraheret castella trans Euphraten amnemque, ut olim, medium faceret. Ille Armeniam quoque diversis praesidiis vacuam fieri expostulabat. Et postremo concessit rex : dirutaque quae Euphraten ultra communiverat Corbulo, et Armenii sine arbitro relicti sunt.

XVIII. At Romae tropaea de Parthis arcusque medio Capitolini montis sistebantur, decreta ab senatu integro adhuc bello neque tum omissa, dum aspectui consulitur spreta conscientia. Quin et dissimulandis rerum externarum curis Nero frumentum plebis vetustate corruptum in Tiberim iecit,

---

[1] conquerente *Faërnus* : conquerentium.

---

[1] By the dating followed in the notes, the reference here is to the winter already mentioned as impending (*instante iam hieme*) in chap. 8, and the whole of the events related from that point of the narrative to this must have taken place in the brief interval. The assumption has its difficulties, but that considerable military operations were feasible in the neighbourhood of Nisibis, when they had ceased to be so in that of Artaxata, is shown by Plut. *Luc.* 32.

XVII. Between the leaders followed a brief conversation, Corbulo complaining that his labour had been wasted—" the campaign might have been settled by a Parthian flight." Paetus replied that with each of them the position was quite uncompromised; they had only to turn the eagles round, join forces, and invade Armenia, now enfeebled by the withdrawal of Vologeses. Corbulo " had no orders to that effect from the emperor: only because he was moved by the danger of the legions had he left his province; and, as the Parthian designs were quite uncertain, he would make his way back to Syria. Even so, he must pray for fortune to be at her kindest, if his infantry, outworn by their long marches, were to come up with active cavalry, almost sure to outstrip him along level and easy ground." Paetus then took up his winter quarters in Cappadocia:[1] Vologeses sent emissaries to Corbulo, proposing that he should withdraw his posts across the Euphrates and make the river as formerly a line of delimitation. The Roman demanded that Armenia should be similarly cleared of the various scattered garrisons. In the long run, the king gave way: Corbulo demolished his defensive works beyond the Euphrates, and the Armenians were left to their own devices.

XVIII. But at Rome trophies over the Parthians and arches were being erected in the middle of the Capitoline Hill: they had been voted by the senate while the issue of the war was still open, and now they were not abandoned—appearances being consulted, though known truth had to be ignored. Moreover, to cloak his uneasiness as to the situation abroad, Nero had the grain for the populace—which had been spoilt by age—thrown into the Tiber, as proof that

243

quo securitatem annonae ostentaret.[1] Cuius pretio
nihil additum est, quamvis ducentas ferme naves
portu in ipso violentia tempestatis et centum alias
Tiberi subvectas fortuitus ignis absumpsisset. Tris
dein consulares, L. Pisonem, Ducenium Geminum,
Pompeium Paulinum vectigalibus publicis praeposuit, cum insectatione priorum principum, qui
gravitate sumptuum iustos reditus anteissent: se
annuum sexcentiens sestertium rei publicae largiri.

XIX. Percrebruerat ea tempestate praviss*imus*
mos, cum propinquis comitiis aut sorte provinciarum
plerique orbi fictis adoptionibus adsciscerent filios,
praeturasque et provincias inter patres sortiti statim
emitterent manu, quos adoptaverant. . . .[2] Magna
cum invidia senatum adeunt, ius naturae, labores
educandi adversus fraudem et artes et brevitatem
adoptionis enumerant. Satis pretii esse orbis, quod
multa securitate, nullis oneribus gratiam honores
cuncta prompta et obvia haberent. Sibi promissa
legum diu exspectata in ludibrium verti, quando
quis sine sollicitudine parens, sine luctu orbus longa

---

[1] ostentaret *Agricola* : sustentaret.
[2] . . . *Nipperdey.*

---

[1] Not exactly at Ostia, where no serviceable harbour was
possible through silting due to the Tiber, but in the remarkable
portus Claudii (later, *portus Romae*; now *Porto*), two miles to
the north.

[2] The expression seems to cover the whole revenues of the
senatorial treasury.

[3] Occasional grants to the *aerarium* from the *fiscus* are fairly
often mentioned: see, for instance, XIII. 31. Here the
language points to a fixed annual contribution, as to which all
details are lacking.

[4] In order to circumvent the *lex Papia Poppaea* (9 A.D.),

the corn-supply was not a matter for anxiety. The price was not raised, though some two hundred vessels actually in port[1] had been destroyed by a raging tempest, and a hundred more, which had made their way up the Tiber, by a chance outbreak of fire. He proceeded to appoint three consulars, Lucius Piso, Ducenius Geminus, and Pompeius Paulinus, to supervise the contributions to the national treasury,[2] adding a stricture on the previous emperors, " who with their ruinous expenditure had forestalled the legal revenue : personally, he was making the state a yearly present of sixty million sesterces."[3]

XIX. There was a perverse custom in vogue at that period for childless candidates, shortly before an election or an allotment of provinces, to procure themselves sons by fictitious acts of adoption,[4] then, after obtaining in their quality of fathers a praetorship or governorship, to emancipate immediately the adopted persons. ⟨The consequence was that the authentic heads of families⟩ made an embittered appeal to the senate. They dwelt on the rights of nature—the anxieties entailed by rearing children —as against the calculated frauds and ephemeral character of adoption. " It was ample compensation for the childless that, almost without a care and quite without responsibilities, they should have influence, honours, anything and everything, ready to their hand. In their own case, the promises of the law, for which they had waited so long, were converted into a mockery, when some person who had known parenthood without anxiety and childlessness without bereavement could overtake in a moment

which gave priority to the father of a family over a childless competitor. See III. 25–28 and the instance in II. 51.

patrum vota repente adaequaret. Factum ex eo
senatus consultum, ne simulata adoptio in ulla parte
muneris publici iuvaret ac ne usurpandis quidem
hereditatibus prodesset.

XX. Exim Claudius Timarchus Cretensis reus
agitur, ceteris criminibus, ut solent praevalidi provincialium et opibus nimiis ad iniurias minorum elati :
una vox eius usque ad contumeliam senatus pene-
traverat, quod dictitasset in sua potestate situm, an
proconsulibus, qui Cretam obtinuissent, grates
agerentur. Quam occasionem Paetus Thrasea ad
bonum publicum vertens, postquam de reo censuerat
provincia Creta depellendum, haec addidit :—" Vsu
probatum est, patres conscripti, leges egregias,
exempla honesta apud bonos ex delictis aliorum
gigni. Sic oratorum licentia Cinciam rogationem,
candidatorum ambitus Iulias leges, magistratuum
avaritia Calpurnia scita pepererunt; nam culpa
quam poena tempore prior, emendari quam peccare
posterius est. Ergo adversus novam provincialium
superbiam dignum fide constantiaque Romana capia-
mus consilium, quo tutelae sociorum nihil derogetur,
nobis opinio decedat, qualis quisque habeatur, alibi
quam in civium iudicio esse.

----

[1] Celibates were prohibited by the *lex Papia Poppaea* from
entering upon any bequest except from a relative within a
specified degree of nearness : married but childless legatees
received half the amount bequeathed.

[2] For the *lex Cincia*, see XI. 5 n.; for the *leges Iuliae* of
Augustus (the plural seems to be only rhetorical), Suet. *Aug.*
34. The *lex Calpurnia de repetundis* was passed in 149 B.C.

the long-cherished hopes of genuine fathers." A senatorial decree was thereupon passed, ruling that a feigned adoption should not be a qualification for public office in any form, nor even a valid title for the acquiry of an inheritance.[1]

XX. Now came the trial of the Cretan, Claudius Timarchus. The rest of the charges were those usual in the case of provincial magnates, whose excessive wealth prompts them to oppress their inferiors; but one remark of his had gone far enough to constitute an insult to the senate, as he was reported to have said more than once that it rested within his competency to determine whether the proconsuls who had been administering Crete should receive the thanks of the province. Turning the occasion to the profit of the state, Thrasea Paetus, after giving his opinion that the defendant should be exiled from Crete, proceeded :—" It has been proved by experience, Conscript Fathers, that in a community of honourable men excellent laws and salutary precedents may have their rise in the delinquencies of others. So, the licence of the advocates bore fruit in the Cincian rogation; the corruption of candidates, in the Julian laws; and the cupidity of officials, in the Calpurnian plebiscites;[2] for, in the order of time, the fault must precede the chastisement, the reform follow the abuse. Let us, then, meet this new development of provincial arrogance by framing a decision consonant with Roman honour and firmness : a decision which, without detriment to the protection we owe to our allies, shall disabuse us of the idea that the reputation of a Roman may be settled elsewhere than in the judgement of his countrymen.

XXI. Olim quidem non modo praetor aut consul, sed privati etiam mittebantur, qui provincias viserent et quid de cuiusque obsequio videretur referrent, trepidabantque gentes de aestimatione singulorum: at nunc colimus externos et adulamur, et quo modo ad nutum alicuius grates, ita promptius accusatio decernitur. Decernaturque et maneat provincialibus *ius* potentiam [1] suam tali modo ostentandi: sed laus falsa et precibus expressa perinde cohibeatur quam malitia, quam crudelitas. Plura saepe peccantur, dum demeremur quam dum offendimus. Quaedam immo virtutes odio sunt, severitas obstinata, invictus adversum gratiam animus. Inde initia magistratuum nostrorum meliora ferme et finis inclinat, dum in modum candidatorum suffragia conquirimus: quae si arceantur, aequabilius atque constantius provinciae regentur. Nam ut metu repetundarum infracta avaritia est, ita vetita gratiarum actione ambitio cohibebitur."

XXII. Magno adsensu celebrata sententia, non tamen senatus consultum perfici potuit, abnuentibus consulibus ea de re relatum. Mox auctore principe sanxere, ne quis ad concilium sociorum referret agendas apud senatum pro praetoribus prove consulibus gratis, neu quis ea legatione fungeretur.

Isdem consulibus gymnasium ictu fulminis con-

[1] <ius> potentiam *A. Schmidt*: potentiam *Med.*, pote-<stas sente>ntiam *Madvig*.

[1] Furneaux instances the cases of Pilate, Herod Agrippa (*Acts xii.* 2), Felix (XXIV. 27), Festus (XXV. 9).

[2] XIV. 47 n.

XXI. " There was a day, indeed, when we sent not merely a praetor or a consul, but private citizens, to visit the provinces and report upon the loyalty of each; and nations awaited in trepidation the verdict of an individual. But now we court foreigners; we flatter them; and, as at the nod of one or other among them, there is decreed a vote of thanks, so— with more alacrity—is decreed an impeachment. And let it be decreed! Leave the provincials the right to advertise their power in that fashion; but see that these hollow compliments, elicited by the entreaties of the receiver, are repressed as sternly as knavery or cruelty. Often we go further astray while we oblige than while we offend.[1] In fact, certain virtues are a ground for hatred—unbending strictness and a breast impregnable to favouritism. Hence, the early days of our officials are usually the best; the falling off is at the end, when we begin, like candidates, to cast about for votes; and if that practice is vetoed, the provinces will be governed with more steadiness and consistency. For as rapacity has been tamed by fear of a trial for extortion, so will canvassing for popularity be curbed by the prohibition of votes of thanks."

XXII. The proposal was greeted with loud assent: it proved impossible, however, to complete a decree, as the consuls declined to admit that there was a motion on the subject. Later, at the suggestion of the emperor, a rule was passed that no person should at a provincial diet propose the presentation in the senate of an address of thanks to a Caesarian or senatorial governor, and that no one should undertake the duties of such a deputation.

In the same consulate, the Gymnasium [2] was struck

flagravit, effigiesque in eo Neronis ad informe aes
liquefacta. Et motu terrae celebre Campaniae
oppidum Pompei magna ex parte proruit. De-
functaque virgo Vestalis Laelia, in cuius locum
Cornelia ex familia Cossorum capta est.

XXIII. Memmio Regulo et Verginio Rufo consulibus natam sibi ex Poppaea filiam Nero ultra mortale
gaudium accepit appellavitque Augustam dato et
Poppaeae eodem cognomento. Locus puerperio
colonia Antium fuit, ubi ipse generatus erat. Iam
senatus uterum Poppaeae commendaverat dis vota-
que publice susceperat, quae multiplicata exsoluta-
que. Et additae supplicationes templumque Fe-
cunditati et certamen ad exemplar Actiacae religionis
decretum, utque Fortunarum effigies aureae in solio
Capitolini Iovis locarentur, ludicrum circense, ut
Iuliae genti apud Bovillas, ita Claudiae Domitiaeque
apud Antium ederetur. Quae fluxa fuere, quartum
intra mensem defuncta infante. Rursusque exortae
adulationes censentium honorem divae et pulvinar
aedemque et sacerdotem. Atque ipse ut laetitiae,

---

[1] Seneca, writing shortly after the event, gives the date as
Feb. 5, 63 A.D. (*Regulo et Verginio consulibus*, N.Q. VI. 1).

[2] Son or nephew of the more notable P. Memmius Regulus
(V. 11 n.).

[3] The famous legatus of Upper Germany, who, after crushing
the rising of Vindex, "*imperium asseruit, non sibi sed patriae.*"
Consul for the third time in 97 A.D.—*ut summum fastigium
privati hominis impleret, cum principis noluisset*, says the
younger Pliny, once his ward—he was succeeded in the office
by Tacitus, who pronounced his funeral panegyric.

[4] Quinquennial games, athletic and musical, instituted by
Augustus to commemorate his victory at Actium (Sept. 2,
31 B.C.), and celebrated at Nicopolis (II. 53 n.). They ranked,
like the four national festivals of Greece, as a ἱερὸς ἀγών.

by lightning and burned to the ground, a statue of
Nero, which it contained, being melted into a shape-
less piece of bronze.   An earthquake also demolished
to a large extent the populous Campanian town of
Pompeii;[1] and the debt of nature was paid by the
Vestal Virgin Laelia, whose place was filled by the
appointment of Cornelia, from the family of the Cossi.

XXIII. In the consulate of Memmius Regulus[2] and
Verginius Rufus,[3] Nero greeted a daughter, presented
to him by Poppaea, with more than human joy,
named the child Augusta, and bestowed the same
title on Poppaea.   The scene of her delivery was
the colony of Antium, where the sovereign himself
had seen the light.   The senate had already commended the travail of Poppaea to the care of Heaven
and formulated vows in the name of the state: they
were now multiplied and paid.   Public thanksgivings were added, and a Temple of Fertility was
decreed, together with a contest on the model of
the Actian festival;[4] while golden effigies of the Two
Fortunes[5] were to be placed on the throne of Capitoline Jove, and, as the Julian race had its Circus Games
at Bovillae,[6] so at Antium should the Claudian and
Domitian houses.   But all was transitory, as the
infant died in less than four months.   Then fresh
forms of adulation made their appearance, and she
was voted the honour of deification, a place in the
pulvinar,[7] a temple, and a priest.   The emperor,

A.V.C. 816 =
A.D. 63

---

[5] The two *Fortunae Antiates*, regarded as sisters.   Their cult,
associated with an oracle, appears to have persisted till the
time of Theodosius (Macrob. *Sat.* I. 23).

[6] II. 41 n.

[7] Her image was to rank with those of other divinities at
lectisternia.

ıta maeroris inmodicus egit. Adnotatum est, omni senatu Antium sub recentem partum effuso, Thraseam prohibitum inmoto animo praenuntiam inminentis caedis contumeliam excepisse. Secutam dehinc vocem Caesaris ferunt qua reconciliatum se Thraseae apud Senecam iactaverit, ac Senecam Caesari gratulatum : unde gloria egregiis viris et pericula gliscebant.

XXIV. Inter quae veris principio legati Parthorum mandata regis Vologesis litterasque in eandem formam attulere : se priora et totiens iactata super optinenda Armenia nunc omittere, quoniam di, quamvis potentium populorum arbitri, possessionem Parthis non sine ignominia Romana tradidissent. Nuper clausum Tigranen ; post Paetum legionesque, cum opprimere posset, incolumis dimisisse. Satis adprobatam vim ; datum et lenitatis experimentum. Nec recusaturum Tiridaten accipiendo diademati in urbem venire, nisi sacerdotii religione attineretur. Iturum ad signa et effigies principis, ubi legionibus coram regnum auspicaretur.

XXV. Talibus Vologesis litteris, quia Paetus diversa tamquam rebus integris scribebat, interrogatus centurio, qui cum legatis advenerat, quo in statu Armenia esset, omnis inde Romanos excessisse respondit. Tum intellecto barbarum inrisu, qui

---

[1] As a Magian he objected to crossing the sea, *quoniam expuere in maria aliisque mortalium necessitatibus violare naturam eam fas non putant* (Plin. *H.N.* XXX. 2, 16).

[2] See chap. 29 below.

too, showed himself as incontinent in sorrow as in joy. It was noted that when the entire senate streamed towards Antium shortly after the birth, Thrasea, who was forbidden to attend, received the affront, prophetic of his impending slaughter, without emotion. Shortly afterwards, they say, came a remark of the Caesar, in which he boasted to Seneca that he was reconciled to Thrasea; and Seneca congratulated the Caesar: an incident which increased the fame, and the dangers, of those eminent men.

XXIV. Meanwhile, at the beginning of spring, a Parthian legation brought a message from King Vologeses and a letter to the same purport:—" He was now dropping his earlier and often-vented claims to the possession of Armenia, since the gods, arbiters of the fate of nations however powerful, had transferred the ownership to Parthia, not without some humiliation to Rome. Only recently he had besieged Tigranes: a little later, when he might have crushed them, he had released Paetus and the legions with their lives. He had sufficiently demonstrated his power; he had also given an example of his clemency. Nor would Tiridates have declined to come to Rome and receive his diadem, were he not detained by the scruples attaching to his priesthood;[1] he would visit the standards and the effigies of the emperor, there to inaugurate his reign in the presence of the legions."[2]

XXV. As this missive from Vologeses could not be reconciled with Paetus' report, which spoke of the situation as still uncompromised, the centurion who had arrived with the deputies was examined on the condition of Armenia, and replied that all Romans had left the country. The irony of the barbarians in

peterent quod eripuerant, consuluit inter primores
civitatis Nero, bellum anceps an pax inhonesta
placeret. Nec dubitatum de bello. Et Corbulo
militum atque hostium tot per annos gnarus gerendae
rei praeficitur, ne cuius alterius inscitia rursum
peccaretur, quia Paeti piguerat. Igitur inriti re-
mittuntur, cum donis tamen, unde spes fieret non
frustra eadem oraturum Tiridaten, si preces ipse
attulisset. Suriaeque executio[1] C. Cestio,[2] copiae
militares Corbuloni permissae, et quinta decuma legio
ducente Mario Celso e Pannonia adiecta est. Scribi-
tur tetrarchis ac regibus praefectisque et procura-
toribus et qui praetorum finitimas provincias regebant, iussis Corbulonis obsequi, in tantum ferme
modum aucta potestate, quem populus Romanus
Cn. Pompeio bellum piraticum gesturo dederat.
Regressum Paetum, cum graviora metueret, facetiis
insectari satis habuit Caesar, his ferme verbis:
ignoscere se statim, ne tam promptus in pavorem
longiore solicitudine aegresceret.

XXVI. At Corbulo quarta et duodecuma legionibus, quae fortissimo quoque amisso et ceteris exterri-

---

[1] executio] iurisdictio *Madvig.*
[2] <C.> *Nipperdey,* Cestio *Pighius* : citio.

---

[1] Probably son of the previous year's consul. He served
first Galba, then Otho, with equal courage, ability and honour,
and was allowed his consulate even by Vitellius (*Hist.* I-II.
passim.).
[2] Vassal princes below the rank of the " kings "—for whom
see XIII. 7, XIV. 6. The " prefects " are the commanders of
cohortes and *alae* in the smaller provinces; the " procurators,"
the governors of Judaea and Cappadocia. The term " praetors "
includes the governors of the more important provinces—not
only the *legati pro praetore* of Cilicia, Lycia, Pamphylia and

asking for what had been taken was now obvious, and Nero held a council of state to decide the choice between a hazardous war and an ignominious peace. There was no hesitation about the verdict for war. Corbulo, familiar for years with his troops and his enemy, was put at the head of operations, lest there should be a fresh blunder from the incompetence of another substitute, seeing that Paetus had inspired complete disgust. The deputation was therefore sent back with its purpose unachieved, but with presents leaving room for hope that Tiridates would not make the same requests in vain, if he brought his suit in person. The administration of Syria was entrusted to Gaius Cestius, the military forces to Corbulo, with the addition of the fifteenth legion from Pannonia under the command of Marius Celsus.[1] Instructions in writing were given to the tetrarchs [2] and kings, the prefects and procurators, and the praetors in charge of the neighbouring provinces, to take their orders from Corbulo, whose powers were raised to nearly the same level as that allowed by the Roman nation to Pompey for the conduct of the Pirate War.[3] When Paetus returned, with apprehensions of a graver cast, the Caesar contented himself with a jocular reprimand, the wording of which was roughly, that " he was pardoning him on the spot, lest a person with such a tendency to panic might fall ill if his suspense were protracted."

XXVI. Meanwhile Corbulo, who regarded the fourth and twelfth legions as incapacitated for active service by the loss of their bravest men and the

Galatia, but also the proconsul of Bithynia, a senatorial province administered by an ex-praetor.

[3] In 67 B.C.

tis parum habiles proelio videbantur, in Suriam translatis, sextam inde ac tertiam legiones, integrum militem et crebris ac prosperis laboribus exercitum, in Armeniam ducit. Addiditque legionem quintam, quae per Pontum agens expers cladis fuerat, simul quintadecumanos recens adductos et vexilla delectorum ex Illyrico et Aegypto, quodque alarum cohortiumque, et auxilia regum in unum conducta apud Melitenen, qua tramittere Euphraten parabat. Tum lustratum rite exercitum ad contionem vocat orditurque magnifica de auspiciis imperatoris rebusque a se gestis, adversa in inscitiam Paeti declinans, multa auctoritate, quae viro militari pro facundia erat.

XXVII. Mox iter L. Lucullo quondam penetratum, apertis quae vetustas obsaepserat, pergit. Et venientis Tiridatis Vologesisque de pace legatos haud aspernatus, adiungit iis centuriones cum mandatis non inmitibus : nec enim adhuc eo ventum, ut certamine extremo opus esset. Multa Romanis secunda, quaedam Parthis evenisse, documento adversus superbiam. Proinde et Tiridati conducere intactum vastationibus regnum dono accipere, et Vologesen melius societate Romana quam damnis mutuis genti Parthorum consulturum. Scire, quan-

---

[1] In his advance on Tigranocerta in 69 B.C. His route is only vaguely indicated in Plut. *Luc.* 24 fin.

demoralization of the rest, transferred them to Syria; whence he took the sixth and third legions, fresh troops, seasoned by numerous and successful labours, and led them into Armenia. He reinforced them with the fifth, which through being stationed in Pontus had escaped the disaster; also with the men of the fifteenth, recently brought up, and picked detachments from Illyricum and Egypt; with the whole of the allied horse and foot; and with the auxiliaries of the tributary princes, concentrated at Melitene, where he was making ready for the passage of the Euphrates. Then, after the usual lustration, he convoked the army for an address, and opened with a florid reference to the auspices of the emperor and his own exploits, the reverses being attributed to the incompetence of Paetus: all with a weight which in a professional soldier was a fair substitute for eloquence.

XXVII. Soon, he took the road along which Lucius Lucullus had once penetrated,[1] first clearing the parts which time had obstructed. On the arrival of envoys from Vologeses and Tiridates to discuss a peace, instead of rejecting their overtures, he sent back in their company a few centurions with instructions not unconciliatory in tone:—" For matters had not yet come to a pass where war to the bitter end was necessary. Rome had been favoured with many successes, Parthia with a few, so that both had received a lesson against arrogance. Not only, therefore, was it to the advantage of Tiridates to accept the free gift of a realm untouched by the ravager, but Vologeses would better consult the interest of the Parthian nation by an alliance with Rome than by a policy of reciprocal injury. He

tum intus discordiarum quamque indomitas et praeferoces nationes regeret : contra imperatori suo immotam ubique pacem et unum id bellum esse. Simul consilio terrorem adicere, et megistanes Armenios, qui primi a nobis defecerant, pellit sedibus, castella eorum excindit, plana edita, validos invalidosque pari metu complet.

XXVIII. Non infensum nec cum hostili odio Corbulonis nomen etiam barbaris habebatur, eoque consilium eius fidum credebant. Ergo Vologeses neque atrox in summam, et quibusdam praefecturis indutias petit : Tiridates locum diemque conloquio poscit. Tempus propinquum, locus, in quo nuper obsessae cum Paeto legiones erant, barbaris [1] delectus est ob memoriam laetioris ibi [2] rei, Corbuloni [3] non vitatus ut dissimilitudo fortunae gloriam augeret. Neque infamia Paeti angebatur, quod eo maxime patuit, quia filio eius tribuno ducere manipulos atque operire reliquias malae pugnae imperavit. Die pacta Tiberius Alexander, inlustris eques Romanus, minister bello datus, et Vinicianus Annius, gener Corbulonis, nondum senatoria aetate, set pro legato

[1] barbaris *Doederlein* : cum barbaris.
[2] laetioris ibi] laetiori sibi *Med.*[1], laetioris sibi *Med.*
[3] Corbuloni *Agricola* : Corbulo.

---

[1] XI. 9 n.
[2] Ti. Julius Alexander, nephew of Philo Judaeus, but a pagan; procurator of Judaea in 46 A.D., prefect of Egypt twenty-one years later; took the initiative in proclaiming Vespasian (July 1, 69 A.D.); lieutenant-general of Titus at the sieeg of Jerusalem. He is the "Arabarches"—*cuius ad effigiem non tantum meiere fas est*—of Juv. I. 30, though the title in reality was borne by his father Alexander Lysimachus.

knew how many were the internal discords of his kingdom—how intractable and fierce the peoples over whom he ruled. In contrast, his own emperor enjoyed unshaken peace everywhere, and this was his solitary war." At the same time, he reinforced persuasion by terror, expelled from their homes the Armenian grandees who had been the first to rebel against us, and razed their strongholds, filling plain and mountain, strong and weak, with equal consternation.

XXVIII. The name of Corbulo was regarded by the barbarians themselves without bitterness and with no rancour of hostility: consequently they believed his advice to be trustworthy. Hence Vologeses, without showing himself inexorable on the main question, asked for a truce for certain prefectures:[1] Tiridates demanded a place and day for an interview. The date was to be early; for the place, the scene of the recent investment of Paetus and the legions was chosen by the barbarians in memory of their success there; and it was not avoided by Corbulo, who wished the contrast in fortune to enhance his fame. The slur upon Paetus gave him no qualms, as was very clearly shown by the fact that he ordered the defeated general's son, a tribune, to put himself at the head of a few maniples and bury the relics of the disastrous field. On the day fixed upon, Tiberius Alexander,[2] a Roman knight of the first rank, who had been appointed a commissioner for the campaign, and Annius Vinicianus,[3] a son-in-law of Corbulo, still under senatorial age,[4]

[3] Sent later to Rome in attendance on Tiridates, and perhaps implicated in the obscure "Vinician conspiracy" at Beneventum (Suet. *Ner.* 36).

[4] Twenty-five years.—A *legatus legionis* was necessarily a senator, usually an ex-praetor.

quintae legioni inpositus, in castra Tiridatis venere, honori eius ac ne metueret insidias tali pignore; viceni dehinc equites adsumpti. Et viso Corbulone rex prior equo desiluit; nec cunctatus Corbulo, sed pedes uterque dexteras miscuere.

XXIX. Exim Romanus laudat iuvenem omissis praecipitibus tuta et salutaria capessentem. Ille de nobilitate generis multum praefatus, cetera temperanter adiungit: iturum quippe Romam laturumque novum Caesari decus, non adversis Parthorum rebus supplicem Arsaciden. Tum placuit Tiridaten ponere apud effigiem Caesaris insigne regium nec nisi manu Neronis resumere; et conloquium osculo finitum. Dein paucis diebus interiectis, magna utrimque specie, inde eques compositus per turmas et insignibus patriis, hinc agmina legionum stetere fulgentibus aquilis signisque et simulacris deum in modum templi: medio tribunal sedem curulem et sedes effigiem Neronis sustinebat. Ad quam progressus Tiridates, caesis ex more victimis, sublatum capiti diadema imagini subiecit, magnis apud cunctos animorum motibus, quos augebat insita adhuc oculis exercituum Romanorum caedes aut obsidio. At nunc versos casus: iturum Tiridaten ostentui gentibus, quanto minus quam captivum?

and acting legate in command of the fifth legion, entered the camp of Tiridates, partly out of compliment to him, but also, by such a pledge, to remove all fear of treachery. On each side twenty mounted men were then taken into attendance. On descrying Corbulo, the king was the first to leap from his horse; Corbulo was not slow to follow, and the pair clasped hands on foot.

XXIX. The Roman then praised the young monarch, who had rejected adventure and was choosing the safe and salutary course: the other, after a long preface on the nobility of his family, proceeded temperately:—" He would go," he said, " to Rome and carry the Caesar a new distinction—an Arsacid in the guise of a suppliant, though the fortunes of Parthia were unclouded." It was then arranged that Tiridates should lay the emblem of his royalty before the statue of the emperor, to resume it only from the hand of Nero; and the dialogue was closed by a kiss. Then, after a few days' interval, came an impressive pageant on both sides: on the one hand, cavalry ranged in squadrons and carrying their national decorations; on the other, columns of legionaries standing amid a glitter of eagles and standards and effigies of gods which gave the scene some resemblance to a temple: in the centre, the tribunal sustained a curule chair, and the chair a statue of Nero. To this Tiridates advanced, and, after the usual sacrifice of victims, lifted the diadem from his head and placed it at the feet of the image; arousing among all present a deep emotion increased by the picture of the slaughter or siege of Roman armies which was still imprinted on their eyes:—" But now the tide had turned: Tiridates was about to depart (how little less than a captive!) to be a gazing-stock to the nations! "

XXX. Addidit gloriae Corbulo comitatem epulas-
que; et rogitante rege causas, quotiens novum
aliquid adverterat, ut initia vigiliarum per centurionem nuntiari, convivium bucina dimitti et structam
ante augurale aram subdita face accendi, cuncta in
maius attollens admiratione prisci moris adfecit.
Postero die spatium oravit, quo tantum itineris
aditurus fratres ante matremque viseret; obsidem
interea filiam tradit litterasque supplices ad Neronem.

XXXI. Et digressus Pacorum apud Medos, Vologesen Ecbatanis repperit, non incuriosum fratris:
quippe et propriis nuntiis a Corbulone petierat, ne
quam imaginem servitii Tiridates perferret neu
ferrum traderet aut complexu provincias optinentium
arceretur foribusve eorum adsisteret, tantusque ei
Romae quantus consulibus honor esset. Scilicet
externae superbiae sueto non inerat notitia nostri,
apud quos vis imperii valet, inania tramittuntur.

XXXII. Eodem anno Caesar nationes Alpium
maritimarum in ius Latii transtulit. Equitum
Romanorum locos sedilibus plebis anteposuit apud
circum; namque ad eam diem indiscreti inibant,

---

[1] In his own kingdom : see chap. 2 n.

[2] The summer residence of the Arsacids, in Greater Media;
now Hamadan.

[3] The national sabre—*Medus acinaces*. Tiridates contrived
to retain it even in the presence of Nero, though he first gave
security for his intentions by nailing the blade to the scabbard
(D. Cass. LXIII. 2 fin.).

[4] A diminutive procuratorial province, dating from 14 B.C.
and lying north of Nice on each side of the Var.

[5] A partial citizenship, which had ceased since the Social
War to exist in Italy but was valued in the provinces as a stage
towards the full franchise.

[6] Claudius *propria senatoribus constituit loca, promisce
spectare solitis* (Suet. *Claud.* 21; D. Cass. LX. 7), and Nero

XXX. To his glories Corbulo added courtesy and a banquet; and upon the inquiries of the king, whenever he observed some novelty—the announcement, for instance, by a centurion of the beginning of the watches; the dismissal of the company by bugle-note; the application of a torch to fire the altar raised in front of the general's pavilion—he so far exaggerated each point as to inspire him with admiration for our ancient customs. On the next day, Tiridates applied for a respite in which to visit his brothers and his mother before embarking upon so long a journey: in the interval, he handed over his daughter as a hostage, together with a letter of petition to Nero.

XXXI. On his departure, he found Pacorus in Media[1] and Vologeses at Ecbatana[2]—the latter not inattentive to his brother; for he had even requested Corbulo by special couriers that Tiridates should be exposed to none of the outward signs of vassalage, should not give up his sword,[3] should not be debarred from embracing the provincial governors or be left to stand and wait at their doors, and in Rome should receive equal distinction with the consuls. Evidently, accustomed as he was to foreign pride, he lacked all knowledge of ourselves who prize the essentials of sovereignty and ignore its vanities.

XXXII. In the same year, the Caesar placed the tribes of the Maritime Alps[4] in possession of Latin privileges.[5] To the Roman knights he assigned a place in the Circus in front of the popular seats— up to that date, the orders entered indiscriminately[6]

now does as much for the knights : the *lex Roscia* (VI. 3 n.) applied only to the theatre.

quia lex Roscia nihil nisi de quattuordecim ordinibus sanxit. Spectacula gladiatorum idem annus habuit pari magnificentia ac priora; sed feminarum inlustrium senatorumque plures per arenam foedati sunt.

XXXIII. C. Laecanio M. Licinio consulibus acriore in dies cupidine adigebatur Nero promiscas scaenas frequentandi. Nam adhuc per domum aut hortos cecinerat [1] Iuvenalibus ludis, quos ut parum celebres et tantae voci angustos spernebat. Non tamen Romae incipere ausus Neapolim quasi Graecam urbem delegit: inde initium fore, ut transgressus in Achaiam insignisque et antiquitus sacras coronas adeptus maiore fama studia civium eliceret. Ergo contractum oppidanorum vulgus, et quos e proximis coloniis et muncipiis eius rei fama acciverat, quique Caesarem per honorem aut varios usus sectantur, etiam militum manipuli, theatrum Neapolitanorum complent.

XXXIV. Illic, plerique ut arbitrabantur, triste, ut ipse, providum potius et secundis numinibus evenit: nam egresso qui adfuerat populo vacuum et sine ullius noxa theatrum conlapsum est. Ergo per conpositos cantus grates dis atque ipsam recentis casus fortunam celebrans petiturusque maris Hadriae

---

[1] cecinerat <aut> *Haase.*

---

[1] In his private theatre (XIV. 15 init.).

[2] " Celestial," according to his admirers (XVI. 22); " weak and husky," according to Dio and Suetonius (LXI. 20; *Ner.* 20). The Philostratean *Nero*, printed with Lucian, is more judicial:—Μεν. Ἡ φωνὴ δέ, Μουσώνιε, δἰ ἦν μουσομανεῖ . . ., πῶς ἔχει τῷ τυράννῳ; . . . Μουσ. Ἀλλ᾽ ἐκεῖνός γε, ὦ Μενέκρατες, οὔτε θαυμασίως ἔχει τοῦ φθέγματος οὔτε γελοίως κτέ.

[3] The town was a foundation of the Chalcidian colony

as the provisions of the Roscian law applied only to the " fourteen rows." The same year witnessed a number of gladiatorial shows, equal in magnificence to their predecessors, though more women of rank and senators disgraced themselves in the arena.

XXXIII. In the consulate of Gaius Laecanius A.V.C. 817 = and Marcus Licinius, a desire that grew every day A.D. 64 sharper impelled Nero to appear regularly on the public stage—hitherto he had sung in his palace or his gardens at the Juvenile Games,[1] which now he began to scorn as thinly attended functions, too circumscribed for so ample a voice.[2] Not daring, however, to take the first step at Rome, he fixed upon Naples as a Greek city :[3] after so much preface, he reflected, he might cross into Achaia, win the glorious and time-hallowed crowns of song, and then, with heightened reputation, elicit the plaudits of his countrymen. Accordingly, a mob which had been collected from the town, together with spectators drawn by rumours of the event from the neighbouring colonies and municipalities, the suite which attends the emperor whether in compliment or upon various duties, and, in addition, a few maniples of soldiers, filled the Neapolitan theatre.

XXXIV. There an incident took place, sinister in the eyes of many, providential and a mark of divine favour in those of the sovereign ; for, after the audience had left, the theatre, now empty, collapsed without injury to anyone. Therefore, celebrating in a set of verses his gratitude to Heaven, together with the happy course of the late accident, Nero—now bent on crossing the Adriatic—came to

Cumae, and retained some of its Greek characteristics even into the Middle Ages.

traiectus apud Beneventum interim consedit, ubi
gladiatorium munus a Vatinio celebre edebatur.
Vatinius inter foedissima eius aulae ostenta fuit,
sutrinae tabernae alumnus, corpore detorto, facetiis
scurrilibus; primo in contumelias adsumptus, dehinc
optimi cuiusque criminatione eo usque valuit, ut
gratia, pecunia, vi nocendi etiam malos praemineret.

XXXV. Eius munus frequentanti Neroni ne inter
voluptates quidem a sceleribus cessabatur. Isdem
quippe illis diebus Torquatus Silanus mori adigitur,
quia super Iuniae familiae claritudinem divum
Augustum abavum ferebat. Iussi accusatores obicere prodigum largitionibus, neque aliam spem
quam in rebus novis esse: quin inter libertos [1]
habere, quos ab epistulis et libellis et rationibus
appellet, nomina summae curae et meditamenta.
Tum intimus quisque libertorum vincti abreptique.
Et cum damnatio instaret, brachiorum venas Torquatus interscidit. Secutaque Neronis oratio ex more,
quamvis sontem et defensioni merito diffisum
victurum tamen fuisse, si clementiam iudicis
exspectasset.

XXXVI. Nec multo post omissa in praesens Achaia
(causae in incerto fuere) urbem revisit, provincias
Orientis, maxime Aegyptum, secretis imaginationibus

---

[1] quin inter libertos *Andresen*: quine innobiles *Med.*, *alii
alia.*

---

[1] In Samnium on the Appian Way, by which Nero was
travelling to Brundisium.
[2] Little else is known of him: see *Hist.* I. 37, *Dial.* 11, D.
Cass. LXIII. 15. His name was attached to a cheap and presumably grotesque type of *calix* (Juv. V. 46; Mart. X. 3,
XIV. 96).
[3] XII. 58 n.   [4] See XI. 29, with the notes, and XVI. 8.

rest for the moment at Beneventum;[1] where a largely attended gladiatorial spectacle was being exhibited by Vatinius. Vatinius ranked among the foulest prodigies of that court; the product of a shoemaker's shop, endowed with a misshapen body and a scurrile wit, he had been adopted at the outset as a target for buffoonery; then, by calumniating every man of decency, he acquired a power which made him in influence, in wealth, and in capacity for harm, pre-eminent even among villains.[2]

XXXV. But though Nero might attend his show, even in the midst of the diversions there was no armistice from crime; for in those very days Torquatus Silanus[3] was driven to die, because, not content with the nobility of the Junian house, he could point to the deified Augustus as his grandsire's grandsire. The accusers had orders to charge him with a prodigal munificence which left him no hope but in revolution, and to insist, further, that he had officials among his freedmen whom he styled his Masters of Letters, Petitions, and Accounts[4]—titles and rehearsals of the business of empire. Next, his confidential freedmen were arrested and removed; and Torquatus, finding his condemnation imminent, severed the arteries in his arms. There followed the usual speech from Nero, stating that, however guilty the defendant, however well founded his misgivings as to his defence, he should none the less have lived, if he had awaited the clemency of his judge.

XXXVI. Before long, giving up for the moment the idea of Greece (his reasons were a matter of doubt), he revisited the capital, his secret imaginations being now occupied with the eastern provinces,

agitans. Dehinc edicto testificatus non longam sui absentiam et cuncta in re publica perinde immota ac prospera fore, super ea profectione adiit Capitolium. Illic veneratus deos, cum Vestae quoque templum inisset, repente cunctos per artus tremens, seu numine exterrente, seu facinorum recordatione numquam timore vacuus, deseruit inceptum, cunctas sibi curas amore patriae leviores dictitans. Vidisse maestos civium vultus, audire secretas querimonias, quod tantum *itineris* [1] aditurus esset, cuius ne modicos quidem egressus tolerarent, sueti adversum fortuita aspectu principis refoveri. Ergo ut in privatis necessitudinibus proxima pignora praevalerent, ita *in re publica* [2] populum Romanum vim plurimam habere parendumque retinenti. Haec atque talia plebi volentia fuere, voluptatum cupidine et, quae praecipua cura est, rei frumentariae angustias si abesset, metuenti. Senatus et primores in incerto erant, procul an coram atrocior haberetur: dehinc, quae natura magnis timoribus, deterius credebant quod evenerat.

XXXVII. Ipse quo fidem adquireret nihil usquam perinde laetum sibi, publicis locis struere convivia

[1] <itineris> *Halm (after Heinsius).*
[2] <in re p.> *Wurm.*

Egypt in particular. Then after asseverating by edict that his absence would not be for long, and that all departments of the state would remain as stable and prosperous as ever, he repaired to the Capitol in connection with his departure. There he performed his devotions; but, when he entered the temple of Vesta also, he began to quake in every limb, possibly from terror inspired by the deity, or possibly because the memory of his crimes never left him devoid of fear. He abandoned his project, therefore, with the excuse that all his interests weighed lighter with him than the love of his fatherland:—" He had seen the dejected looks of his countrymen: he could hear their whispered complaints against the long journey soon to be undertaken by one whose most limited excursions were insupportable to a people in the habit of drawing comfort under misfortune from the sight of their emperor. Consequently, as in private relationships the nearest pledges of affection were the dearest, so in public affairs the Roman people had the first call, and he must yield if it wished him to stay." These and similar professions were much to the taste of the populace with its passion for amusements and its dread of a shortage of corn (always the chief preoccupation) in the event of his absence. The senate and high aristocracy were in doubt whether his cruelty was more formidable at a distance or at close quarters: in the upshot, as is inevitable in all great terrors, they believed the worse possibility to be the one which had become a fact.

XXXVII. He himself, to create the impression that no place gave him equal pleasure with Rome, began to serve banquets in the public places and to

totaque urbe quasi domo uti. Et celeberrimae luxu famaque epulae fuere, quas a Tigellino paratas ut exemplum referam, ne saepius eadem prodigentia narranda sit. Igitur in stagno Agrippae fabricatus est ratem, cui superpositum convivium navium aliarum tractu moveretur. Naves auro et ebore distinctae, remigesque exoleti per aetates et scientiam libidinum componebantur. Volucris et feras diversis e terris et animalia maris Oceano abusque petiverat. Crepidinibus stagni lupanaria adstabant inlustribus feminis completa, et contra scorta visebantur nudis corporibus. Iam gestus motusque obsceni; et postquam tenebrae incedebant, quantum iuxta nemoris et circumiecta tecta consonare cantu et luminibus clarescere. Ipse per licita atque inlicita foedatus nihil flagitii reliquerat, quo corruptior ageret, nisi paucos post dies uni ex illo contaminatorum grege (nomen Pythagorae fuit) in modum sollemnium coniugiorum denupsisset. Inditum imperatori flammeum, missi [1] auspices, dos et genialis torus et faces nuptiales, cuncta denique spectata, quae etiam in femina nox operit.

XXXVIII. Sequitur clades, forte an dolo principis incertum (nam utrumque auctores prodidere), sed omnibus, quae huic urbi per violentiam ignium

[1] missi *Frobeniana* : misit *Med.*, visi *Rhenanus.*

---

[1] The exact site is not determined.
[2] II. 14 n.
[3] Those who survive follow the more sensational version (Suet. *Ner.* 38; D. Cass. LXII. 16; Plin. *H.N.* XVII. 1, 5; [Sen.] *Oct.* 831 sqq.). There is obviously no possibility of deciding the question.

treat the entire city as his palace. In point of extravagance and notoriety, the most celebrated of the feasts was that arranged by Tigellinus; which I shall describe as a type, instead of narrating time and again the monotonous tale of prodigality. He constructed, then, a raft on the Pool of Agrippa,[1] and superimposed a banquet, to be set in motion by other craft acting as tugs. The vessels were gay with gold and ivory, and the oarsmen were catamites marshalled according to their ages and their libidinous attainments. He had collected birds and wild beasts from the ends of the earth, and marine animals from the ocean itself. On the quays of the lake stood brothels, filled with women of high rank; and, opposite, naked harlots met the view. First came obscene gestures and dances; then, as darkness advanced, the whole of the neighbouring grove, together with the dwelling-houses around, began to echo with song and to glitter with lights. Nero himself, defiled by every natural and unnatural lust had left no abomination in reserve with which to crown his vicious existence; except that, a few days later, he became, with the full rites of legitimate marriage, the wife of one of that herd of degenerates,[2] who bore the name of Pythagoras. The veil was drawn over the imperial head, witnesses were despatched to the scene; the dowry, the couch of wedded love, the nuptial torches, were there: everything, in fine, which night enshrouds even if a woman is the bride, was left open to the view.

XXXVIII. There followed a disaster, whether due to chance or to the malice of the sovereign is uncertain—for each version has its sponsors [3]—but graver and more terrible than any other which has

acciderunt, gravior atque atrocior. Initium in ea parte circi ortum, quae Palatino Caelioque montibus contigua est, ubi per tabernas, quibus id mercimonium inerat, quo flamma alitur, simul coeptus ignis et statim validus ac vento citus longitudinem circi corripuit. Neque enim domus munimentis saeptae vel templa muris cincta aut quid aliud morae interiacebat. Impetu pervagatum incendium plana primum, deinde in edita adsurgens et rursus inferiora populando, anteiit remedia velocitate mali et obnoxia urbe artis itineribus hucque et illuc flexis atque enormibus vicis, qualis vetus Roma fuit. Ad hoc lamenta paventium feminarum, fessa[1] aut rudis pueritiae[2] aetas, quique sibi quique aliis consulebant, dum trahunt invalidos aut opperiuntur, pars mora, pars festinans, cuncta impediebant. Et saepe, dum in tergum respectant, lateribus aut fronte circumveniebantur, vel si in proxima evaserant, illis quoque igni correptis, etiam quae longinqua crediderant in eodem casu reperiebant. Postremo, quid vitarent quid peterent ambigui, complere vias, sterni per agros; quidam amissis omnibus fortunis, diurni quoque victus,[3] alii caritate suorum, quos eripere nequiverant, quamvis patente effugio interiere. Nec quisquam defendere audebat, crebris

---

[1] fessa *Lipsius :* fessa aetate. [2] [pueritiae] *Haase.*
[3] victus <egeni> ?

---

[1] Similar descriptions are common. The town, in fact, was, as Livy puts it, " built promiscuously " after the Gallic disaster of 390 B.C. (V. fin.), and the meanness of its appearance struck the Greeks forcibly (XL. 5).

befallen this city by the ravages of fire. It took its
rise in the part of the Circus touching the Palatine
and Caelian Hills; where, among the shops packed
with inflammable goods, the conflagration broke out,
gathered strength in the same moment, and, impelled by the wind, swept the full length of the
Circus: for there were neither mansions screened
by boundary walls, nor temples surrounded by stone
enclosures, nor obstacles of any description, to bar
its progress. The flames, which in full career over-
ran the level districts first, then shot up to the heights,
and sank again to harry the lower parts, kept ahead
of all remedial measures, the mischief travelling
fast, and the town being an easy prey owing to the
narrow, twisting lanes and formless streets typical
of old Rome.¹ In addition, shrieking and terrified
women; fugitives stricken or immature in years;
men consulting their own safety or the safety of
others, as they dragged the infirm along or paused
to wait for them, combined by their dilatoriness or
their haste to impede everything. Often, while
they glanced back to the rear, they were attacked
on the flanks or in front; or, if they had made their
escape into a neighbouring quarter, that also was
involved in the flames, and even districts which they
had believed remote from danger were found to be
in the same plight. At last, irresolute what to avoid
or what to seek, they crowded into the roads or threw
themselves down in the fields: some who had lost
the whole of their means—their daily bread included
—chose to die, though the way of escape was open,
and were followed by others, through love for the
relatives whom they had proved unable to rescue.
None ventured to combat the fire, as there were

multorum minis restinguere prohibentium, et quia
alii palam faces iaciebant atque esse sibi auctorem
vociferabantur, sive ut raptus licentius exercerent
seu iussu.

XXXIX. Eo in tempore Nero Antii agens non
ante in urbem regressus est, quam domui eius, qua
Palatium et Maecenatis hortos continuaverat, ignis
propinquaret. Neque tamen sisti potuit, quin et
Palatium et domus et cuncta circum haurirentur.
Sed solacium populo exturbato ac profugo campum
Martis ac monumenta Agrippae, hortos quin etiam
suos patefecit et subitaria aedificia exstruxit, quae
multitudinem inopem acciperent; subvectaque uten-
silia ab Ostia et propinquis municipiis, pretiumque
frumenti minutum usque ad ternos nummos. Quae
quamquam popularia in inritum cadebant, quia
pervaserat rumor ipso tempore flagrantis urbis inisse
eum domesticam scaenam et cecinisse Troianum
excidium, praesentia mala vetustis cladibus
adsimulantem.

XL. Sexto demum die apud imas Esquilias finis
incendio factus, prorutis per inmensum aedificiis, ut

---

[1] Suetonius is more circumstantial :— . . . *incendit urbem,
tam palam ut plerique consulares cubicularios eius, cum stuppa
taedaque in praediis suis deprehensos, non attigerint* (*Ner.* 38).
Whatever the worth of the statements, it is clear that, if the
town was fired deliberately, no particular secrecy was
attempted : for there must have been a full moon on the night
before the outbreak (July 17–18).

[2] On the Esquiline, and now imperial property. The house
—*domus transitoria* (Suet. *Ner.* 31)—rose from its ashes as the
Golden House : see chap. 42.

[3] The great buildings erected by Agrippa, at the height of

reiterated threats from a large number of persons who
forbade extinction, and others were openly throwing
firebrands[1] and shouting that "they had their
authority"—possibly in order to have a freer hand
in looting, possibly from orders received.

XXXIX. Nero, who at the time was staying in
Antium, did not return to the capital until the fire
was nearing the house by which he had connected
the Palatine with the Gardens of Maecenas.[2] It
proved impossible, however, to stop it from engulfing
both the Palatine and the house and all their surround
ings. Still, as a relief to the homeless and fugitive
populace, he opened the Campus Martius, the
buildings[3] of Agrippa, even his own Gardens, and
threw up a number of extemporized shelters to accommodate the helpless multitude. The necessities
of life were brought up from Ostia and the neighbouring municipalities, and the price of grain was
lowered to three sesterces. Yet his measures,
popular as their character might be, failed of their
effect; for the report had spread that, at the very
moment when Rome was aflame, he had mounted
his private stage,[4] and, typifying the ills of the
present by the calamities of the past, had sung the
destruction of Troy.

XL. Only on the sixth day, was the conflagration
brought to an end at the foot of the Esquiline,
by demolishing the buildings over a vast area and

his power, in the Campus Martius—the Pantheon, Diribi-
torium, Saepta Iulia, etc.

[4] See the beginning of chap. 33. Suetonius and Dio give
him more conspicuous eminences : the former, the Tower of
Maecenas on the Esquiline; the latter, the palace-roof. The
verses, if there is truth in the story, were doubtless from the
Troica which Juvenal regarded as his crowning atrocity.

continuae violentiae campus et velut vacuum caelum
occurreret. Necdum positus [1] metus aut redierat
plebi spes: [2] rursum grassatus ignis patulis magis
urbis locis, eoque strages hominum minor: delubra
deum et porticus amoenitati dicatae latius procidere.
Plusque infamiae id incendium habuit, quia praediis
Tigellini Aemilianis proruperat; videbaturque Nero
condendae urbis novae et cognomento suo appel-
landae gloriam quaerere. Quippe in regiones quattuordecim Roma dividitur, quarum quattuor integrae
manebant, tres solo tenus deiectae: septem reliquis
pauca tectorum vestigia supererant, lacera et
semusta.

XLI. Domuum et insularum et templorum, quae
amissa sunt, numerum inire haud promptum fuerit:
sed vetustissima religione, quod Servius Tullius
Lunae, et magna ara fanumque, quae praesenti
Herculi Arcas Evander sacraverat, aedesque Statoris
Iovis vota Romulo Numaeque regia et delubrum
Vestae cum Penatibus populi Romani exusta; iam
opes tot victoriis quaesitae et Graecarum artium
decora, exim monumenta ingeniorum antiqua et
incorrupta, ut [3] quamvis in tanta resurgentis urbis

---

[1] positus *Jacob* : post.
[2] redierat plebi s<pes> *Madvig* : rediebat lebis *Med.*
(*with space for three letters left vacant*).
[3] <ut> *Halm.*

---

[1] The exact site is uncertain.
[2] The title contemplated was supposed to be *Neronopolis*
(Suet. *Ner.* 55). Commodus, faced by a similar problem, decided with more originality for *Colonia Commodiana*.
[3] Both the archaeological and the literary evidence show this
assertion to be too sweeping.
[4] The temple of Luna stood on the Aventine; the Ara
Maxima and temple of Hercules, in the Forum Boarium; that

opposing to the unabated fury of the flames a clear
tract of ground and an open horizon. But fear had
not yet been laid aside, nor had hope yet returned
to the people, when the fire resumed its ravages;
in the less congested parts of the city, however;
so that, while the toll of human life was not so great,
the destruction of temples and of porticoes dedicated
to pleasure was on a wider scale. The second fire
produced the greater scandal of the two, as it had
broken out on the Aemilian property [1] of Tigellinus
and appearances suggested that Nero was seeking
the glory of founding a new capital and endowing it
with his own name.[2] Rome, in fact, is divided into
fourteen regions, of which four remained intact,
while three were laid level with the ground: in the
other seven nothing survived but a few dilapidated
and half-burned relics of houses.[3]

XLI. It would not be easy to attempt an estimate
of the private dwellings, tenement-blocks, and
temples, which were lost; but the flames consumed,
in their old-world sanctity, the temple dedicated
to Luna by Servius Tullius, the great altar and chapel
of the Arcadian Evander to the Present Hercules,
the shrine of Jupiter Stator vowed by Romulus, the
Palace of Numa, and the holy place of Vesta with the
Penates of the Roman people.[4] To these must be
added the precious trophies won upon so many
fields, the glories of Greek art, and yet again the
primitive and uncorrupted memorials of literary
genius; [5] so that, despite the striking beauty of the

of Jupiter Stator, the Regia, and the shrine of Vesta, on the
northern side of the Palatine.

[5] The natural inference, though direct evidence is lacking,
is that the Palatine Library had suffered in the fire.

pulchritudine multa seniores meminerint, quae
reparari nequibant. Fuere qui adnotarent XIIII Kal.
Sextiles principium incendii huius ortum, quo et
Senones captam urbem inflammaverint. Alii eo
usque cura progressi sunt, ut totidem annos mensisque et dies inter utraque incendia numerent.

XLII. Ceterum Nero usus est patriae ruinis
exstruxitque domum, in qua haud perinde gemmae
et aurum miraculo essent, solita pridem et luxu
vulgata, quam arva et stagna et in modum soli-
tudinum hinc silvae, inde aperta spatia et prospectus,
magistris et machinatoribus Severo et Celere, quibus
ingenium et audacia erat etiam, quae natura dene-
gavisset, per artem temptare et viribus principis
inludere. Namque ab lacu Averno navigabilem
fossam usque ad ostia Tiberina depressuros promiserant, squalenti litore aut per montis adversos.
Neque enim aliud umidum gignendis aquis occurrit
quam Pomptinae paludes: cetera abrupta aut
arentia, ac si perrumpi possent, intolerandus labor

---

[1] Rome was fired by the Gauls after Allia in 390 B.C., and
the 454 years separating the two conflagrations may be resolved, though not exactly, into 418 years, 418 months,
418 days. The sentence, which had baffled Lipsius and
succeeding editors, was explained in 1843 by Grotefend.

[2] The celebrated *Domus Aurea*, which moved the emperor
to the admission that he " had begun to be housed like a human
being." Its short-lived splendours are catalogued by Suetonius
(*Ner.* 31) : a modern monograph is Weege's *Das Goldene Haus
des Nero*, 1913. It was demolished by Vespasian, and his
Colosseum now occupies perhaps one-tenth of its area.

rearisen city, the older generation recollects much that it proved impossible to replace. There were those who noted that the first outbreak of the fire took place on the nineteenth of July, the anniversary of the capture and burning of Rome by the Senones : others have pushed their researches so far as to resolve the interval between the two fires into equal numbers of years, of months, and of days.[1]

XLII. However, Nero turned to account the ruins of his fatherland by building a palace,[2] the marvels of which were to consist not so much in gems and gold, materials long familiar and vulgarized by luxury, as in fields and lakes and the air of solitude given by wooded ground alternating with clear tracts and open landscapes. The architects and engineers were Severus and Celer, who had the ingenuity and the courage to try the force of art even against the veto of nature and to fritter away the resources of a Caesar. They had undertaken to sink a navigable canal[3] running from Lake Avernus to the mouths of the Tiber along a desolate shore or through intervening hills ; for the one district along the route moist enough to yield a supply of water is the Pomptine Marsh ;[4] the rest being cliff and sand, which could be cut through, if at all, only by intolerable exertions for which no

[3] The lake could be made accessible from the Bay of Baiae by repairing the Julian Harbour (see XIV. 5 n.). The canal was then to have been carried northwards to the Tiber by convict labour drawn from every quarter of the empire, the estimated length being 160 Roman miles (Suet. *Ner.* 31).

[4] The water-logged, fever-ridden tract, some 30 miles long and from 6 to 11 broad, in S. Latium between the Volscian hills and the sea. The problem of its reclamation seems to have been definitely solved by Mussolini.

nec satis causae. Nero tamen, ut erat incredibilium cupitor, effodere proxima Averno iuga conisus est, manentque vestigia inritae spei.

XLIII. Ceterum urbis quae domui supererant non, ut post Gallica incendia, nulla distinctione nec passim erecta, sed dimensis vicorum ordinibus et latis viarum spatiis cohibitaque aedificiorum altitudine ac patefactis areis additisque porticibus, quae frontem insularum protegerent. Eas porticus Nero sua pecunia exstructurum purgatasque areas dominis traditurum pollicitus est. Addidit praemia pro cuiusque ordine et rei familiaris copiis, finivitque tempus, intra quod effectis domibus aut insulis apiscerentur. Ruderi accipiendo Ostiensis paludes destinabat, utique naves, quae frumentum Tiberi subvectassent, onustae rudere decurrerent, aedificiaque ipsa certa sui parte sine trabibus saxo Gabino Albanove solidarentur, quod is lapis ignibus impervius est; iam aqua privatorum licentia intercepta quo largior et pluribus locis in publicum flueret, custodes *adessent*;[1] et subsidia reprimendis ignibus in propatulo quisque haberet; nec communione parietum, sed propriis quaeque muris ambirentur.[2] Ea ex utilitate accepta decorem quoque novae urbi attulere.

---

[1] <adessent> *Jackson,* <essent> *Madvig.*

[2] nec . . . ambirentur]. *Plausibly transposed by Nipperdey, to follow* impervius est *above.*

---

[1] The object, apart from the draining of the Marshes was to enable the grainships to avoid 125 miles of open and dangerous coast.

[2] Two kinds of the volcanic *peperino* of the Campagna—the latter quarried in the Alban hills, the former in the level between Tivoli and Frascati.

sufficient motive existed.[1] None the less, Nero, with his passion for the incredible, made an effort to tunnel the heights nearest the Avernus, and some evidences of that futile ambition survive.

XLIII. In the capital, however, the districts spared by the palace were rebuilt, not, as after the Gallic fire, indiscriminately and piecemeal, but in measured lines of streets, with broad thoroughfares, buildings of restricted height, and open spaces, while colonnades were added as a protection to the front of the tenement-blocks. These colonnades Nero offered to erect at his own expense, and also to hand over the building-sites, clear of rubbish, to the owners. He made a further offer of rewards, proportioned to the rank and resources of the various claimants, and fixed a term within which houses or blocks of tenements must be completed, if the bounty was to be secured. As the receptacle of the refuse he settled upon the Ostian Marshes, and gave orders that vessels which had carried grain up the Tiber must run down-stream laden with débris. The buildings themselves, to an extent definitely specified, were to be solid, untimbered structures of Gabine or Alban stone,[2] that particular stone being proof against fire. Again, there was to be a guard to ensure that the water-supply—intercepted by private lawlessness—should be available for public purposes in greater quantities and at more points; appliances for checking fire were to be kept by everyone in the open; there were to be no joint partitions between buildings, but each was to be surrounded by its own walls. These reforms, welcomed for their utility, were also beneficial to the appearance of the new capital. Still, there were

Erant tamen qui crederent, veterem illam formam
salubritati magis conduxisse, quoniam angustiae
itinerum et altitudo tectorum non perinde solis
vapore perrumperentur: at nunc patulam lati-
tudinem et nulla umbra defensam graviore aestu
ardescere.

XLIV. Et haec quidem humanis consiliis pro-
videbantur. Mox petita dis piacula aditique Sibullae
libri, ex quibus supplicatum Volcano et Cereri Pro-
serpinaeque, ac propitiata Iuno per matronas, primum
in Capitolio, deinde apud proximum mare, unde
hausta aqua templum et simulacrum deae per-
spersum est; et sellisternia ac pervigilia celebravere
feminae, quibus mariti erant. Sed non ope humana,
non largitionibus principis aut deum placamentis
decedebat infamia, quin iussum incendium crederetur. Ergo abolendo rumori Nero subdidit reos et
quaesitissimis poenis adfecit, quos per flagitia invisos
vulgus Christianos appellabat. Auctor nominis eius
Christus Tiberio imperitante per procuratorem
Pontium Pilatum supplicio adfectus erat; repressa-
que in praesens exitiabilis superstitio rursum erumpe-
bat, non modo per Iudaeam, originem eius mali, sed
per urbem etiam, quo cuncta undique atrocia aut
pudenda confluunt celebranturque. Igitur primum
correpti qui fatebantur, deinde indicio eorum multi-

---

[1] The charges bandied about in the next century were those
always favoured in such cases: ritual murder, nameless
abominations with extinguished lights, *et hoc genus omne*
(Just. Mart. *Apol.* I. 26, etc.).

[2] About twenty years had elapsed since the name arose in
Antioch (*Acts* xi. 26).—For a clear statement of the main
problems of this " Neronian persecution," the reader may be
referred to Furneaux' Excursus (II[2]. 416–427).

those who held that the old form had been the more salubrious, as the narrow streets and high-built houses were not so easily penetrated by the rays of the sun; while now the broad expanses, with no protecting shadows, glowed under a more oppressive heat.

XLIV. So far, the precautions taken were suggested by human prudence: now means were sought for appeasing deity, and application was made to the Sibylline books; at the injunction of which public prayers were offered to Vulcan, Ceres, and Proserpine, while Juno was propitiated by the matrons, first in the Capitol, then at the nearest point of the sea-shore, where water was drawn for sprinkling the temple and image of the goddess. Ritual banquets and all-night vigils were celebrated by women in the married state. But neither human help, nor imperial munificence, nor all the modes of placating Heaven, could stifle scandal or dispel the belief that the fire had taken place by order. Therefore, to scotch the rumour, Nero substituted as culprits, and punished with the utmost refinements of cruelty, a class of men, loathed for their vices,[1] whom the crowd styled Christians.[2] Christus, the founder of the name, had undergone the death penalty in the reign of Tiberius, by sentence of the procurator Pontius Pilatus,[3] and the pernicious superstition was checked for a moment, only to break out once more, not merely in Judaea, the home of the disease, but in the capital itself, where all things horrible or shameful in the world collect and find a vogue. First, then, the confessed members of the sect were arrested; next, on their disclosures, vast

[3] The only mention in heathen Latin.

tudo ingens haud perinde in crimine incendii quam
odio humani generis convicti sunt. Et pereuntibus
addita ludibria, ut ferarum tergis contecti laniatu
canum interirent, † aut crucibus adfixi aut flammandi †, atque ubi defecisset dies, in usum nocturni
luminis urerentur.[1] Hortos suos ei spectaculo Nero
obtulerat et circense ludicrum edebat, habitu aurigae
permixtus plebi vel curriculo insistens. Unde quamquam adversus sontis et novissima exempla meritos
miseratio oriebatur, tamquam non utilitate publica,
sed in saevitiam unius absumerentur.

XLV. Interea conferendis pecuniis pervastata
Italia, provinciae eversae sociique populi et quae civitatium liberae vocantur. Inque eam praedam etiam
di cessere, spoliatis in urbe templis egestoque auro,
quod triumphis, quod votis omnis populi Romani
aetas prospere aut in metu sacraverat. Enimvero
per Asiam atque Achaiam non dona tantum, sed
simulacra numinum abripiebantur, missis in eas
provincias Acrato ac Secundo Carrinate. Ille libertus
cuicumque flagitio promptus, hic Graeca doctrina
ore tenus exercitus animum bonis artibus non
inbuerat.[2] Ferebatur Seneca, quo invidiam sacrilegii

---

[1] *So the Mediceus, corruptly and, it would seem, defectively;
nor is it possible to restore the original with the help of the
version of Sulpicius Severus (about* 400 A.D.)*:—interirent, multi
crucibus adfixi aut flamma usti, plerique in id reservati ut,
cum defecisse e.q.s. (Chron. ii. 29). Nipperdey cut the knot
by cancelling* aut crucibus . . . flammandi.

[2] imbuerat *Lipsius :* induerat.

---

[1] The expression, of course, may mean anything. Gibbon
compared the terms applied by Livy to the 7,000 people
involved in the Bacchanalian scandals—*multitudinem ingen-
tem, alterum iam populun* (XXXIX. 13), *multa milia hominum*
(ib. 15).

[2] Jewish "misanthropy"—which was proverbial—may have

numbers [1] were convicted, not so much on the count of arson as for hatred of the human race.[2] And derision accompanied their end: they were covered with wild beasts' skins and torn to death by dogs; or they were fastened on crosses, and, when daylight failed were burned to serve as lamps by night. Nero had offered his Gardens for the spectacle, and gave an exhibition in his Circus, mixing with the crowd in the habit of a charioteer, or mounted on his car. Hence, in spite of a guilt which had earned the most exemplary punishment, there arose a sentiment of pity, due to the impression that they were being sacrificed not for the welfare of the state but to the ferocity of a single man.

XLV. Meanwhile, Italy had been laid waste for contributions of money; the provinces, the federate communities, and the so-called free states, were ruined. The gods themselves formed part of the plunder, as the ravaged temples of the capital were drained of the gold dedicated in the triumphs or the vows, the prosperity or the fears, of the Roman nation at every epoch. But in Asia and Achaia, not offerings alone but the images of deity were being swept away, since Acratus and Carrinas Secundus had been despatched into the two provinces. The former was a freedman prepared for any enormity; the latter, as far as words went, was a master of Greek philosophy, but his character remained untinctured by the virtues. Seneca, it was rumoured, to divert the odium of sacrilege from

partly suggested the charge; though from a passage of Sulpicius Severus, almost certainly transcribed from the *Histories* (see vol. ii. p. 220 of this edition), it is evident that the gulf between Jew and Christian had been clearly recognized by the Roman high command in 70 A.D.

a semet averteret, longinqui ruris secessum oravisse,
et postquam non concedebatur, ficta valetudine, quasi
aeger nervis, cubiculum non egressus. Tradidere
quidam venenum ei per libertum ipsius, cui nomen
Cleonicus, paratum iussu Neronis vitatumque a
Seneca proditione liberti seu propria formidine, dum
persimplici victu et agrestibus pomis, ac si sitis
admoneret, profluente aqua vitam tolerat.

XLVI. Per idem tempus gladiatores apud oppidum
Praeneste temptata eruptione praesidio militis, qui
custos adesset,[1] coerciti sunt, iam Spartacum et
vetera mala rumoribus ferente populo, ut est novarum
rerum cupiens pavidusque. Nec multo post clades
rei navalis accipitur, non bello (quippe haud alias
tam immota pax), sed certum ad diem in Campaniam redire classem Nero iusserat, non exceptis
maris casibus. Ergo gubernatores, quamvis sae-
viente pelago, a Formiis movere; et gravi Africo,
dum promunturium Miseni superare contendunt,
Cumanis litoribus inpacti triremium plerasque et
minora navigia passim amiserunt.

XLVII. Fine anni vulgantur prodigia, inminentium
malorum nuntia. Vis fulgurum non alias crebrior,
et sidus cometes, sanguine inlustri semper Neroni
expiatum. Bicipites hominum aliorumve animalium
partus abiecti in publicum aut in sacrificiis, quibus

---

[1] adesset] adest *Nipperdey.*

---

[1] Palestrina. That the gladiators belonged to an imperial
school (XI. 35 n.) is shown by the presence of the military
guard.

[2] III. 73 n.

[3] The fleet was to return from Formiae (Mola di Gaëta)
on the Latian coast to its base at Misenum.

himself, had asked leave to retire to a distant estate in the country, and, when it was not accorded, had feigned illness—a neuralgic affection, he said—and declined to leave his bedroom. Some have put it on record that, by the orders of Nero, poison had been prepared for him by one of his freedmen, Cleonicus by name; and that, owing either to the man's revelations or to his own alarms, it was avoided by Seneca, who supported life upon an extremely simple diet of field fruits and, if thirst was insistent, spring water.

XLVI. About the same time, an attempted outbreak of the gladiators at the town of Praeneste[1] was quelled by the company of soldiers stationed as a guard upon the spot; not before the populace, allured and terrified as always by revolution, had turned its conversation to Spartacus[2] and the calamities of the past. Not long afterwards, news was received of a naval disaster. War was not the cause (for at no other time had peace been so completely undisturbed), but Nero had ordered the fleet to return to Campania[3] by a given date, no allowance being made for hazards of the sea. The helmsmen, therefore, in spite of a raging storm, stood out from Formiae; and, while attempting to round the promontory of Misenum, were driven by a south-west gale on to the beach at Cumae, losing a considerable number of triremes and smaller vessels in crowds.

XLVII. At the close of the year, report was busy with portents heralding disaster to come—lightning-flashes in numbers never exceeded, a comet (a phenomenon to which Nero always made atonement in noble blood); two-headed embryos, human or of the other animals, thrown out in public or discovered

gravidas hostias inmolare mos est, reperti. Et in agro Placentino viam propter natus vitulus, cui caput in crure esset; secutaque haruspicum interpretatio, parari rerum humanarum aliud caput, sed non fore validum neque occultum, quia in utero repressum et [1] iter iuxta editum sit.

XLVIII. Ineunt deinde consulatum Silius Nerva et Atticus Vestinus, coepta simul et aucta coniuratione, in quam certatim nomina dederant senatores eques miles, feminae etiam, cum odio Neronis, tum favore in C. Pisonem. Is Calpurnio genere ortus ac multas insignisque familias paterna nobilitate complexus, claro apud vulgum rumore erat per virtutem aut species virtutibus similis. Namque facundiam tuendis civibus exercebat, largitionem adversum amicos, et ignotis quoque comi sermone et congressu; aderant etiam fortuita, corpus procerum, decora facies: sed procul gravitas morum aut voluptatum parsimonia; levitati [2] ac magnificentiae et aliquando luxu indulgebat. Idque pluribus probabatur, qui in tanta vitiorum dulcedine summum imperium non restrictum nec perseverum volunt.

---

[1] et *Ernesti:* aut.   [2] levitati *Ernesti:* lenitati.

---

[1] Piacenza.

[2] To judge from the last sentence of XIV. 65, it must have been at least in contemplation by 63 A.D.: if the reading *ardente domo* is correct two chapters below, it was already mature at the time of the fire.

[3] His parents, curiously enough, cannot be identified. It is known that he was married in 37 A.D., though his wedding-guest Caligula appropriated the bride (Suet. *Cal.* 25); that he was banished two years (?) later (*biennio post* Suet. *l.l.*, πρὶν δύο μῆνας ἐξελθεῖν, D. Cass. LIX. 8); and that he returned under Claudius, held a consulate, and subsequently inherited a fortune from his mother (Σ. Juv. V. 109).

in the sacrifices where it is the rule to kill pregnant victims. Again, in the territory of Placentia,[1] a calf was born close to the road with the head grown to a leg; and there followed an interpretation of the sooth-sayers, stating that another head was being pre-pared for the world; but it would be neither strong nor secret, as it had been repressed in the womb, and had been brought forth at the wayside.

XLVIII. Silius Nerva and Vestinus Atticus then entered upon their consulate—the year of a con-spiracy, no sooner hatched than full-grown,[2] for which senators, knights, soldiers, and women themselves had vied in giving in their names, not simply through hatred of Nero, but also through partiality for Gaius Piso.[3] Piso, sprung from the Calpurnian house, and, by his father's high descent, uniting in his own person many families of distinction, enjoyed with the multitude a shining reputation for virtue, or for spectacular qualities resembling virtues.[4] For he exercised his eloquence in the defence of his fellow-citizens, his liberality in the service of his friends; and even with strangers his conversation and inter-course were marked by courtesy. He was favoured also with those gifts of chance, a tall figure and handsome features. But weight of character and continence in pleasure were absent: he gave full scope to frivolity, to ostentation, and at times to debauchery—a trait which was approved by that majority of men, who, in view of the manifold allure-ments of vice, desire no strictness or marked austerity in the head of the state.

[4] They are enumerated in the *Laus Pisonis* (Baehrens, *P.L.M.* i. 220 sqq.)—261 hexameters by a young and indigent author, whom Maurice Haupt and Lachmann identified with the pastoral poet Calpurnius.

XLIX. Initium coniurationi non a cupidine ipsius fuit: nec tamen facile memoraverim, quis primus auctor, cuius instinctu concitum sit quod tam multi sumpserunt. Promptissimos Subrium Flavum [1] tribunum praetoriae cohortis et Sulpicium Asprum centurionem extitisse constantia exitus docuit; et Lucanus Annaeus Plautiusque Lateranus [2] vivida odia intulere. Lucanum propriae causae accendebant, quod famam carminum eius premebat Nero prohibueratque ostentare, vanus adsimulatione: [3] Lateranum consulem designatum nulla iniuria, sed amor rei publicae sociavit. At Flavius Scaevinus et Afranius Quintianus, uterque senatorii ordinis, contra famam sui principium tanti facinoris capessivere. Nam Scaevino dissoluta luxu mens et proinde vita somno languida: Quintianus mollitia corporis infamis et a Nerone probroso carmine diffamatus contumelias ultum ibat.

L. Ergo dum scelera principis, et finem adesse imperio deligendumque, qui fessis rebus succurreret, inter se aut inter amicos iaciunt, adgregavere Claudium [4] Senecionem, Cervarium Proculum, Vulcacium [5] Araricum, Iulium Augurinum, Munatium Gratum, An-

[1] Flavum *Bekker* : Flavium.
[2] Lateranus *Bekker* : lateranus consul designatus.
[3] vanus adsimulatione] vanissima aemulatione *Ruperti (after Lipsius).*
[4] Claudium *Ritter* : tullium.
[5] Vulcacium *Andresen* (Vulcatium *Rhenanus*) : vulgacium.

---

[1] Nephew of Claudius' commander in Britain, A. Plautius Silvanus; implicated in the scandal of Messalina and Silius, but spared out of consideration for his uncle (XI. 36); restored

XLIX. The beginning of the conspiracy did not
come from his own wish. At the same time, it is
not easy for me to say who was its original author,
whose the initiative that called into being a project
which so many embraced. That its most resolute
adherents had been found in Subrius Flavus, the
tribune of a praetorian cohort, and the centurion
Sulpicius Asper, was proved by the firmness of
their end; while Annaeus Lucanus and Plautius
Lateranus [1] contributed the vivacity of their hatreds.
Lucan had private motives to inflame him, since
Nero was stifling the reputation of his poems and had
ordered him not to seek publicity—for he had the
vanity to count himself his peer. Lateranus, a
consul designate, was brought to the cause, not by
an injury, but by affection for the commonwealth.
On the other hand, Flavius Scaevinus and Afranius
Quintianus, both of senatorial rank, belied their
repute when they took the lead in so desperate an
enterprise. For the mental powers of Scaevinus
had been wrecked by debauchery, and his life was
one of corresponding languor and somnolence;
Quintianus, a notorious degenerate, had been
attacked by Nero in a scurrilous poem, and was now
intent upon avenging the affront.

L. Scattering allusions, therefore, among themselves or their friends to the crimes of the sovereign,
the approaching dissolution of the empire, the need
of choosing the saviour of an outworn society, they
gathered to their number Claudius Senecio, Cervarius Proculus, Vulcacius Araricus, Julius Augurinus,

to the senate by Nero (XIII. 11). His great mansion on the
Coelian Hill passed, by gift of Constantine to the Popes, and
the Lateran palace and church perpetuate his name.

tonium Natalem, Marcium Festum, equites Romanos.
Ex quibus Senecio, e praecipua familiaritate Neronis,
speciem amicitiae etiam tum retinens eo pluribus
periculis conflictabatur: Natalis particeps ad omne
secretum Pisoni erat, ceteris spes ex novis rebus
petebatur. Adscitae sunt super Subrium et Sulpicium, de quibus rettuli, militares manus, Gavius
Silvanus et Statius Proxumus tribuni cohortium
praetoriarum, Maximus Scaurus et Venetus Paulus
centuriones. Sed summum robur in Faenio Rufo
praefecto videbatur, quem vita famaque laudatum
per saevitiam inpudicitiamque Tigellinus in animo
principis anteibat. Fatigabatque criminationibus ac
saepe in metum adduxerat quasi adulterum Agrippinae et desiderio eius ultioni intentum. Igitur ubi
coniuratis praefectum quoque praetorii in partes
descendisse crebro ipsius sermone facta fides,
promptius iam de tempore ac loco caedis agitabant.
Et cepisse impetum Subrius Flavus ferebatur in
scaena canentem Neronem adgrediendi, aut cum
ardente domo[1] per noctem huc illuc cursaret
incustoditus. Hic occasio solitudinis, ibi ipsa fre-
quentia tanti decoris testis pulcherrima[2] animum
exstimulaverant, nisi impunitatis cupido retinuisset,
magnis semper conatibus adversa.

LI. Interim cunctantibus prolatantibusque spem

---

[1] ardente domo]. *The words are doubted, but there is no
plausible emendation.*
[2] pulcherrima *Urlichs :* pulcherrimum.

---

[1] XIII. 12.   [2] XIV. 51.

Munatius Gratus, Antonius Natalis, and Marcius Festus, all Roman knights. Of these, Senecio, one of Nero's chief familiars,[1] maintained even then a semblance of friendship, and was exposed in consequence to a larger variety of dangers: Natalis was the partner of Piso in all his secret counsels; the rest were seeking hope from revolution. In addition to Subrius and Sulpicius, who have been noticed already, Gavius Silvanus and Statius Proxumus, tribunes of the praetorian cohorts, together with the centurions Maximus Scaurus and Venetus Paulus, were called in as men of the sword. Their main strength, however, was considered to lie in Faenius Rufus,[2] the prefect, whose estimable life and character were, in the prince's favour, outweighed by the ferocity and lust of Tigellinus; who persecuted him with calumnies and had repeatedly awakened his alarm by describing him as the paramour of Agrippina, still mourning her, and determined upon vengeance. Hence, when his own reiterated statements had convinced the plotters that the commander of the Praetorian Guard had himself entered the lists, they began to show more alacrity in debating the time and place of the assassination. It was asserted that Subrius Flavus had conceived an impulse to attack Nero while he was singing on the stage, or while, during the burning of the palace, he was rushing unguarded from place to place in the night. In one case, there were the opportunities of solitude: in the other, the very presence of a crowd, to be the fairest witness of such an exploit, had fired his imagination; only the desire of escape, that eternal enemy of high emprises, gave him pause.

LI. In the meantime, while they were still hesi-

ac metum Epicharis quaedam, incertum quonam
modo sciscitata (neque illi ante ulla rerum hone-
starum cura fuerat), accendere et arguere coniuratos,
ac postremum lenitudinis eorum pertaesa et in
Campania agens primores classiariorum Misenensium
labefacere et conscientia inligare conisa est tali
initio.   Erat navarchus in ea classe Volusius Proculus,
occidendae matris Neroni [1] inter ministros, non ex
magnitudine sceleris provectus, ut rebatur. Is
mulieri olim cognitus, seu recens orta amicitia, dum
merita erga Neronem sua et quam in inritum ceci-
dissent aperit adicitque questus et destinationem
vindictae, si facultas oreretur, spem dedit posse
inpelli et pluris conciliare: nec leve auxilium in
classe, crebras occasiones, quia Nero multo apud
Puteolos et Misenum maris usu laetabatur.   Ergo
Epicharis plura; et omnia scelera principis orditur,
neque senatui *neque populo* [2] quid*quam* [3] manere.
Sed provisum, quonam modo poenas eversae rei
publicae daret: accingeretur modo navare operam et
militum acerrimos ducere in partis, ac digna pretia
exspectaret; nomina tamen coniuratorum reticuit.
Unde Proculi indicium inritum fuit, quamvis ea, quae

[1] Neroni *Heinsius* : neronis.
[2] <neque populo> *Halm (after Madvig)*.
[3] quidquam *Madvig* : quod.

tating, reluctant to abridge the period of hope and
fear, a certain Epicharis, who had gained her information by means unknown—she had never previously
shown interest in anything honourable—began to
animate and upbraid the conspirators. Finally,
wearied of their slowness and happening to be in
Campania, she made an effort to undermine the
loyalty of the fleet officers at Misenum and to
implicate them in the plot. The beginning of the
intrigue was this. In the squadron was a ship-
captain, Volusius Proculus, one of Nero's agents
in the assassination of his mother, but not (he
considered) promoted as the importance of the
crime deserved. This person, as a former acquaintance of the woman (or possibly the friendship
may have been of recent growth), disclosed what his
services to Nero had been, and how thankless they
had proved, then proceeded to complaints and to a
declared intention of settling the account, should
occasion offer. He thus gave hope that he might
be influenced and win fresh adherents. The help
of the fleet, it was reflected, was no slight matter;
and opportunities must be plentiful, as Nero delighted in frequent excursions by sea in the neighbourhood of Puteoli and Misenum. Epicharis therefore went further, and entered upon a catalogue of
the emperor's crimes:—Nothing was left either for
the senate ⟨or for the people⟩! But a way had been
provided by which he might pay the penalty for the
ruin of his country. Proculus had only to gird
himself to do his part, bring over his most resolute
men to the cause, and look forward to a worthy reward." On the names of the conspirators, however,
she observed silence; with the result that Proculus

audierat, ad Neronem detulisset. Accita quippe Epicharis et cum indice composita nullis testibus innisum facile confutavit. Sed ipsa in custodia retenta est, suspectante Nerone haud falsa esse etiam quae vera non probabantur.

LII. Coniuratis tamen metu proditionis permotis placitum maturare caedem apud Baias in villa Pisonis, cuius amoenitate captus Caesar crebro ventitabat balneasque et epulas inibat omissis excubiis et fortunae suae mole. Sed abnuit Piso, invidiam praetendens, si sacra mensae dique hospitales caede qualiscumque principis cruentarentur: melius apud urbem in illa invisa et spoliis civium extructa domo vel in publico patraturos quod pro re publica suscepissent. Haec in commune, ceterum timore occulto, ne L. Silanus eximia nobilitate disciplinaque C. Cassii, apud quem educatus erat, ad omnem claritudinem sublatus imperium invaderet, prompte daturis, qui a coniuratione integri essent quique miserarentur Neronem tamquam per scelus interfectum. Plerique Vestini quoque consulis acre ingenium vitavisse Pisonem crediderunt, ne ad libertatem oreretur, vel delecto imperatore alio sui

---

[1] A son of M. Silanus (the " Golden Sheep" of XIII. 1), and the last lineal descendant of Augustus, apart from Nero.— Cassius is the jurist (XII. 11, etc.).

though he reported what he had heard to Nero, made his disclosure in vain. For Epicharis was summoned, confronted with the informer, and in the absence of corroborating evidence silenced him with ease. Still, she was herself detained in custody, Nero having a suspicion that the statements, even if not demonstrated to be true, were not therefore false.

LII. The plotters, however, moved by the fear of betrayal, decided to hasten on the murder at Baiae in a villa belonging to Piso—its charms had a fascination for the Caesar, who came frequently and indulged in the bath or the banquet, dispensing with his guards and the tedious magnificence of his rank. But Piso refused, his pretext being the odium which must be faced, " if they stained with the blood of an emperor, however contemptible, the sanctities of the guest-table and the gods of hospitality. Better in the capital, in that hated palace reared from the spoils of his countrymen, or under the public gaze, to do the deed they had undertaken for the public good." This was for the general ear : actually he had an unconfessed misgiving that Lucius Silanus [1]—who, thanks to his exalted lineage and to the training of Gaius Cassius, with whom he had been educated, stood high enough for any dignity—might grasp at the empire; which would be promptly offered to him by the persons who had held aloof from the plot or who pitied Nero as the victim of a murder. It was commonly believed that Piso had intended at the same time to evade the energy of the consul Vestinus, lest he should arise as the champion of liberty, or, by selecting another as emperor, convert the state into a gift of

muneris rem publicam faceret. Etenim expers coniurationis erat, quamvis super eo crimine Nero vetus adversum insontem odium expleverit.

LIII. Tandem statuere circensium ludorum die, qui Cereri celebratur, exsequi destinata, quia Caesar rarus egressu domoque aut hortis clausus ad ludicra circi ventitabat promptioresque aditus erant laetitia spectaculi. Ordinem insidiis composuerant, ut Lateranus, quasi subsidium rei familiari oraret, deprecabundus et genibus principis accidens prosterneret incautum premeretque, animi validus et corpore ingens. Tum iacentem et impeditum tribuni et centuriones et ceterorum, ut quisque audentiae habuisset, adcurrerent trucidarentque, primas sibi partis expostulante Scaevino, qui pugionem templo Salutis [1] sive, ut alii tradidere, Fortunae Ferentino in oppido detraxerat gestabatque velut magno operi sacrum. Interim Piso apud aedem Cereris opperiretur, unde eum praefectus Faenius et ceteri accitum ferrent in castra, comitante Antonia, Claudii Caesaris filia, ad eliciendum vulgi favorem, quod C. Plinius memorat. Nobis quoquo modo traditum non occultare in animo fuit, quamvis absurdum videretur

---

[1] Salutis *Ernesti* : salutis in etruria.

---

[1] The date of the Cerialia was Apr. 12–19, the games being circensian on the opening and closing days.

[2] Hardly the Latian town of the name (Ferentino, near Anagni), but the Etrurian Ferentinum, or Ferentium (Ferento, between Viterbo and Bomarzo). In that case, " Fortuna " is certainly, and " Salus " possibly, the Etruscan goddess Nortia (Juv. X. 74).

[3] By his marriage with Aelia Paetina (XII. 2). Wife first of Cn. Pompeius, then of Faustus Sulla, she refused Nero's

his own bestowing. For in the conspiracy he had no part, though conspiracy was the charge on which Nero satisfied his old hatred of an innocent man.

LIII. At last they resolved to execute their purpose on the day of the Circensian Games when the celebration is in honour of Ceres;[1] as the emperor, who rarely left home and secluded himself in his palace or gardens, went regularly to the exhibitions in the Circus and could be approached with comparative ease owing to the gaiety of the spectacle. They had arranged a set programme for the plot. Lateranus, as though asking financial help, would fall in an attitude of entreaty at the emperor's feet, overturn him while off his guard, and hold him down, being as he was a man of intrepid character and a giant physically. Then, as the victim lay prostrate and pinned, the tribunes, the centurions, and any of the rest who had daring enough, were to run up and do him to death; the part of protagonist being claimed by Scaevinus, who had taken down a dagger from the temple of Safety—of Fortune, according to other accounts—in the town of Ferentinum,[2] and wore it regularly as the instrument sanctified to a great work. In the interval, Piso was to wait in the temple of Ceres; from which he would be summoned by the prefect Faenius and the others and carried to the camp: he would be accompanied by Claudius' daughter[3] Antonia, with a view to eliciting the approval of the crowd. This is the statement of Pliny. For my own part, whatever his assertion may be worth, I was not inclined to suppress it, absurd as it may seem that either

hand after the death of Poppaea, and was later executed on a charge of seditious activities (Suet. *Ner.* 35).

aut inanem ad spem Antoniam nomen et periculum commodavisse, aut Pisonem notum amore uxoris alii matrimonio se obstrinxisse, nisi si cupido dominandi cunctis adfectibus flagrantior est.

LIV. Sed mirum quam inter diversi generis ordinis, aetatis sexus, ditis pauperes taciturnitate omnia cohibita sint, donec proditio coepit e domo Scaevini; qui pridie insidiarum multo sermone cum Antonio Natale, dein regressus domum testamentum obsignavit, promptum vagina pugionem, de quo supra rettuli, vetustate obtusum increpans, asperari saxo et in mucronem ardescere iussit eamque curam liberto Milicho mandavit. Simul adfluentius solito convivium initum, servorum carissimi libertate et alii pecunia donati. Atque ipse maestus et magnae cogitationis manifestus erat, quamvis laetitiam vagis sermonibus simularet. Postremo vulneribus ligamenta quibusque sistitur sanguis parari iubet, *id*que [1] eundem Milichum monet, sive gnarum coniurationis et illuc usque fidum, seu nescium et tunc primum arreptis suspicionibus, ut plerique tradidere. De consequentibus *consentitur*.[2] Nam cum secum servilis animus praemia perfidiae reputavit simulque inmensa pecunia et potentia obversabantur, cessit fas et salus patroni et acceptae libertatis

---

[1] parari iubet, idque *Nipperdey-Andresen*: partiebatque.
[2] <consentitur> *Mueller.*

[1] A conflicting account, included by Plutarch among his examples of the ills of garrulity (*Mor.* 505 CD), seems to be negligible.

Antonia should have staked her name and safety on an empty expectation, or Piso, notoriously devoted to his wife, should have pledged himself to another marriage—unless, indeed, the lust of power burns more fiercely than all emotions combined.

LIV. It is surprising, none the less, how in this mixture of ranks and classes, ages and sexes, rich and poor, the whole affair was kept in secrecy, till the betrayal came from the house of Scaevinus.[1] On the day before the attempt, he had a long conversation with Antonius Natalis, after which he returned home, sealed his will, and taking the dagger, mentioned above, from the sheath, complained that it was blunt from age, and gave orders that it was to be rubbed on a whetstone till the edge glittered: this task he entrusted to his freedman Milichus. At the same time, he began a more elaborate dinner than usual, and presented his favourite slaves with their liberty, or, in some cases, with money. He himself was moody, and obviously deep in thought, though he kept up a disconnected conversation which affected cheerfulness. At last, he gave the word that bandages for wounds and appliances for stopping haemorrhage were to be made ready. The instructions were again addressed to Milichus: possibly he was aware of the conspiracy, and had so far kept faith; possibly, as the general account goes, he knew nothing, and caught his first suspicions at that moment. About the sequel there is unanimity. For when his slavish brain considered the wages of treason, and unbounded wealth and power floated in the same instant before his eyes, conscience, the safety of his patron, the memory of the liberty he had received, withdrew into the background.

memoria. Etenim uxoris quoque consilium adsump-
serat muliebre ac deterius: quippe ultro metum
intentabat, multosque adstitisse libertos ac servos,
qui eadem viderint: nihil profuturum unius silentium,
at praemia penes unum fore, qui indicio praevenisset.

LV. Igitur coepta luce Milichus in hortos Ser-
vilianos pergit; et cum foribus arceretur, magna et
atrocia adferre dictitans deductusque ab ianitoribus
ad libertum Neronis Epaphroditum, mox ab eo ad
Neronem, urguens periculum, gravis coniuratos et
cetera, quae audierat coniectaverat, docet. Telum
quoque in necem eius paratum ostendit accirique
reum iussit. Is raptus per milites et defensionem
orsus, ferrum, cuius argueretur, olim religione patria
cultum et in cubiculo habitum ac fraude liberti
subreptum respondit, tabulas testamenti saepius
a se et incustodita dierum observatione signatas.
Pecunias et libertates servis et ante dono datas,
sed ideo tunc largius, quia tenui iam re familiari et
instantibus creditoribus testamento diffideret. Enimvero liberalis semper epulas struxisse, vitam amoe-
nam et duris iudicibus parum probatam. Fomenta

---

[1] Their position can only be vaguely inferred from *Hist.*
III. 38 and Suet. *Ner.* 47.

[2] *Libertus a libellis* in succession to Doryphorus (XIV. 65);
accompanied the fallen Nero to Phaon's villa, and assisted
him in his suicide (Suet. *Ner.* 49; D. Cass. LXIII. 29); executed
on that account by Domitian (Suet. *Dom.* 14; D. Cass. LXVII.
14).—He was the owner of Epictetus, and can hardly have
been other than the Epaphroditus addressed by Josephus in
the *Life*, the *Antiquities* and the *Apion*, though in the case
of the *Life* there is a difficulty turning on the date of death
of Agrippa II.

For he had also taken his wife's counsel. It was feminine and baser; for she held before him the further motive of fear, and pointed out that numbers of freedmen and slaves had been standing by, who had witnessed the same incidents as himself:—" One man's silence would profit nothing; but one man would handle the rewards—he who won the race to give information."

LV. At the break of day, then, Milichus went straight to the Servilian Gardens.[1] He was turned from the door; but, on insisting that he was the bearer of great and terrible news, was escorted by the porters to Nero's freedman Epaphroditus,[2] and by him in due course to Nero, whom he informed of the urgency of the danger, of the desperate character of the conspirators, and of all else that he had heard or conjectured. He also showed the weapon prepared for the assassination, and demanded that the accused should be summoned. Scaevinus was hurried to the spot by soldiers, and opened his defence by replying that " the weapon charged against him had long been regarded with veneration by his family, had been kept in his bedroom, and had been purloined by the knavery of his freedman. The tablets of his will he had quite often sealed, and without taking any particular notice of the days. He had previously made grants of money or freedom to his slaves; but this time more liberally, for the simple reason that his means were now slender, and, with his creditors pressing, he had misgivings about his will. As to his table, it had always been generously provided: his life had been on pleasant lines, and hardly to the taste of austere critics. There had been no bandages

vulneribus nulla iussu suo, sed quia cetera palam
vana obiecisset, adiungere crimen, cuius se pariter
indicem et testem faceret. Adicit dictis constantiam; incusat ultro intestabilem et conscelera-
tum, tanta vocis ac vultus securitate, ut labaret
indicium, nisi Milichum uxor admonuisset Antonium
Natalem multa cum Scaevino ac secreta conlocutum et
esse utrosque C. Pisonis intimos.

LVI. Ergo accitur Natalis, et diversi interro-
gantur, quisnam is sermo, qua de re fuisset. Tum
exorta suspicio, quia non congruentia responderant,
inditaque vincla. Et tormentorum aspectum ac
minas non tulere: prior tamen Natalis, totius con-
spirationis magis gnarus, simul arguendi peritior,
de Pisone primum fatetur, deinde adicit Annaeum
Senecam, sive internuntius inter eum Pisonemque
fuit, sive ut Neronis gratiam pararet, qui infensus
Senecae omnis ad eum opprimendum artis conquire-
bat. Tum cognito Natalis indicio Scaevinus quoque
pari inbecillitate, an cuncta iam patefacta credens
nec ullum silentii emolumentum, edidit ceteros. Ex
quibus Lucanus Quintianusque et Senecio diu
abnuere: post promissa inpunitate corrupti, quo
tarditatem excusarent, Lucanus Aciliam matrem
suam, Quintianus Glitium Gallum, Senecio Annium
Pollionem, amicorum praecipuos, nominavere.

for wounds of his ordering, but the accuser—whose other allegations had been patently futile—was adding a charge in which he could play informer and witness alike." He followed up his words with a display of spirit, and attacked the freedman as an unspeakable villain, with so much assurance of look and tone that the informer's tale was on the point of collapse, had not his wife reminded Milichus that Antonius Natalis had had a long and secret interview with Scaevinus, and that both were on intimate terms with Gaius Piso.

LVI. Natalis accordingly was summoned, and the two were separately questioned as to the nature and the subject of the conversation. Suspicion was now awakened, as their answers had failed to tally, and they were thrown into irons. At the sight and threat of torture they broke down. Natalis, however, took the lead. Better acquainted with the conspiracy as a whole, and at the same time more adroit as an accuser, he first admitted the case against Piso, then went on to name Annaeus Seneca, perhaps because he had acted as intermediary between him and Piso, or perhaps to win the good graces of Nero; who, in his hatred of Seneca, grasped at all methods of suppressing him. Then, when Natalis' disclosure became known, Scaevinus himself, with similar weakness,—or else in the belief that all had now been told and there was no profit in silence, —divulged the rest of the confederates. Of these, Lucan, Quintianus, and Senecio, long denied the charge: at last, bribed by a promise of impunity, and by way of excuse for their slowness, they gave the names, Lucan of his mother Acilia; Quintianus and Senecio, of their principal friends—Glitius Gallus and Annius Pollio respectively.

LVII. Atque interim Nero recordatus Volusii
Proculi indicio Epicharim attineri ratusque muliebre
corpus impar dolori tormentis dilacerari iubet. At
illam non verbera, non ignes, non ira eo acrius
torquentium, ne a femina spernerentur, pervicere,
quin obiecta denegaret. Sic primus quaestionis dies
contemptus. Postero cum ad eosdem cruciatus
retraheretur gestamine sellae (nam dissolutis membris insistere nequibat), vinclo fasciae, quam pectori
detraxerat, in modum laquei ad arcum sellae restricto
indidit cervicem et corporis pondere conisa tenuem
iam spiritum expressit, clariore exemplo libertina
mulier in tanta necessitate alienos ac prope ignotos
protegendo, cum ingenui et viri et equites Romani
senatoresque intacti tormentis carissima suorum
quisque pignorum proderent. Non enim omittebant
Lucanus quoque et Senecio et Quintianus passim
conscios edere, magis magisque pavido Nerone,
quamquam multiplicatis excubiis semet saepsisset.

LVIII. Quin et urbem per manipulos occupatis
moenibus, insesso etiam mari et amne, velut in
custodiam dedit. Volitabantque per fora, per domos,
rura quoque et proxima municipiorum pedites
equitesque, permixti Germanis, quibus fidebat

---

[1] A mounted corps, chiefly of Batavians, formed by
Augustus to replace his Spanish guard (Suet. *Aug.* 49);
disbanded " in spite of its tried fidelity " by Galba (Suet. *Galb.*
12).

LVII. In the meantime, Nero recollected that Epicharis was in custody on the information of Volusius Proculus; and, assuming that female flesh and blood must be unequal to the pain, he ordered her to be racked. But neither the lash nor fire, nor yet the anger of the torturers, who redoubled their efforts rather than be braved by a woman, broke down her denial of the allegations. Thus the first day of torment had been defied. On the next, as she was being dragged back in a chair to a re-petition of the agony—her dislocated limbs were unable to support her—she fastened the breast-band (which she had stripped from her bosom) in a sort of noose to the canopy of the chair, thrust her neck into it, and, throwing the weight of her body into the effort, squeezed out such feeble breath as remained to her. An emancipated slave and a woman, by shielding, under this dire coercion, men unconnected with her and all but unknown, she had set an example which shone the brighter at a time when persons freeborn and male, Roman knights and senators, untouched by the torture, were betraying each his nearest and his dearest. For Lucan himself, and Senecio and Quintianus, did not omit to disclose their confederates wholesale; while Nero's terror grew from more to more, though he had multiplied the strength of the guards surrounding his person.

LVIII. He went further, and laid the very capital under a species of arrest: maniples held the walls; the sea and the river themselves were occupied. And through squares and houses, even through the country districts and nearest towns, flitted footmen and horsemen, interspersed with Germans,[1] trusted

princeps quasi externis. Continua hinc et vincta
agmina trahi ac foribus hortorum adiacere. Atque
ubi dicendam ad causam introissent, laetatum [1]
erga coniuratos et fortuitus sermo et subiti occursus,
si convivium, si spectaculum simul inissent, pro
crimine accipi, cum super Neronis ac Tigellini saevas
percontationes Faenius quoque Rufus violenter
urgueret, nondum ab indicibus nominatus, et quo
fidem inscitiae pararet, atrox adversus socios. Idem
Subrio Flavo adsistenti adnuentique, an inter ipsam
cognitionem destringeret gladium caedemque pa-
traret, renuit infregitque impetum iam manum ad
capulum referentis.

LIX. Fuere qui prodita coniuratione, dum auditur
Milichus, dum dubitat Scaevinus, hortarentur Pisonem pergere in castra aut rostra escendere studiaque
militum et populi temptare. Si conatibus eius
conscii adgregarentur, secuturos etiam integros;
magnamque motae rei famam, quae plurimum in
novis consiliis valeret. Nihil adversum haec Neroni
provisum. Etiam fortes viros subitis terreri, nedum
ille scaenicus, Tigellino scilicet cum paelicibus suis
comitante, arma contra cieret. Multa experiendo
confieri, quae segnibus ardua videantur. Frustra
silentium et fidem in tot consciorum animis et

---

[1] laetatum *dett.*: latatum *Med. The corruption, however,
must be far deeper. The sense could be given approximately
by something like*:—introissent, ⟨non benivolent⟩ia tantum
erga coniuratos set (*Med.*: et *Bipontina* fortuitus e.q.s.

---

[1] Of the *horti Serviliani* (chap. 55).

by the emperor because they were foreign. Then
followed continuous columns of manacled men,
dragged and deposited at the garden doors.[1] And
when they entered to plead their cause, cheerfulness towards a plotter, a chance conversation, an
unforeseen meeting, an appearance at a banquet or
spectacle in his company, were taken as crimes;
while, over and above the pitiless cross-questioning
of Nero and Tigellinus, there were the truculent
attacks of Faenius Rufus, not yet named by the
informers, and struggling to demonstrate his ignorance by browbeating his allies. It was the same
Rufus who, when Subrius Flavus at his side inquired by a motion if he should draw his sword and do
the bloody deed during the actual inquiry, shook his
head and checked the impulse which was already
carrying his hand to his hilt.

LIX. There were those who, after the betrayal
of the plot, while Milichus was still in audience,
Scaevinus still wavering, urged Piso to make his
way to the camp, or mount the Rostra, and sound the
dispositions of the troops and the people:—" If his
confederates rallied to his attempt, outsiders too
would follow; and the movement so started would be
trumpeted abroad—a point of prime importance in
planning revolutions. Nero had taken no precautions
against a step of this kind. Even brave men could
lose their nerve in emergencies: what likelihood
that this play-actor, accompanied no doubt by
Tigellinus and his lemans, would answer force with
force? Many things which to the timid looked
arduous were accomplished on attempt. It was idle
to look for silence and good faith in the minds
and persons of so many accomplices: torture

corporibus sperare: cruciatui aut praemio cuncta
pervia esse. Venturos qui ipsum quoque vincirent,
postremo indigna nece adficerent. Quanto lauda-
bilius periturum, dum amplectitur rem publicam,
dum auxilia libertati invocat. Miles potius deesset
et plebes desereret, dum ipse maioribus, dum posteris,
si vita praeriperetur, mortem adprobaret. Inmotus
his et paululum in publico versatus, post domi secre-
tus, animum adversum suprema firmabat, donec
manus militum adveniret, quos Nero tirones aut
stipendiis recentis delegerat: nam vetus miles
timebatur tamquam favore inbutus. Obiit abruptis
brachiorum venis. Testamentum foedis adversus
Neronem adulationibus amori uxoris dedit, quam
degenerem et sola corporis forma commendatam
amici matrimonio abstulerat. Nomen mulieri
Satria[1] Galla, priori marito Domitius Silus: hic
patientia, illa inpudicitia Pisonis infamiam propa-
gavere.

LX. Proximam necem Plautii Laterani consulis
designati Nero adiungit, adeo propere, ut non
complecti liberos, non illud breve mortis arbitrium
permitteret. Raptus in locum servilibus poenis
sepositum manu Statii tribuni trucidatur, plenus
constantis silentii nec tribuno obiciens eandem
conscientiam.

Sequitur caedes Annaei Senecae, laetissima princi-

---

[1] mulieri Satria *Andresen :* mulieris atria.

---

[1] The point of the remark is obscure.
[2] Known as the *Sessorium*, in the Campus Esquilinus.
It was here that Galba's head was thrown by the slaves of
Patrobius (Plut. *Galb.* 28—where the definition of the place
is :—ἡ τοὺς ὑπὸ τῶν Καισάρων κολαζομένους θανατοῦσιν).—
Lateranus' courage is noticed also by Epictetus (*Diss.* I. 1,
19-20).

or gold would find a way through anything! The men would come who would bind him also and put him at the last to an unworthy death. How much more honourably would he perish in the act of taking his country to his heart—of invoking help for liberty! Sooner let the soldiers hold aloof and the commons forsake him, provided that he himself, were his life to be cut short, justified his death in the sight of his ancestors and of his descendants." Piso, unmoved by all this, spent a short time in public, then secluded himself at home, and steeled his spirit against the end, until a body of troops arrived, recruits or men new to the service, and chosen as such by Nero, the veterans being distrusted as tainted with partisanship. His mode of death was to sever the arteries of each arm. His will, marked by disgusting flatteries of Nero, was a concession to his love for his wife, whom, low-born as she was and recommended only by physical beauty, he had stolen from the bed of one of his friends. The woman was named Satria Galla, her former husband Domitius Silius; and by the complaisance of the latter and the profligacy of the former Piso's infamy was kept alive.[1]

LX. The next killing, that of the consul designate Plautius Lateranus, was added by Nero to the list with such speed that he allowed him neither to embrace his children nor the usual moment's respite in which to choose his death. Dragged to the place reserved for the execution of slaves,[2] he was slaughtered by the hand of the tribune Statius, resolutely silent and disdaining to reproach the tribune with his complicity in the same affair.

There followed the murder of Annaeus Seneca, a

pi, non quia coniurationis manifestum compererat, sed ut ferro grassaretur, quando venenum non processerat. Solus quippe Natalis et hactenus prompsit, missum se ad aegrotum Senecam, uti viseret conquerereturque, cur Pisonem aditu arceret: melius fore, si amicitiam familiari congressu exercuissent. Et respondisse Senecam sermones mutuos et crebra conloquia neutri conducere; ceterum salutem suam incolumitate Pisonis inniti. Haec ferre Gavius [1] Silvanus tribunus praetoriae cohortis, et an dicta Natalis suaque responsa nosceret percontari Senecam iubetur. Is forte an prudens ad eum diem ex Campania remeaverat quartumque apud lapidem suburbano rure substiterat. Illo propinqua vespera tribunus venit et villam globis militum saepsit; tum ipsi cum Pompeia Paulina uxore et amicis duobus epulanti mandata imperatoris edidit.

LXI. Seneca missum ad se Natalem conquestumque nomine Pisonis, quod a visendo eo prohiberetur, seque rationem valetudinis et amorem quietis excusavisse respondit. Cur salutem privati hominis incolumitati suae anteferret, causam non habuisse; nec sibi promptum in adulationes ingenium. Idque nulli magis gnarum quam Neroni, qui saepius libertatem Senecae quam servitium expertus esset. Ubi haec a tribuno relata sunt Poppaea et Tigellino coram, quod erat saevienti principi intimum con-

---

[1] Gavius *Bekker* : gravius.

---

[1] Seneca denies the possibility of his having said *salutem suam incolumitate Pisonis inniti* :—He cannot have made the remark in earnest, for the only person whose safety he ranks above his own is the emperor : he cannot have made it out of empty civility, for such complaisances are alien to his nature.

joyful event to the sovereign: not that he had established his connection with the plot, but, as poison had not worked, he was anxious to proceed by the sword. Only Natalis, in fact, mentioned Seneca; nor did his statement go further than that he had been sent to visit him when sick and to make a complaint:—" Why did he close his door on Piso? It would be better if they cultivated their friendship by meeting on intimate terms." Seneca's answer had been that " spoken exchanges and frequent interviews were to the advantage of neither: still, his own existence depended on the safety of Piso." Gavius Silvanus, tribune of a praetorian cohort, was instructed to take this report and ask Seneca if he admitted Natalis' words and his own reply. By accident or design, Seneca that day had returned from Campania and broke his journey at one of his country-houses four miles out of Rome. Evening was near when the tribune arrived and surrounded the villa with pickets of soldiers: then he delivered the imperial message to the owner, who was dining with his wife Pompeia Paulina and two friends.

LXI. Seneca rejoined that " Natalis had been sent to him, and had remonstrated in Piso's name against his refusal to receive his visits. By way of excuse, he had pleaded considerations of health and love of quiet. He had had no reason for ranking the security of a private person higher than his own safety, and his temper was not one which was quick to flattery: no one was better aware of that than Nero, who had more often experienced the frankness of Seneca than his servility." [1] When the tribune made his report in the presence of Poppaea and Tigellinus—the emperor's privy council in his

313

siliorum, interrogat an Seneca voluntariam mortem
pararet. Tum tribunus nulla pavoris signa, nihil
triste in verbis eius aut vultu deprensum confirmavit.
Ergo regredi et indicere mortem iubetur. Tradit
Fabius Rusticus non eo quo venerat itinere reditum,
sed flexisse ad Faenium praefectum, et expositis
Caesaris iussis an obtemperaret interrogavisse,
monitumque ab eo ut exsequeretur, fatali omnium
ignavia. Nam et Silvanus inter coniuratos erat
augebatque scelera, in quorum ultionem con-
senserat. Voci tamen et aspectui pepercit intromi-
sitque ad Senecam unum ex centurionibus, qui
necessitatem ultimam denuntiaret.

LXII. Ille interritus poscit testamenti tabulas;
ac denegante centurione conversus ad amicos,
quando meritis eorum referre gratiam prohiberetur,
quod unum iam et tamen pulcherrimum habeat,
imaginem vitae suae relinquere testatur, cuius si
memores essent, bonarum artium famam *pretium* [1]
tam constantis amicitiae laturos. Simul lacrimas
eorum modo sermone, modo intentior in modum
coercentis ad firmitudinem revocat, rogitans ubi
praecepta sapientiae, ubi tot per annos meditata
ratio adversum imminentia? Cui enim ignaram
fuisse saevitiam Neronis? Neque aliud superesse
post matrem fratremque [2] interfectos, quam ut
educatoris praeceptorisque necem adiceret.

[1] <pretium> *Nipperdey.*
[2] fratremque] fratresque *Nipperdey.*

[1] XIII. 20 n.

ferocious moods—Nero demanded if Seneca was preparing for a voluntary death. The officer then assured him that there were no evidences of alarm, and that he had not detected any sadness in his words or looks. He was therefore directed to go back and pronounce the death-sentence. Fabius Rusticus[1] states that, instead of returning by the road he had come, the tribune went out of his way to the prefect Faenius, and, after recapitulating the Caesar's orders, asked if he should obey them; only to be advised by Faenius to carry them out. Fate had made cowards of them all. For Silvanus, too, was numbered with the plotters; and now he was engaged in adding to the crimes he had conspired to avenge. However, he was so far considerate of his voice and his eyes as to send one of his centurions in to Seneca, to announce the last necessity.

LXII. Seneca, nothing daunted, asked for the tablets containing his will. The centurion refusing, he turned to his friends, and called them to witness that " as he was prevented from showing his gratitude for their services, he left them his sole but fairest possession—the image of his life. If they bore it in mind, they would reap the reward of their loyal friendship in the credit accorded to virtuous accomplishments." At the same time, he recalled them from tears to fortitude, sometimes conversationally, sometimes in sterner, almost coercive tones. " Where," he asked, " were the maxims of their philosophy? Where that reasoned attitude towards impending evils which they had studied through so many years? For to whom had Nero's cruelty been unknown? Nor was anything left him, after the killing of his mother and his brother, but to add the murder of his guardian and preceptor."

315

LXIII. Ubi haec atque talia velut in commune disseruit, complectitur uxorem, et paululum adversus praesentem formidinem[1] mollitus rogat oratque temperaret dolori neu aeternum susciperet, sed in contemplatione vitae per virtutem actae desiderium mariti solaciis honestis toleraret. Illa contra sibi quoque destinatam mortem adseverat manumque percussoris exposcit. Tum Seneca gloriae eius non adversus, simul amore, ne sibi unice dilectam ad iniurias relinqueret, " Vitae " inquit " delenimenta monstraveram tibi, tu mortis decus mavis: non invidebo exemplo. Sit huius tam fortis exitus constantia penes utrosque par, claritudinis plus in tuo fine." Post quae eodem ictu brachia ferro exsolvunt. Seneca, quoniam senile corpus et parco victu tenuatum lenta effugia sanguini praebebat, crurum quoque et poplitum venas abrumpit; saevisque cruciatibus defessus, ne dolore suo animum uxoris infringeret atque ipse visendo eius tormenta ad inpatientiam delaberetur, suadet in aliud cubiculum abscedere. Et novissimo quoque momento suppeditante eloquentia advocatis scriptoribus pleraque tradidit, quae in vulgus edita eius verbis invertere supersedeo.

LXIV. At Nero nullo in Paulinam proprio odio, ac

---

[1] formidinem *dett.* : fortitudinem.

---

[1] The road of freedom was longer than it seemed when he wrote the words :—*Scalpello aperitur ad illam magnam libertatem via, et puncto securitas constat* (Ep. 70).

LXIII. After these and some similar remarks,
which might have been meant for a wider audience,
he embraced his wife, and, softening momentarily
in view of the terrors at present threatening her,
begged her, conjured her, to moderate her grief—
not to take it upon her for ever, but in contemplating
the life he had spent in virtue to find legitimate solace
for the loss of her husband. Paulina replied by
assuring him that she too had made death her
choice, and she demanded her part in the executioner's stroke. Seneca, not wishing to stand in
the way of her glory, and influenced also by his
affection, that he might not leave the woman who
enjoyed his whole-hearted love exposed to outrage,
now said : " I had shown you the mitigations of life,
you prefer the distinction of death : I shall not
grudge your setting that example. May the
courage of this brave ending be divided equally
between us both, but may more of fame attend your
own departure ! " After this, they made the
incision in their arms with a single cut. Seneca,
since his aged body, emaciated further by frugal
living, gave slow escape to the blood, severed as
well the arteries in the leg and behind the knee.[1]
Exhausted by the racking pains, and anxious lest
his sufferings might break down the spirit of his
wife, and he himself lapse into weakness at the
sight of her agony, he persuaded her to withdraw
into another bedroom. And since, even at the last
moment his eloquence remained at command, he
called his secretaries, and dictated a long discourse,
which has been given to the public in his own words,
and which I therefore refrain from modifying.

LXIV. Nero, however, who had no private ani-

ne glisceret invidia crudelitatis, *iubet*[1] inhiberi mortem. Hortantibus militibus servi libertique obligant brachia, premunt sanguinem, incertum an ignarae. Nam, ut est vulgus ad deteriora promptum, non defuere qui crederent, donec inplacabilem Neronem timuerit, famam sociatae cum marito mortis petivisse, deinde oblata mitiore spe blandimentis vitae evictam; cui addidit paucos postea annos, laudabili in maritum memoria et ore ac membris in eum pallorem albentibus, ut ostentui esset multum vitalis spiritus egestum. Seneca interim, durante tractu et lentitudine mortis, Statium Annaeum, diu sibi amicitiae fide et arte medicinae probatum, orat provisum pridem venenum, quo damnati publico Atheniensium iudicio extinguerentur, promeret; adlatumque hausit frustra, frigidus iam artus et cluso corpore adversum vim veneni. Postremo stagnum calidae aquae introiit, respergens proximos servorum addita voce, libare se liquorem illum Iovi liberatori. Exim balneo inlatus et vapore eius exanimatus, sine ullo funeris sollemni crematur. Ita codicillis praescripserat, cum etiam tum praedives et praepotens supremis suis consuleret.

LXV. Fama fuit Subrium Flavum[2] cum centurioni

---

[1] ⟨iubet⟩ *Heinsius.*   [2] Flavum *Bekker*: flavium.

---

[1] Hemlock—a choice to be expected.

[2] The same remark is made by Thrasea at XVI. 35—the only other place, it is said, apart from coins of Nero and a calendar, in which this Latin version of Ζεὺς Ἐλευθέριος occurs.

mosity against Paulina, and did not wish to increase the odium of his cruelty, ordered her suicide to be arrested. Under instructions from the military, her slaves and freedmen bandaged her arms and checked the bleeding—whether without her knowledge is uncertain. For, with the usual readiness of the multitude to think the worst, there were those who believed that, so long as she feared an implacable Nero, she had sought the credit of sharing her husband's fate, and then, when a milder prospect offered itself, had succumbed to the blandishments of life. To that life she added a few more years—laudably faithful to her husband's memory and blanched in face and limb to a pallor which showed how great had been the drain upon her vital powers. Seneca, in the meantime, as death continued to be protracted and slow, asked Statius Annaeus, who had long held his confidence as a loyal friend and a skilful doctor, to produce the poison—it had been provided much earlier—which was used for despatching prisoners condemned by the public tribunal of Athens.[1] It was brought, and he swallowed it, but to no purpose; his limbs were already cold, and his system closed to the action of the drug. In the last resort, he entered a vessel of heated water, sprinkling some on the slaves nearest, with the remark that he offered the liquid as a drink-offering to Jove the Liberator.[2] He was then lifted into a bath, suffocated by the vapour, and cremated without ceremony. It was the order he had given in his will, at a time when, still at the zenith of his wealth and power, he was already taking thought for his latter end.

LXV. It was rumoured that Subrius Flavus and the centurions had decided in private conference,

bus occulto consilio, neque tamen ignorante Seneca, destinavisse, ut post occisum opera Pisonis Neronem Piso quoque interficeretur tradereturque imperium Senecae, quasi insontibus claritudine virtutum ad summum fastigium delecto. Quin et verba Flavi [1] vulgabantur, non referre dedecori, si citharoedus demoveretur et tragoedus succederet, quia ut Nero cithara, ita Piso tragico ornatu canebat.

LXVI. Ceterum militaris quoque conspiratio non ultra fefellit, accensis indicibus ad prodendum Faenium Rufum, quem eundem conscium et inquisitorem non tolerabant. Ergo instanti minitantique renidens Scaevinus neminem ait plura scire quam ipsum, hortaturque ultro redderet tam bono principi vicem. Non vox adversum ea Faenio, non silentium, sed verba sua praepediens et pavoris manifestus, ceterisque et maxime Cervario Proculo equite Romano [2] ad convincendum eum conisis, iussu imperatoris a Cassio milite, qui ob insigne corporis robur adstabat, corripitur vinciturque.

LXVII. Mox eorundem indicio Subrius Flavus tribunus pervertitur, primo dissimilitudinem morum ad defensionem trahens, neque se armatum cum inermibus et effeminatis tantum facinus consociaturum; dein, postquam urguebatur, confessionis

---

[1] Flavi *Bekker* : flavii.
[2] equite R. *Orelli :* equiter.

---

[1] He took the title part in lyrical tragedies, as was constantly done by the emperor himself : cf. *e.g.* Suet. *Ner.* 21, *inter cetera cantavit Canacen parturientem, Oresten matricidam, Oedipodem occaecatum, Herculem insanum.* The details of these performances are largely uncertain.

though not without Seneca's knowledge, that, once
Nero had been struck down by the agency of Piso,
Piso should be disposed of in his turn, and the empire
made over to Seneca; who would thus appear to
have been chosen for the supreme power by innocent
men, as a consequence of his distinguished virtues.
More than this, there was a saying of Flavus
in circulation, that " so far as disgrace went, it was
immaterial if a harper was removed and a tragic
actor took his place "; for Nero singing to his
instrument was matched by Piso singing in his stage
costume.[1]

LXVI. But the military conspiracy itself no longer
evaded detection; for the informers were stung into
denouncing Faenius Rufus, whom they could not
tolerate in the double part of accomplice and inquisi-
tor. Accordingly, in the midst of Faenius' browbeating and threats, Scaevinus observed with a
civil sneer that no one knew more than himself, and
presented him with the advice to show his gratitude
to so kindly a prince. Faenius was unable to retort
either by speech or by silence. Tripping over his
words, and patently terrified, while the rest—and
notably the Roman knight Cervarius Proculus—
strained every nerve for his conviction, he was
seized and bound, at the emperor's order, by the
private soldier Cassius, who was standing near in
consideration of his remarkable bodily strength.

LXVII. Before long, the evidence of the same
group destroyed the tribune Subrius Flavus. At
first he sought to make unlikeness of character a
ground of defence: a man of the sword, like himself,
would never have shared so desperate an enterprise
with unarmed effeminates. Then, as he was pressed

gloriam amplexus. Interrogatusque a Nerone, quibus causis ad oblivionem sacramenti processisset, " Oderam te " inquit, " nec quisquam tibi fidelior militum fuit, dum amari meruisti. Odisse coepi, postquam parricida matris [1] et uxoris, auriga et histrio et incendiarius extitisti." Ipsa rettuli verba, quia non, ut Senecae, vulgata erant, nec minus nosci decebat militaris viri sensus incomptos et validos. Nihil in illa coniuratione gravius auribus Neronis accidisse constitit, qui ut faciendis sceleribus promptus, ita audiendi quae faceret insolens erat. Poena Flavi Veianio Nigro tribuno mandatur. Is proximo in agro scrobem effodi iussit, quam visam [2] Flavus ut humilem et angustam increpans, circumstantibus militibus, " Ne hoc quidem " inquit " ex disciplina." Admonitusque fortiter protendere cervicem, " Utinam " ait " tu tam fortiter ferias ! " Et ille multum tremens, cum vix duobus ictibus caput amputavisset, saevitiam apud Neronem iactavit, sesquiplaga interfectum a se dicendo.

LXVIII. Proximum constantiae exemplum Sulpicius Asper centurio praebuit, percontanti Neroni, cur in caedem suam conspiravisset, breviter respondens non aliter tot flagitiis eius subveniri potuisse. Tum iussam poenam subiit. Nec ceteri centuriones in perpetiendis suppliciis degeneravere : at non Faenio

[1] matris <et fratris> *Nipperdey.*
[2] quam visam *Walther* : quamvis.

more closely, he embraced the glory of confession. Questioned by Nero as to the motives which had led him so far as to forget his military oath :— " I hated you," he answered, " and yet there was not a man in the army truer to you, as long as you deserved to be loved. I began to hate you when you turned into the murderer of your mother and wife—a chariot-driver, an actor, a fire-raiser." I have reported his exact words; for, unlike those of Seneca, they were given no publicity; and the plain, strong sentiments of the soldier were not the less worth knowing. It was notorious that nothing in this conspiracy fell more harshly on the ears of Nero, who was equally ready to commit crimes and unaccustomed to be informed of what he was committing. The execution of Flavus was entrusted to the tribune Veianius Niger. Niger gave orders for a grave to be dug in a neighbouring field; where it was criticized by Flavus as neither deep nor broad enough :— "Faulty discipline even here," he observed to the soldiers around. When admonished to hold his neck out firmly :— " I only hope," he said, " that you will strike as firmly ! " Shaking violently, the tribune severed the head with some difficulty at two blows, and boasted of his brutality to Nero by saying that he had killed with a stroke and a half.

LXVIII. The next example of intrepidity was furnished by Sulpicius Asper; who to Nero's question, why he had conspired to murder him, rejoined curtly that it was the only service that could be rendered to his many infamies. He then underwent the ordained penalty. The other centurions, as well, met their fate without declining from their traditions; but such resolution was not for Faenius

Rufo par animus, sed lamentationes suas etiam in testamentum contulit.

Opperiebatur Nero, ut Vestinus quoque consul in crimen attraheretur, violentum et infensum ratus: sed ex coniuratis consilia cum Vestino non miscuerant, quidam vetustis in eum simultatibus, plures, quia praecipitem et insociabilem credebant. Ceterum Neroni odium adversus Vestinum ex intima sodalitate coeperat, dum hic ignaviam principis penitus cognitam despicit, ille ferociam amici metuit, saepe asperis facetiis inlusus, quae ubi multum ex vero traxere, acrem sui memoriam relinquunt. Accesserat repens causa, quod Vestinus Statiliam Messalinam matrimonio sibi iunxerat, haud nescius inter adulteros eius et Caesarem esse.

LXIX. Igitur non crimine, non accusatore existente, quia speciem iudicis induere non poterat, ad vim dominationis conversus Gerellanum tribunum cum cohorte militum inmittit iubetque praevenire conatus consulis, occupare velut arcem eius, opprimere delectam iuventutem, quia Vestinus inminentis foro aedes decoraque servitia et pari aetate habebat. Cuncta eo die munia consulis impleverat conviviumque celebrabat, nihil metuens an dissimulando metu, cum ingressi milites vocari eum a tribuno dixere. Ille nihil demoratus exsurgit et omnia simul properantur: clauditur cubiculo, praesto est medicus,

---

[1] Great-great-granddaughter of the Statilius Taurus mentioned at VI. 11. After the death of Poppaea, she became the wife of Nero, her fifth husband, " *post quem interemptum et opibus et fama et ingenio plurimum valuit* " (Σ. Juv. VI. 434). Otho had destined her for his wife, and his two last letters were for her and his sister (Suet. *Oth.* 10).

Rufus, who imported his lamentations even into his will.

Nero was waiting for the consul Vestinus to be also incriminated, regarding him as a violent character and an enemy. But the conspirators had not shared their plans with Vestinus—some through old animosities, the majority because they considered him headstrong and impossible as a partner. Nero's hatred of him had grown out of intimate companionship—Vestinus understanding perfectly, and despising, the pusillanimity of the sovereign; the sovereign afraid of the masterful friend who so often mocked him with that rough humour which, if it draws too largely on truth, leaves pungent memories behind. An additional, and recent, motive was that Vestinus had contracted a marriage with Statilia Messalina,[1] though well aware that the Caesar also was among her paramours.

LXIX. Accordingly, with neither a charge nor an accuser forthcoming, Nero, precluded from assuming the character of judge, turned to plain despotic force, and sent out the tribune Gerellanus with a cohort of soldiers, under orders to " forestall the attempts of the consul, seize what might be termed his citadel, and suppress his chosen corps of youths ": Vestinus maintained a house overlooking the forum, and a retinue of handsome slaves of uniform age. On that day, he had fulfilled the whole of his consular functions, and was holding a dinner-party, either apprehending nothing or anxious to dissemble whatever he apprehended, when soldiers entered and said the tribune was asking for him. He rose without delay, and all was hurried through in a moment. He shut himself in his bedroom, the

abscinduntur venae, vigens adhuc balneo infertur, calida aqua mersatur, nulla edita voce, qua semet miseraretur. Circumdati interim custodia qui simul discubuerant, nec nisi provecta nocte omissi sunt, postquam pavorem eorum, ex mensa exitium opperientium, et imaginatus et inridens Nero satis supplicii luisse ait pro epulis consularibus.

LXX. Exim Annaei [1] Lucani caedem imperat. Is profluente sanguine ubi frigescere pedes manusque et paulatim ab extremis cedere spiritum fervido adhuc et compote mentis pectore intellegit, recordatus carmen a se compositum, quo vulneratum militem per eius modi mortis imaginem obisse tradiderat, versus ipsos rettulit, eaque illi suprema vox fuit. Senecio posthac et Quintianus et Scaevinus non e priore vitae mollitia, mox reliqui coniuratorum periere, nullo facto dictove memorando.

LXXI. Sed compleri interim urbs funeribus, Capitolium victimis; alius filio, fratre alius aut propinquo aut amico interfectis, agere grates deis, ornare lauru domum genua ipsius advolvi et dextram osculis fatigare. Atque ille gaudium id credens Antonii Natalis et Cervarii Proculi festinata indicia inpunitate remuneratur. Milichus praemiis ditatus conservatoris sibi nomen, Graeco eius rei vocabulo,

---

[1] Annaei *Ritter* (M. Annaei *Rhenanus*) : mane na et.

---

[1] Unfortunately, few worse passages can have revisited the memory of a dying man. The most relevant and least absurd lines are (III. 642 sqq.) :—*pars ultima trunci Tradidit in letum vacuos vitalibus artus*; *At tumidus qua pulmo iacet, qua viscera fervent, Haeserunt ibi fata diu, luctataque multum Hac cum parte viri vix omnia membra tulerunt.* In Suetonius, the ruling passion finds another vent :—*Codicillos ad patrem de corrigendis quibusdam versibus suis exaravit, epulatusque largiter brachia ad secandas venas medico praebuit* (vit. Luc. ad fin.).

doctor was at hand, the arteries were cut: still
vigorous, he was carried into the bath and plunged
in hot water, without letting fall a word of self-pity.
In the meantime, the guests who had been at table
with him were surrounded by guards; nor were
they released till a late hour of the night, when
Nero, laughing at the dismay, which he had been
picturing in his mind's eye, of the diners who were
awaiting destruction after the feast, observed that
they had paid dearly enough for their consular
banquet.

LXX. He next ordained the despatch of Lucan.
When his blood was flowing, and he felt his feet and
hands chilling and the life receding little by little
from the extremities, though the heart retained
warmth and sentience, Lucan recalled a passage in
his own poem, where he had described a wounded
soldier dying a similar form of death, and he recited
the very verses.[1] Those were his last words. Then
Senecio and Quintianus and Scaevinus, belying their
old effeminacy of life, and then the rest of the conspirators, met their end, doing and saying nothing
that calls for remembrance.

LXXI. Meanwhile, however, the city was filled
with funerals, and the Capitol with burnt offerings.
Here, for the killing of a son; there, for that of a
brother, a kinsman, or a friend; men were addressing
their thanks to Heaven, bedecking their mansions
with bays, falling at the knees of the sovereign, and
persecuting his hand with kisses. And he, imagining
that this was joy, recompensed the hurried informations of Antonius Natalis and Cervarius Proculus by
a grant of immunity. Milichus, grown rich on
rewards, assumed in its Greek form the title of

adsumpsit. E tribunis Gavius Silvanus, quamvis absolutus, sua manu cecidit; Statius Proxumus veniam, quam ab imperatore acceperat, vanitate exitus corrupit. Exuti dehinc tribunatu . . . [1] Pompeius, Cornelius Martialis, Flavius Nepos, Statius Domitius, quasi principem non quidem odissent, sed tamen existimarentur. Novio Prisco per amicitiam Senecae et Glitio Gallo atque Annio Pollioni infamatis magis quam convictis data exilia. Priscum Artoria Flaccilla coniunx comitata est, Gallum Egnatia Maximilla, magnis primum et integris opibus, post ademptis, quae utraque gloriam eius auxere. Pellitur et Rufrius Crispinus occasione coniurationis, sed Neroni invisus, quod Poppaeam quondam matrimonio tenuerat. Verginium *Flavum et Musonium* [2] Rufum claritudo nominis expulit: nam Verginius studia iuvenum eloquentia, Musonius praeceptis sapientiae fovebat. Cluvidieno Quieto, Iulio Agrippae, Blitio Catulino, Petronio Prisco, Iulio Altino, velut in agmen et numerum, Aegaei maris insulae permittuntur. At Caedicia [3] uxor Scaevini et Caesennius [4] Maximus Italia prohibentur, reos fuisse se tantum poena experti. Acilia mater Annaei Lucani sine absolutione, sine supplicio dissimulata.

[1] . . . *Ritter.—A praenomen or cognomen is missing.*
[2] <Flavum et Musonium> *Ruperti,* <et Musonium *Lipsius*>
[3] Caedicia *Orelli* : cadicia.
[4] Caesennius] Caesonius *Mart. VII, 44.*

---

[1] Commanders of praetorian cohorts. The number involved or under suspicion—six mentioned here, and Subrius Flavus—is remarkable.
[2] What the end may have been, is unknown.

Saviour. Of the tribunes,[1] Gavius Silvanus, though acquitted, fell by his own hand; Statius Proxumus stultified the pardon he had received from the emperor by the folly of his end.[2] Then . . . Pompeius, Cornelius Martialis, Flavius Nepos, and Statius Domitius, were deprived of their rank, on the ground that, without hating the Caesar, they had yet the reputation of doing so. Novius Priscus, as a friend of Seneca, Glitius Gallus and Annius Pollio as discredited if hardly convicted, were favoured with sentences of exile. Priscus was accompanied by his wife Artoria Flaccilla, Gallus by Egnatia Maximilla,[3] the mistress of a great fortune, at first left intact but afterwards confiscated—two circumstances which redounded equally to her fame. Rufrius Crispinus was also banished: the conspiracy supplied the occasion, but he was detested by Nero as a former husband of Poppaea. To Verginius Flavus[4] and Musonius Rufus expulsion was brought by the lustre of their names; for Verginius fostered the studies of youth by his eloquence, Musonius by the precepts of philosophy. As though to complete the troop and a round number, Cluvidienus Quietus, Julius Agrippa, Blitius Catulinus, Petronius Priscus, and Julius Altinus were allowed the Aegean islands. But Scaevinus' wife Caedicia and Caesennius Maximus[5] were debarred from Italy, and by their punishment—and that alone—discovered that they had been on trial. Lucan's mother Acilia was ignored, without acquittal and without penalty.

[3] The pair spent their exile in Andros, where an inscription has survived to attest their popularity.

[4] A rhetorician and tutor of Persius.—For Musonius, see XIV. 59 n.

[5] A friend of Seneca (*Ep.* 87 : cf. Mart. VII. 44, 45).

THE ANNALS OF TACITUS

LXXII. Quibus perpetratis Nero et contione militum habita bina nummum milia viritim manipularibus divisit addiditque sine pretio frumentum, quo ante ex modo annonae utebantur. Tum, quasi gesta bello expositurus, vocat senatum et triumphale decus Petronio Turpiliano consulari, Cocceio Nervae praetori designato, Tigellino praefecto praetorii tribuit, Tigellinum et Nervam ita extollens, ut super triumphalis in foro imagines apud Palatium quoque effigies eorum sisteret. Consularia insignia Nymphidio, . . .[1] quia nunc primum oblatus est, pauca repetam : nam et ipse pars Romanarum cladium erit. Igitur matre libertina ortus, quae corpus decorum inter servos libertosque principum vulgaverat, ex Gaio Caesare se genitum ferebat, quoniam forte quadam habitu procerus et torvo vultu erat, sive Gaius Caesar, scortorum quoque cupiens, etiam matri eius inlusit . . .[2]

LXXIII. Sed Nero[3] oratione inter patres habita, edictum apud populum et conlata in libros indicia confessionesque damnatorum adiunxit. Etenim crebro vulgi rumore lacerabatur, tamquam viros *claros* et insontis ob invidiam aut metum extinxisset.

---

[1] . . . *Ritter.*
[2] . . . *Wurm.*
[3] Nero *Nipperdey* : Nero vocato senatu.

---

[1] The praetorians.—The corn-ration of the legionaries seems to have been already gratuitous : at all events, there is no mention of it as a charge on their pay, in the list of grievances at I. 17.

[2] See XIV. 29 n. : Nerva is the future emperor.

[3] He now replaced Faenius Rufus as Tigellinus' colleague in the praetorian prefectship, an appointment which must have been mentioned either in this lacuna or in the next. The only detailed account of his treachery, first to Nero, then to Galba,

LXII. Now that all was over, Nero held a meeting of the troops,[1] and made a distribution of two thousand sesterces a man, remitting in addition the price of the grain ration previously supplied to them at the current market rate. Then, as if to recount the achievements of a war, he convoked the senate and bestowed triumphal distinctions on the consular Petronius Turpilianus,[2] the praetor designate Cocceius Nerva, and the praetorian prefect Tigellinus: Nerva and Tigellinus he exalted so far that, not content with triumphal statues in the Forum, he placed their effigies in the palace itself. Consular insignia were decreed to Nymphidius ⟨Sabinus[3] . . .⟩. As Nymphidius now presents himself for the first time, I notice him briefly; for he too will be part of the tragedies of Rome. The son, then, of a freedwoman[4] who had prostituted her handsome person among the slaves and freedmen of emperors, he described himself as the issue of Gaius Caesar: for some freak of chance had given him a tall figure and a lowering brow; or, possibly, Gaius, whose appetite extended even to harlots, had abused this man's mother with the rest . . .

LXXIII. However, after he had spoken in the senate, Nero followed by publishing an edict to the people and a collection, in writing, of the informations laid and the avowals of the condemned; for in the gossip of the multitude he was being commonly attacked for procuring the destruction of great and guiltless citizens from motives of jealousy or of fear.

and his killing by the guards is furnished by Plutarch (*Galb.* 2; 8 sq.; 13 sqq.).

[4] Daughter, according to Plutarch, of Callistus (XI. 29 n.) by an ἀκέστρια ἐπιμίσθιος. The probable father of the new prefect he gives as an eminent gladiator, Martianus.

Ceterum coeptam adultamque et revictam coniurationem neque tunc dubitavere, quibus verum noscendi cura erat, et fatentur, qui post interitum Neronis in urbem regressi sunt. At in senatu cunctis, ut cuique plurimum maeroris, in adulationem demissis, Iunium Gallionem, Senecae fratris morte pavidum et pro sua incolumitate supplicem, increpuit Salienus Clemens, hostem et parricidam vocans, donec consensu patrum deterritus est, ne publicis malis abuti ad occasionem privati odii videretur, neu composita aut oblitterata mansuetudine principis novam ad saevitiam retraheret.

LXXIV. Tum dona[1] et grates deis decernuntur, propriusque honos Soli, cui est vetus aedes apud circum, in quo facinus parabatur, qui occulta coniurationis numine retexisset; utque circensium Cerealium ludicrum pluribus equorum cursibus celebraretur mensisque Aprilis Neronis cognomentum acciperet; templum Saluti exstrueretur eo loci . . .[2] ex quo Scaevinus ferrum prompserat. Ipse eum pugionem apud Capitolium sacravit inscripsitque Iovi Vindici: in praesens haud animadversum post

---

[1] dona *J. F. Gronovius*: decreta dona.
[2] . . . *Nipperdey.*

---

[1] Originally M. Annaeus Novatus; then, after his adoption (VI. 3 n.), L. Annaeus Iunius Gallio. He owes his celebrity to the proconsulate of Achaia which brought him into contact with St. Paul (*Acts* xviii. 12 sqq.). He perished a year after the Pisonian conspiracy—by suicide, according to Jerome.

[2] XVI. 12 n.

Still, that a conspiracy was initiated, matured, and brought home to its authors, was neither doubted at the period by those who were at pains to ascertain the facts, nor is denied by the exiles who have returned to the capital since the death of Nero. But in the senate, whilst all members, especially those with most to mourn, were stooping to syco-phancy, Junius Gallio,[1] dismayed by the death of his brother Seneca, and petitioning for his own existence, was attacked by Salienus Clemens, who styled him the enemy and parricide of his country; until he was deterred by the unanimous request of the Fathers that he would avoid the appearance of abusing a national sorrow for the purposes of a private hatred, and would not reawaken cruelty by recurring to matters either settled or cancelled by the clemency of the sovereign.

LXXIV. Offerings and thanks were then voted to Heaven, the Sun, who has an old temple in the Circus, where the crime was to be staged, receiving special honour for revealing by his divine power the secrets of the conspiracy. The Circensian Games of Ceres were to be celebrated with an increased number of horse-races; the month of April was to take the name of Nero;[2] a temple of Safety was to be erected on the site . . .[3] from which Scaevinus had taken his dagger. That weapon the emperor himself consecrated in the Capitol, and inscribed it :— *To Jove the Avenger*. At the time, the incident passed unnoticed : after the armed rising of the other

[3] In the lacuna were specified, first the point of Rome at which a new temple was to be erected to *Salus*, then the memorial to be placed in her old temple at Ferentinum (chap. 53).

arma Iulii Vindicis ad auspicium et praesagium futurae ultionis trahebatur. Reperio in commentariis senatus Cerialem Anicium consulem designatum pro sententia dixisse, ut templum divo Neroni quam maturrime publica pecunia poneretur. Quod quidem ille decernebat tamquam mortale fastigium egresso et venerationem hominum merito, *sed ipse prohibuit, ne interpretatione*[1] quorundam ad omen ac votum[2] sui exitus verteretur: nam deum honor principi non ante habetur, quam agere inter homines desierit.

[1] <sed . . . interpretatione> *Halm.*
[2] omen ac votum *Heinisch, R. Seyffert*: omnia dolum. *Med.,* omen malum *Heinsius.—No emendation is entirely satisfactory.*

" avenger," Julius Vindex,[1] it was read as a token
and a presage of coming retribution. I find in the
records of the senate that Anicius Cerialis, consul
designate, gave it as his opinion that a temple should
be built to Nero the Divine, as early as possible and
out of public funds. His motion, it is true, merely
implied that the prince had transcended mortal
eminence and earned the worship of mankind;
but it was vetoed by that prince, because by
other interpreters it might be wrested into an omen
of, and aspiration for, his decease; for the honour
of divinity is not paid to the emperor until he has
ceased to live and move among men.[2]

[1] C. Iulius Vindex, member of a princely family of Aqui-
taine, and legatus of Gallia Lugdunensis in 68 A.D. His rising
in that year—the ulterior object is uncertain—was suppressed
by Verginius Rufus, but set in motion the train of events which
led up to the fall of Nero and the outbreak of the civil war.

[2] By Roman citizens. The deification and worship of a
living emperor by provincials was regular.

BOOK XVI

LIBER XVI

I. Inlusit dehinc Neroni fortuna per vanitatem ipsius et promissa Caeselli Bassi, qui origine Poenus, mente turbida, nocturnae quietis imaginem ad spem haud dubiae rei traxit,[1] vectusque Romam, principis aditum emercatus, expromit repertum in agro suo specum altitudine inmensa, quo magna vis auri contineretur, non in formam pecuniae, sed rudi et antiquo pondere. Lateres quippe praegravis iacere, adstantibus parte alia columnis; quae per tantum aevi occulta [2] augendis praesentibus bonis. Ceterum, ut [3] coniectura demonstrabat,[4] Dido Phoenissam Tyro profugam condita Carthagine illas opes abdidisse, ne novus populus nimia pecunia lasciviret, aut reges Numidarum, et alias infensi, cupidine auri ad bellum accenderentur.

II. Igitur Nero, non auctoris, non ipsius negotii fide satis spectata nec missis, per quos nosceret an vera adferrentur, auget ultro rumorem mittitque, qui velut paratam praedam adveherent. Dantur

---

[1] dubiae rei traxit *Doederlein* : dubie retraxit.
[2] occulta] occultata *Nipperdey.*
[3] [ut] *Madvig.*
[4] demonstrabat *Halm* : demonstrat.

BOOK XVI

I. Nero now became the sport of fortune as a result of his own credulity and the promises of Caesellius Bassus. Punic by origin and mentally deranged, Bassus treated the vision he had seen in a dream by night as a ground of confident expectation, took ship to Rome, and, buying an interview with the emperor, explained that he had found on his estate an immensely deep cavern, which contained a great quantity of gold, not transformed into coin but in unwrought and ancient bullion. For there were ponderous ingots on the floor; while, in another part, the metal was piled in columns—a treasure which had lain hidden through the centuries in order to increase the prosperity of the present era. The Phoenician Dido, so his argument ran, after her flight from Tyre and her foundation of Carthage, had concealed the hoard, for fear that too much wealth might tempt her young nation to excess, or that the Numidian princes, hostile on other grounds as well, might be fired to arms by the lust of gold.

II. Accordingly, Nero, without sufficiently weighing the credibility either of his informant or of the affair in itself, and without sending to ascertain the truth of the tale, deliberately magnified the report and despatched men to bring in the spoils lying, he thought, ready to his hand. The party were given

triremes et delectum remigium [1] iuvandae festina-
tioni. Nec aliud per illos dies populus credulitate,
prudentes [2] diversa fama tulere. Ac forte quinquennale ludicrum secundo lustro celebrabatur, ab
oratoribusque [3] praecipua materia in laudem principis
adsumpta est. Non enim solitas tantum fruges nec
confusum metallis [4] aurum gigni, sed nova ubertate
provenire terram et obvias opes deferre deos, quaeque alia summa facundia nec minore adulatione
servilia fingebant, securi de facilitate credentis.

III. Gliscebat interim luxuria spe inani, consume-
banturque veteres opes quasi oblatis, quas multos
per annos prodigeret. Quin et inde iam largi-
ebatur; et divitiarum exspectatio inter causas pau-
pertatis publicae erat. Nam Bassus, effosso agro
suo latisque circum arvis, dum hunc illum locum pro-
missi specus adseverat, sequunturque non modo
milites, sed populus agrestium efficiendo operi
adsumptus, tandem posita vaecordia, non falsa antea
somnia sua seque tunc primum elusum admirans,
pudorem et metum morte voluntaria effugit. Quidam vinctum ac mox dimissum tradidere ademptis
bonis in locum regiae gazae.

---

[1] remigium *Boxhorn* : navigium.
[2] prudentes *Boxhorn* : prodentis.
[3] ab oratoribusque *Baiter* : avaratoribus oratoribusque.
[4] metallis <aliis> *Nipperdey*.

---

[1] The Neronia (XIV. 20 n.).
[2] For the insane extravagance of his last phase, see *Hist.*
I. 20; Suet. *Ner.* 30; Plut. *Galb.* 16.

triremes, and to better their speed, picked oarsmen; and, throughout those days, this one theme
was canvassed, by the populace with credulity, by
the prudent with very different comments. It
happened, too, that this was the second period for
the celebration of the Quinquennial Games,[1] and the
incident was taken by the orators as the principal
text for their panegyrics of the sovereign:—" For
not the customary crops alone, or gold alloyed with
other metals, were now produced: the earth gave
her increase with novel fecundity, and high heaven
sent wealth unsought." And there were other
servilities, which they developed with consummate
eloquence and not inferior sycophancy, assured of
the easy credence of their dupe!

III. Meanwhile, on the strength of this idle hope,
his extravagance grew, and treasures long accumu-
lated were dispersed on the assumption that others
had been vouchsafed which would serve his prodigality for many years. In fact, he was already
drawing on this fund for his largesses;[2] and the
expectation of wealth was among the causes of
national poverty. For Bassus—who had dug up
his own land along with a wide stretch of the adjacent
plains, always insisting that this or that was the site
of the promised cave, and followed not simply by
the soldiers but by a whole people of rustics enlisted
to carry out the work—at last threw off his delusion,
and, with an astonished protest that never before
had his dreams proved fallible and that this was his
first deception, avoided disgrace and danger by a
voluntary death. By some the statement is made
that he was imprisoned, only to be released shortly
afterwards, his property being confiscated to replace the queen's treasure.

IV. Interea senatus, propinquo iam lustrali certamine, ut dedecus averteret, offert imperatori victoriam cantus adicitque facundiae coronam, qua ludicra deformitas velaretur. Sed Nero nihil ambitu nec potestate senatus opus esse dictitans, se aequum adversum aemulos et religione iudicum meritam laudem adsecuturum, primo carmen in scaena recitat; mox flagitante vulgo ut omnia studia sua publicaret (haec enim verba dixere) ingreditur theatrum, cunctis citharae legibus obtemperans, ne fessus resideret, ne sudorem nisi ea, quam indutui gerebat, veste detergeret, ut nulla oris aut narium excrementa viserentur. Postremo flexus genu et coetum illum manu veneratus sententias iudicum opperiebatur ficto pavore. Et plebs quidem urbis, histrionum quoque gestus iuvare solita, personabat certis modis plausuque composito. Crederes laetari, ac fortasse laetabantur per incuriam publici flagitii.

V. Sed qui remotis e municipiis severaque [1] adhuc et antiqui moris retinente Italia,[1] quique per longinquas provincias lascivia inexperti officio legationum aut privata utilitate advenerant, neque aspectum illum tolerare neque labori inhonesto sufficere, cum manibus nesciis fatiscerent, turbarent gnaros ac saepe a militibus verberarentur, qui per cuneos stabant,

---

[1] severaque . . . retinente Italia *Agricola :* severamque . . . retinentes Italiam.

IV. In the meantime, with the Quinquennial Contest hard at hand, the senate attempted to avert a scandal by offering the emperor the victory in song, adding a " crown of eloquence," to cover the stigma inseparable from the stage. Nero protested, however, that he needed neither private interest nor the authority of the senate—he was meeting his competitors on equal terms, and would acquire an honestly earned distinction by the conscientious award of the judges. He began by reciting a poem on the stage: then, as the crowd clamoured for him to " display all his accomplishments" (the exact phrase used), he entered the theatre, observing the full rules of the harp—not to sit down when weary, not to wipe away the sweat except with the robe he was wearing, to permit no discharge from the mouth or nostrils to be visible. Finally, on bended knee, a hand kissed in salutation to that motley gathering, he awaited the verdict of the judges in feigned trepidation. And the city rabble, at least, accustomed to encourage the posturing even of the ordinary actor, thundered approval in measured cadences and regulated plaudits. You might have supposed them to be rejoicing; and possibly rejoicing they were, without a care for the national dishonour!

V. But the spectators from remote country towns in the still austere Italy tenacious of its ancient ways—those novices in wantonness from far-off provinces, who had come on a public mission or upon private business—were neither able to tolerate the spectacle nor competent to their degrading task. They flagged with inexperienced hands; they deranged the experts; often they had to be castigated by the soldiers stationed among the blocks of seats

ne quod temporis momentum inpari clamore aut silentio segni praeteriret. Constitit plerosque equitum, dum per angustias aditus et ingruentem multitudinem enituntur, obtritos, et alios, dum diem noctemque sedilibus continuant, morbo exitiabili correptos. Quippe gravior inerat metus, si spectaculo defuissent, multis palam et pluribus occultis, ut nomina ac vultus, alacritatem tristitiamque coeuntium scrutarentur. Unde tenuioribus statim inrogata supplicia, adversum inlustris dissimulatum ad praesens et mox redditum odium. Ferebantque Vespasianum, tamquam somno coniveret, a Phoebo liberto increpitum aegreque meliorum precibus obtectum, mox inminentem perniciem maiore fato effugisse.

VI. Post finem ludicri Poppaea mortem obiit, fortuita mariti iracundia, a quo gravida ictu calcis adflicta est. Neque enim venenum crediderim, quamvis quidam scriptores tradant, odio magis quam ex fide: quippe liberorum cupiens et amori uxoris obnoxius erat. Corpus non igni abolitum, ut Romanus mos, sed regum externorum consuetudine differtum odoribus conditur tumuloque Iuliorum infertur. Ductae tamen publicae exsequiae, laudavitque ipse apud rostra formam eius et quod divinae infantis parens fuisset aliaque fortunae munera pro virtutibus.

---

[1] By Suetonius and Dio the scene is laid in Greece during the imperial tour (Suet. *Vesp.* 4; D. Cass. LXVI. 11—with which compare Suet. *Vesp.* 14).

[2] Merely an extravagance of remorse. Poppaea's leaning to Judaism—she is called θεοσεβής, a technical term for "proselyte," in Jos. *A.J.* XX. 8, 11—can have had nothing to do with the case.

[3] I. 8 n.

to assure that not a moment of time should be wasted in unmodulated clamour or sluggish silence. It was known that numbers of knights were crushed to death while fighting their way up through the narrow gangway and the inrush of the descending crowd, and that others, through spending day and night on the benches, were attacked by incurable disease. For it was a graver ground of fear to be missing from the spectacle, since there was a host of spies openly present, and more in hiding, to note the names and faces, the gaiety and gloom, of the assembly. Hence, the lot of the humble was punishment, at once inflicted: in the case of the great, the debt of hatred, dissembled for a moment, was speedily repaid; and the story was told that Vespasian, reprimanded by the freedman Phoebus for closing his eyelids, and screened with difficulty by the prayers of the better party, was only saved later from the impending destruction by his predestined greatness.[1]

VI. After the close of the festival, Poppaea met her end through a chance outburst of anger on the part of her husband, who felled her with a kick during pregnancy. That poison played its part I am unable to believe, though the assertion is made by some writers less from conviction than from hatred; for Nero was desirous of children, and love for his wife was a ruling passion. The body was not cremated in the Roman style, but, in conformity with the practice of foreign courts, was embalmed by stuffing with spices,[2] then laid to rest in the mausoleum[3] of the Julian race. Still, a public funeral was held; and the emperor at the Rostra eulogized her beauty, the fact that she had been the mother of an infant daughter now divine, and other favours of fortune which did duty for virtues.

VII. Mortem Poppaeae ut palam tristem, ita
recordantibus laetam ob inpudicitiam eius saevi-
tiamque, nova insuper invidia Nero complevit pro-
hibendo C. Cassium officio exsequiarum, quod primum
indicium mali.   Neque in longum dilatum est, sed
Silanus additur, nullo crimine, nisi quod Cassius
opibus vetustis et gravitate morum, Silanus claritudine generis et modesta iuventa praecellebant.
Igitur missa ad senatum oratione removendos a re
publica utrosque disseruit, obiectavitque Cassio,
quod inter imagines maiorum etiam C. Cassi effigiem
coluisset, ita inscriptam " Duci partium ": quippe
semina belli civilis et defectionem a domo Caesarum
quaesitam.   Ac *ne* memoria tantum infensi nominis
ad discordias uteretur, adsumpsisse L. Silanum,
iuvenem genere nobilem, animo praeruptum, quem
novis rebus ostentaret.

VIII. Ipsum dehinc Silanum increpuit isdem quibus patruum eius Torquatum, tamquam disponeret
iam imperii curas praeficeretque rationibus et libellis
et epistulis libertos, inania simul et falsa: nam
Silanus intentior metu et exitio patrui ad prae-
cavendum exterritus erat.   Inducti posthac vocabulo
indicum, qui in Lepidam, Cassii uxorem, Silani
amitam, incestum cum fratris filio et diros sacrorum

---

[1] XV. 52 n.

[2] The tyrannicide, of whom the jurist was a lineal descendant (XII. 12 n.).—The gravamen of the charge was doubtless
the inscription.   That there was no absolute prohibition of
such effigies is shown by the words of Cremutius Cordus at IV.
35, but the hero-worship of Cassius and the Bruti had its
dangers : see, for instance, III. 76; IV. 34; XVI. 22.

VII. To the death of Poppaea, outwardly regretted, but welcome to all who remembered her profligacy and cruelty, Nero added a fresh measure of odium by prohibiting Gaius Cassius from attendance at the funeral. It was the first hint of mischief. Nor was the mischief long delayed. Silanus [1] was associated with him; their only crime being that Cassius was eminent for a great hereditary fortune and an austere character, Silanus for a noble lineage and a temperate youth. Accordingly, the emperor sent a speech to the senate, arguing that both should be removed from public life, and objecting to the former that, among his other ancestral effigies, he had honoured a bust of Gaius Cassius,[2] inscribed:—" *To the leader of the cause.*" The seeds of civil war, and revolt from the house of the Caesars,—such were the objects he had pursued. And, not to rely merely on the memory of a hated name as an incentive to faction, he had taken to himself a partner in Lucius Silanus, a youth of noble family and headstrong temper, who was to be his figure-head for a revolution.

VIII. He then attacked Silanus himself in the same strain as his uncle Torquatus,[3] alleging that he was already apportioning the responsibilities of empire, and appointing freedmen to the charge of " accounts, documents, and correspondence ": an indictment at once frivolous and false; for the prevalent alarms had made Silanus vigilant, and his uncle's doom had terrified him into especial caution. Next, so-called informers were introduced to forge against Lepida [4]—wife of Cassius, aunt of Silanus—a tale of incest, committed with her brother's son, and of magical

[3] See XII. 58 A and XV. 35.
[4] Junia Lepida, sister of Junia Calvina (XII. 4; 8).

ritus confingerent. Trahebantur ut conscii Vulcacius [1] Tullinus [2] ac Marcellus Cornelius senatores et Calpurnius Fabatus eques Romanus; qui appellato principe instantem damnationem frustrati, mox Neronem circa summa scelera distentum quasi minores evasere.

IX. Tunc consulto senatus Cassio et Silano exilia decernuntur: de Lepida Caesar statueret. Deportatusque in insulam Sardiniam Cassius, et senectus eius expectabatur. Silanus, tamquam Naxum deveheretur, Ostiam amotus, post municipio Apuliae, cui nomen Barium est, clauditur. Illic indignissimum casum sapienter tolerans a centurione ad caedem misso corripitur; suadentique venas abrumpere, animum quidem morti destinatum ait, sed non remittere [3] percussori gloriam ministerii. At centurio quamvis inermem, praevalidum tamen et irae quam timori propiorem cernens premi a militibus iubet. Nec omisit Silanus obniti et intendere ictus, quantum manibus nudis valebat, donec a centurione vulneribus adversis tamquam in pugna caderet.

X. Haud minus prompte L. Vetus socrusque eius Sextia et Pollitta [4] filia necem subiere, invisi principi, tamquam vivendo exprobrarent interfectum esse [5]

---

[1] Vulcacius] volcatius *Med.*
[2] Tullinus] Tertullinus *Hist. IV* 9.
[3] remittere *Med.*[1]: peremittere *Med.*
[4] Pollitta *Nipperdey*: poliitia.
[5] esse] a se *Ernesti.*

---

[1] Grandfather of the wife of the younger Pliny, nine of whose letters are addressed to him.

[2] In spite, however, of his advanced age and blindness, he returned under Vespasian.

ceremonies. The senators Vulcacius Tullinus and
Cornelius Marcellus were brought in as accomplices,
with the Roman knight Calpurnius Fabatus.[1] Their
imminent condemnation they cheated by appealing to
the emperor, and later, as being of minor importance,
made good their escape from Nero, now fully occupied
by crimes of the first magnitude.

IX. Then, by decree of the senate, sentences of
exile were registered against Cassius and Silanus:
on the case of Lepida the Caesar was to pronounce.
Cassius was deported to the island of Sardinia, and
old age left to do its work.[2] Silanus, ostensibly
bound for Naxos, was removed to Ostia, and afterwards confined in an Apulian town by the name of
Barium.[3] There, while supporting with philosophy
his most unworthy fate, he was seized by a centurion
sent for the slaughter. To the suggestion that he
should cut an artery, he replied that he had, in fact,
made up his mind to die, but could not excuse the
assassin his glorious duty. The centurion, however,
noticing that, if unarmed, he was very strongly
built and betrayed more anger than timidity, ordered
his men to overpower him. Silanus did not fail to
struggle, and to strike with what vigour his bare fists
permitted, until he dropped under the sword of the
centurion, as upon a field of battle, his wounds in front.

X. With not less courage Lucius Vetus,[4] his mother-
in-law Sextia, and his daughter Pollitta,[5] met their
doom: they were loathed by the emperor, who took
their life to be a standing protest against the slaying

[3] Bari, on the Adriatic, about 70 miles N.W. of Brindisi;
in the time of Horace, and probably of Nero, little more than
a fishing-village, now a considerable city.

[4] L. Antistius Vetus (XIII. 11, 53; XIV. 58).

[5] The Antistia of XIV. 22.

Rubellium Plautum, generum L. Veteris. Sed
initium detegendae saevitiae praebuit interversis
patroni rebus ad accusandum transgrediens Fortunatus libertus, adscito Claudio Demiano quem ob
flagitia vinctum a Vetere Asiae pro consule exsolvit
Nero in praemium accusationis. Quod ubi cognitum
reo, seque et libertum pari sorte componi, Formianos
in agros digreditur. Illic eum milites occulta
custodia circumdant. Aderat filia, super ingruens
periculum longo dolore atrox, ex quo percussores
Plauti mariti sui viderat; cruentamque cervicem
eius amplexa servabat sanguinem et vestes respersas,
vidua inpexa[1] luctu continuo nec ullis alimentis nisi
quae mortem arcerent. Tum hortante patre Neapolim pergit. Et quia aditu Neronis prohibebatur,
egressus obsidens, audiret insontem neve consulatus
sui quondam collegam dederet liberto, modo muliebri
eiulatu, aliquando sexum egressa voce infensa
clamitabat, donec princeps inmobilem se precibus et
invidiae iuxta ostendit.

XI. Ergo nuntiat patri abicere spem et uti necessitate: simul adfertur parari cognitionem senatus et
trucem sententiam. Nec defuere qui monerent
magna ex parte heredem Caesarem nuncupare atque
ita nepotibus de reliquo consulere. Quod aspernatus,

---

[1] inpexa *Petavius* : inplexa.

---

[1] XIII. 19 n. [2] XIV. 59.
[3] The precaution was usual: a couple of instances are the
will of Prasutagus (XIV. 31) and that of Agricola (*Agr.* 43).

of Rubellius Plautus,[1] the son-in-law of Vetus. But
the opportunity for laying bare his ferocity was supplied by the freedman Fortunatus; who, after em-
bezzling his patron's property, now deserted him to
turn accuser, and called to his aid Claudius Demianus,
imprisoned for heinous offences by Vetus in his
proconsulate of Asia, but now freed by Nero as the
recompense of delation. Apprized of this, and
gathering that he and his freedman were to meet
in the struggle as equals, the accused left for
his estate at Formiae. There be was placed under a
tacit surveillance by the military. He had with him
his daughter, who apart from the impending danger,
was embittered by a grief which had lasted since the
day when she watched the assassins of her husband
Plautus—she had clasped the bleeding neck,[2] and
still treasured her blood-flecked robe, widowed,
unkempt, unconsoled, and fasting except for a little
sustenance to keep death at bay. Now, at the
prompting of her father, she went to Naples; and,
debarred from access to Nero, besieged his doors,
crying to him to give ear to the guiltless and not
surrender to a freedman the one-time partner of
his consulate; sometimes with female lamentations,
and again in threatening accents which went beyond
her sex, until the sovereign showed himself inflexible
alike to prayer and to reproach.

XI. Accordingly, she carried word to her father
to abandon hope and accept the inevitable. At the
same time, news came that arrangements were being
made for a trial in the senate and a merciless verdict.
Nor were there wanting those who advised him to
name the Caesar as a principal heir,[3] and thus safe-
guard the residue for his grandchildren. Rejecting

ne vitam proxime libertatem actam novissimo servitio foedaret, largitur in servos quantum aderat pecuniae; et si qua asportari possent, sibi quemque deducere, tris modo lectulos ad suprema retineri iubet. Tunc eodem in cubiculo, eodem ferro abscindunt venas, properique et singulis vestibus ad verecundiam velati balineis inferuntur, pater filiam, avia neptem, illa utrosque intuens, et certatim precantes labenti animae celerem exitum, ut relinquerent suos superstites et morituros. Servavitque ordinem fortuna, ac seniores prius, tum cui prima aetas extinguuntur. Accusati post sepulturam decretumque ut more maiorum punirentur. Et Nero intercessit, mortem sine arbitro permittens: ea caedibus peractis ludibria adiciebantur.

XII. Publius [1] Gallus eques Romanus, quod Faenio Rufo intimus et Veteri non alienus fuerat, aqua atque igni prohibitus est. Liberto et accusatori praemium operae locus in theatro inter viatores tribunicios datur. Et menses,[2] qui Aprilem eundemque Neroneum sequebantur,[2] Maius Claudii, Iunius [3] Germanici vocabulis mutantur, testificante Cornelio Orfito, qui id censuerat, ideo Iunium

[1] Publius] Rubrius *Nipperdey* (*cf. Hist. II*. 51; 99).
[2] menses . . . sequebantur *Nipperdey :* mensis . . . sequebatur.
[3] Iunius] Iulius *Lipsius* (*Madvig, Halm*).

---

[1] XV. 74.
[2] The names were his own—he was " Claudius Nero Caesar Germanicus "—not those of his adoptive father and grandfather. So Commodus, by drawing upon his farrago of titles, was able to construct a year comprising the months :— *Amazonius, Invictus, Pius, Felix, Lucius, Aelius, Aurelius, Commodus, Augustus, Herculeus, Romanus, Exuperatorius* (D. Cass. LXXII. 15; Lampr. *Comm.* 11 sq.).

the proposal, however, so as not to sully a life, passed in a near approach to freedom, by an act of servility at the close, he distributed among his slaves what money was available : all portable articles he ordered them to remove for their own uses, reserving only three couches for the final scene.   Then, in the same chamber, with the same piece of steel, they severed their veins ; and hurriedly, wrapped in the single garment which decency prescribed, they were carried to the baths, the father gazing on his daughter, the grandmother on her grandchild, and she on both ; all praying with rival earnestness for a quick end to the failing breath, so that they might leave their kith and kin still surviving, and assured of death.   Fate observed the proper order ; and the two eldest passed away the first, then Pollitta in her early youth.   They were indicted after burial ; the verdict was that they should be punished in the fashion of our ancestors ; and Nero, interposing, allowed them to die unsupervised.   Such were the comedies that followed, when the deed of blood was done.

XII. Publius Gallus, a Roman knight, for being intimate with Faenius Rufus and not unacquainted with Vetus, was interdicted from fire and water : the freedman, and accuser, was rewarded for his service by a seat in the theatre among the tribunician runners.   The months following April—otherwise known as " Neroneus " [1]—were renamed, May taking the style of " Claudius," June that of " Germanicus." [2] According to the testimony of Cornelius Orfitus, the author of the proposal, the alteration [3] in the case

[3] The sense given to *transmissum* in the version is unparalleled and totally incredible ; but Lipsius' and Madvig's *Iulium mensem* seems hardly possible, unless, perhaps, *nomen Iunium* is cancelled below.

mensem transmissum, quia duo iam Torquati ob scelera interfecti infaustum nomen Iunium fecissent.

XIII. Tot facinoribus foedum annum etiam di tempestatibus et morbis insignivere. Vastata Campania turbine ventorum, qui villas arbusta fruges passim disiecit pertulitque violentiam ad vicina urbi; in qua omne mortalium genus vis pestilentiae depopulabatur, nulla caeli intemperie, quae occurreret oculis. Sed domus corporibus exanimis, itinera funeribus complebantur; non sexus, non aetas periculo vacua; servitia perinde et ingenua plebes raptim extingui, inter coniugum et liberorum lamenta, qui dum adsident, dum deflent, saepe eodem rogo cremabantur. Equitum senatorumque interitus, quamvis promisci, minus flebiles erant, tamquam communi mortalitate saevitiam principis praevenirent.

Eodem anno dilectus per Galliam Narbonensem Africamque et Asiam habiti sunt supplendis Illyricis legionibus, ex quibus aetate aut valetudine fessi sacramento solvebantur. Cladem Lugdunensem quadragiens¹ sestertio solatus est princeps, ut amissa urbi reponerent; quam pecuniam Lugdunenses ante obtulerant urbis casibus.

¹ Lugdunensem * * quadragiens *Nipperdey.*

---

¹ The gentile name of the two Torquati (XV. 35 and XVI. 8).

² The disaster, it stands to reason, must have happened after the burning of Rome. If, then, it is to be identified with the

of June was due to the fact that already the execution of two Torquati for their crimes had made " Junius " [1] a sinister name.

XIII. Upon this year, disgraced by so many deeds of shame, Heaven also set its mark by tempest and by disease. Campania was wasted by a whirl-wind, which far and wide wrecked the farms, the fruit trees, and the crops, and carried its fury to the neighbourhood of the capital, where all classes of men were being decimated by a deadly epidemic. No outward sign of a distempered air was visible. Yet the houses were filled with lifeless bodies, the streets with funerals. Neither sex nor age gave immunity from danger; slaves and the free-born populace alike were summarily cut down, amid the laments of their wives and children, who, themselves infected while tending or mourning the victims, were often burnt upon the same pyre. Knights and senators, though they perished on all hands, were less deplored—as if, by undergoing the common lot, they were cheating the ferocity of the emperor.

In the same year, levies were held in Narbonese Gaul, Africa, and Asia, to recruit the legions of Illyri-cum, in which all men incapacitated by age or sickness were being discharged the service. The emperor alleviated the disaster at Lugdunum [2] by a grant of four million sesterces to repair the town's losses : the same amount which Lugdunum had previously offered in aid of the misfortunes of the capital.

---

fire known, about this period, to have laid Lyons in ashes, Seneca must be wrong in his date (58 A.D.). Alternatively, he may have been right in his presentiment :—*Nunquam tam infestum exarsit incendium ut nihil alteri superesset incendio* (*Ep.* 91).

XIV. C. Suetonio Luccio [1] Telesino consulibus
Antistius Sosianus, factitatis in Neronem carminibus
probrosis exilio, ut dixi, multatus, postquam id
honoris indicibus tamque promptum ad caedes
principem accepit, inquies animo et occasionum
haud segnis Pammenem, eiusdem loci exulem et
Chaldaeorum arte famosum eoque multorum amicitiis
innexum,[2] similitudine fortunae sibi conciliat. Venti-
tare ad eum nuntios et consultationes non frustra
ratus, simul annuam pecuniam a P. Anteio ministrari
cognoscit. Neque nescium habebat Anteium caritate Agrippinae invisum Neroni opesque eius prae-
cipuas ad eliciendam cupidinem eamque causam
multis exitio esse. Igitur interceptis Antei litteris,
furatus etiam libellos, quibus dies genitalis eius et
eventura secretis Pammenis occultabantur, simul
repertis quae de ortu vitaque Ostorii Scapulae composita erant, scribit ad principem magna se et quae
incolumitati eius conducerent adlaturum, si brevem
exilii veniam inpetravisset: quippe Anteium et
Ostorium inminere rebus et sua Caesarisque fata
scrutari. Exim missae liburnicae advehiturque propere Sosianus. Ac vulgato eius indicio inter damna-
tos magis quam inter reos Anteius Ostoriusque
habebantur, adeo ut testamentum Antei nemo
obsignaret, nisi Tigellinus auctor extitisset, monito

---

[1] Luccio *Rupertus*: L.   [2] innexum *Lipsius* : innixum.

[1] Suetonius Paulinus (XIV. 29 sqq.).

[2] He leaned to philosophy, and makes a few creditable
appearances in Philostratus' *vie romancée* of Apollonius
(*V.A.* IV. 40, 43; VII. 11; VIII. 7, 12). In Martial he is found
declining to make unsecured loans to his " old companion ";
who, like Philostratus, refers to his exile under Domitian
(XII. 25).

[3] XIV. 48.   [4] XIII. 22.   [5] See XIV. 48.

XIV. In the consulate of Gaius Suetonius [1] and
Luccius Telesinus,[2] Antistius Sosianus, who had, as
I have said,[3] been sentenced to exile for composing
scurrilous verses upon Nero, heard of the honour paid
to informers and of the emperor's alacrity for bloodshed. Restless by temperament, with a quick eye
for opportunities, he used the similarity of their
fortunes in order to ingratiate himself with Pammenes,
who was an exile in the same place and, as a noted
astrologer, had wide connections of friendship. He
believed it was not for nothing that messengers were
for ever coming to consult Pammenes, to whom,
as he discovered at the same time, a yearly pension
was allowed by Publius Anteius.[4] He was further
aware that Pammenes' affection for Agrippina had
earned him the hatred of Nero; that his riches were
admirably calculated to excite cupidity; and that
this was a circumstance which proved fatal to many.
He therefore intercepted a letter from Anteius,
stole in addition the papers, concealed in Pammenes'
archives, which contained his horoscope and career,
and, lighting at the same time on the astrologer's
calculations with regard to the birth and life of
Ostorius Scapula,[5] wrote to the emperor that, could
he be granted a short respite from his banishment,
he would bring him grave news conducive to his
safety: for Anteius and Ostorius had designs upon
the empire, and were peering into their destinies
and that of the prince. Fast galleys were at once
sent out, and Sosianus arrived in haste. The moment
his information was divulged, Anteius and Ostorius
were regarded, not as incriminated, but as condemned: so much so, that not a man would become
signatory to the will of Anteius until Tigellinus came

prius Anteio ne supremas tabulas moraretur. Atque
ille hausto veneno, tarditatem eius perosus intercisis
venis mortem adproperavit.

XV. Ostorius longinquis in agris apud finem Ligu-
rum id temporis erat. Eo missus centurio, qui caedem
eius maturaret. Causa festinandi ex eo oriebatur,
quod Ostorius multa militari fama et civicam coronam
apud Britanniam meritus, ingenti corpore [1] armorumque scientia metum Neroni fecerat, ne invaderet
pavidum semper et reperta nuper coniuratione magis
exterritum. Igitur centurio, ubi effugia villae
clausit, iussa imperatoris Ostorio aperit. Is fortitudinem saepe adversum hostes spectatam in se vertit:
et quia venae quamquam interruptae parum sanguinis
effundebant, hactenus manu servi usus, ut inmotum
pugionem extolleret, adpressit dextram eius iugulo-
que occurrit.

XVI. Etiam si bella externa et obitas pro re
publica mortis tanta casuum similitudine memora-
rem, meque ipsum satias cepisset aliorumque taedium exspectarem, quamvis honestos civium exitus,
tristis tamen et continuos aspernantium: at nunc
patientia servilis tantumque sanguinis domi perditum
fatigant animum et maestitia restringunt. Neque
aliam defensionem ab iis, quibus ista noscentur,
exegerim, quam ne oderim [2] tam segniter pereuntis.

---

[1] corpore *dett.*: corporis corporis *Med.*, corporis roboro *Beroaldus*, vi corporis *Wurm*.
[2] oderim] oderint *Agricola*.

forward with his sanction, first warning the testator
not to defer his final dispositions. Anteius swallowed
poison; but, disgusted by its slowness, found a
speedier death by cutting his arteries.

XV. Ostorius, at the moment, was on a remote
estate on the Ligurian frontier; and thither a
centurion was despatched to do the murder quickly.
A motive for speed was given by the fact that
Ostorius, the owner of a considerable military reputation and a civic crown earned in Britain, had, by his
great bodily powers and skill in arms, inspired Nero
with a fear that he might possibly attack his sovereign,
always cowardly and more than ever terrified by the
lately discovered plot. The centurion, then, after
guarding the exits from the villa, disclosed the
imperial orders to Ostorius. The victim turned
against himself the courage which he had often
evinced in face of the enemy. Finding that, although he had opened his veins, the blood ran slowly,
he had recourse to a slave for one service alone,
to hold up a dagger steadily; then he drew his
hand nearer, and met the steel with his throat.

XVI. Even had I been narrating campaigns
abroad and lives laid down for the commonwealth,
and narrating them with the same uniformity of
incident, I should myself have lost appetite for the
task, and I should expect the tedium of others,
repelled by the tale of Roman deaths, honourable
perhaps, but tragic and continuous. As it is, this
slave-like patience and the profusion of blood wasted
at home weary the mind and oppress it with melancholy. The one concession I would ask from those
who shall study these records is that they would
permit me not to hate the men who died with so little

Ira illa numinum in res Romanas fuit, quam non, ut
in cladibus exercituum aut captivitate urbium, semel
edito transire licet. Detur hoc inlustrium virorum
posteritati, ut quo modo exsequiis a promisca
sepultura separantur, ita in traditione supremorum
accipiant habeantque propriam memoriam.

XVII. Paucos quippe intra dies eodem agmine
Annaeus Mela, Cerialis Anicius, Rufrius [1] Crispinus,
T.[2] Petronius cecidere, Mela et Crispinus equites
Romani dignitate senatoria. Nam hic quondam
praefectus praetorii et consularibus insignibus dona-
tus ac nuper crimine coniurationis in Sardiniam
exactus, accepto iussae mortis nuntio semet interfecit.
Mela, quibus Gallio et Seneca parentibus natus,
petitione honorum abstinuerat per ambitionem
praeposteram, ut eques Romanus consularibus potentia aequaretur; simul adquirendae pecuniae
brevius iter credebat per procurationes administrandis
principis negotiis. Idem Annaeum Lucanum genuerat, grande adiumentum claritudinis. Quo interfecto dum rem familiarem eius acriter requirit,

[1] Rufrius *Halm :* rufus.
[2] T. *Haase :* ac *Med.*, C. *Wesenberg, al.—The praenomen is
established by Plin. H.N. XXXVII.* 2, 20 (' T. Petronius
consularis ') *and Plut. Mor.* 60 E (Τίτος Πετρώνιος).

---

[1] The sentence has been variously interpreted, and to very
little effect. The simplest and not impossibly best course is to
acquiesce in the old conjecture *oderint*, with Walther's para-
phrase :—*A lectore non exigimus ut illorum plus quam servilem
patientiam defendat aut excuset, sed hoc tantum, ne istos odio
prosequatur ; nam res fuit plane fatalis.*
[2] For this use of *posteritas*, compare, for instance, Plin. *Ep.*
II. 1, *legit scripta de se carmina, legit historias, et posteritati suae
interfuit.* If the word bears its common meaning, then "the
posterity of the famous" are the *segniter pereuntes,* and the

spirit![1] It was the anger of Heaven against the Roman realm—an anger which you cannot, as in the case of beaten armies or captured towns, mention once and for all and proceed upon your way. Let us make this concession to the memory[2] of the nobly born: that, as in the last rites they are distinguished from the vulgar dead, so, when history records their end, each shall receive and keep his special mention.

XVII. For, in the course of a few days, there fell, in a single band, Annaeus Mela, Anicius Cerialis, Rufrius Crispinus, and Titus Petronius. Mela and Crispinus were Roman knights of senatorial rank.[3] The latter, once commander of the praetorian guards and decorated with the consular insignia,[4] but latterly banished to Sardinia on a charge of conspiracy, committed suicide on reception of the news that his death had been ordered. Mela, son of the same parents as Gallio and Seneca, had refrained from seeking office, as he nursed the paradoxical ambition of equalling the influence of a consular while remaining a simple knight: at the same time, he held that the shorter road to the acquiry of wealth lay in the pro-curatorships handling private business of the sovereign. He was also the father of Lucan—a considerable enhancement of his fame. After his son's death, he called in the debts owing to the estate with a vigour which raised up an accuser

sentiment becomes, in essence, that of Sen. *De benef.* IV. 30, *hic egregiis maioribus ortus est: qualiscumque est, sub umbra suorum lateat.*

[3] They were *laticlavii*—knights possessed of the senatorial property qualification, and wearing the broad purple stripe by permission of the emperor.

[4] His praetorian—not consular—decorations are mentioned at XI. 4: for his exile, see XV. 71.

accusatorem concivit Fabium Romanum, ex intimis
Lucani amicis. Mixta inter patrem filiumque coniurationis scientia fingitur, adsimulatis Lucani litteris:
quas inspectas Nero ferri ad eum iussit, opibus eius
inhians. At Mela, quae tum promptissima mortis
via, exsolvit venas, scriptis codicillis, quibus grandem
pecuniam in Tigellinum generumque eius Cossutianum Capitonem erogabat, quo cetera manerent.
Additur codicillis, tamquam de iniquitate exitii
querens ita scripsisset,[1] se quidem mori nullis supplicii causis, Rufrium autem Crispinum et Anicium
Cerialem vita frui infensos principi. Quae composita
credebantur de Crispino, quia interfectus erat, de
Ceriale, ut interficeretur. Neque enim multo post
vim sibi attulit, minore quam ceteri miseratione,
quia proditam Gaio Caesari coniurationem ab eo
meminerant.

XVIII. De Petronio [2] pauca supra repetenda sunt.
Nam illi dies per somnum, nox officiis et oblectamentis
vitae transigebatur; utque alios industria, ita hunc
ignavia ad famam protulerat, habebaturque non
ganeo et profligator, ut plerique sua haurientium,
sed erudito luxu. Ac dicta factaque eius quanto

---

[1] scripsisset] scripsisse *dett.*
[2] Petronio *Nipperdey :* C. Petronio.

---

[1] XI. 6 n.
[2] XV. 74.
[3] It was apparently suspected that the addition to the
codicil had been forged on behalf of Nero, to vindicate one
execution and supply the pretext for another.
[4] Little is known of it beyond the date (40 A.D.).
[5] He is now universally allowed to be the author of the justly
famous *Satirae*—a sort of picaresque novel interspersed with
verse-pieces, two sadly lacerated books of which survive from
a total of sixteen or over. The objection that some mention

in Fabius Romanus, one of Lucan's intimate friends.
A fictitious charge, that knowledge of the plot had
been shared between father and son, was backed by
a forged letter from Lucan. Nero, after inspecting
it, gave orders that it was to be carried to Mela.
Mela took what was then the favoured way of death,
and opened an artery, first penning a codicil by which
he bequeathed a large sum to Tigellinus and his
son-in-law Cossutianus Capito,[1] in hopes of saving
the rest of the will. A postscript to the codicil,
written in appearance as a protest against the
iniquity of his doom, stated that, while he himself
was dying without a cause for his execution, Rufrius
Crispinus and Anicius Cerialis[2] remained in the
enjoyment of life, though bitterly hostile to the
emperor. The statement was considered to be a
fiction, invented in the case of Crispinus, because
death had been inflicted; in that of Cerialis, to
make certain its infliction.[3] For not long afterwards
he took his own life, exciting less pity than the
others, as memories remained of his betrayal of the
conspiracy[4] to Gaius Caesar.

XVIII. Petronius[5] calls for a brief retrospect. He
was a man whose day was passed in sleep, his nights
in the social duties and amenities of life: others
industry may raise to greatness—Petronius had
idled into fame. Nor was he regarded, like the
common crowd of spendthrifts, as a debauchee and
wastrel, but as the finished artist of extravagance.
His words and actions had a freedom and a stamp of

of his literary powers might, in that case, have been expected
here, is idle: for few works can in the eyes of Tacitus have
borne less resemblance to "literature" than the scandalous
Odyssey of Encolpios, Ascyltos, Giton, and their peers.

solutiora et quandam sui neglegentiam praeferentia, tanto gratius in speciem simplicitatis accipiebantur. Proconsul tamen Bithyniae et mox consul vigentem se ac parem negotiis ostendit. Dein revolutus ad vitia, seu vitiorum imitatione, inter paucos familiarium Neroni adsumptus est, elegantiae arbiter, dum nihil amoenum et molle adfluentia putat, nisi quod ei Petronius adprobavisset. Unde invidia Tigellini quasi adversus aemulum et scientia voluptatum potiorem. Ergo crudelitatem principis, cui ceterae libidines cedebant, adgreditur, amicitiam Scaevini Petronio obiectans, corrupto ad indicium servo ademptaque defensione et maiore parte familiae in vincla rapta.

XIX. Forte illis diebus Campaniam petiverat Caesar, et Cumas usque progressus Petronius illic attinebatur; nec tulit ultra timoris aut spei moras. Neque tamen praeceps vitam expulit, sed incisas venas, ut libitum, obligatas aperire rursum et adloqui amicos, non per seria aut quibus gloriam constantiae peteret. Audiebatque referentes, nihil de inmortalitate animae et sapientium placitis, sed levia

---

[1] The manuscripts of the *Satirae*, and the grammarians, give Arbiter as a cognomen. Whether his court title suggested or was suggested by the surname, it is evidently impossible to say.

[2] XV. 49 sqq.

[3] The other way of thinking perhaps deserves an example :— *Prosequebatur eum philosophus suus* (a Stoic or Cynic chaplain). *Nec iam procul erat tumulus in quo Caesari* (Caligula), *deo nostro, fiebat quotidianum sacrum.* "*Quid,*" *inquit,* "*Cane, nunc*

self-abandonment which rendered them doubly acceptable by an air of native simplicity. Yet as proconsul of Bithynia, and later as consul, he showed himself a man of energy and competent to affairs. Then, lapsing into the habit, or copying the features, of vice, he was adopted into the narrow circle of Nero's intimates as his Arbiter of Elegance;[1] the jaded emperor finding charm and delicacy in nothing save what Petronius had commended. His success awoke the jealousy of Tigellinus against an apparent rival, more expert in the science of pleasure than himself. He addressed himself, therefore, to the sovereign's cruelty, to which all other passions gave pride of place; arraigning Petronius for friendship with Scaevinus,[2] while suborning one of his slaves to turn informer, withholding all opportunity of defence, and placing the greater part of his household under arrest.

XIX. In those days, as it chanced, the Caesar had migrated to Campania; and Petronius, after proceeding as far as Cumae, was being there detained in custody. He declined to tolerate further the delays of fear or hope; yet still did not hurry to take his life, but caused his already severed arteries to be bound up to meet his whim, then opened them once more, and began to converse with his friends, in no grave strain and with no view to the fame of a stout-hearted ending. He listened to them as they rehearsed, not discourses upon the immortality of the soul[3] or the doctrines of philo-

---

cogitas ? Aut quae tibi mens est ?—" Observare," inquit Canus, " proposui, illo velocissimo momento, an sensurus sit animus exire se." Promisitque, si quid explorasset, circumiturum amicos et indicaturum quis esset animarum status (Sen. *De tranquill. animi,* 14).

carmina et facilis versus. Servorum alios largitione, quosdam verberibus adfecit. Iniit epulas,[1] somno indulsit, ut quamquam coacta mors fortuitae similis esset. Ne codicillis quidem, quod plerique pereuntium, Neronem aut Tigellinum aut quem alium potentium adulatus est: sed flagitia principis sub nominibus exoletorum feminarumque et novitatem cuiusque stupri perscripsit atque obsignata misit Neroni. Fregitque anulum, ne mox usui esset ad facienda pericula.

XX. Ambigenti Neroni, quonam modo noctium suarum ingenia notescerent, offertur Silia, matrimonio senatoris haud ignota et ipsi ad omnem libidinem adscita ac Petronio perquam familiaris. Agitur in exilium, tanquam non siluisset quae viderat pertuleratque, proprio odio. At Minucium Thermum praetura functum Tigellini simultatibus dedit, quia libertus Thermi quaedam de Tigellino criminose detulerat, quae cruciatibus tormentorum ipse, patronus eius nece inmerita luere.

XXI. Trucidatis tot insignibus viris, ad postremum Nero virtutem ipsam excindere concupivit interfecto Thrasea Paeto et Barea Sorano, olim utrisque infensus, et accedentibus causis in Thraseam, quod senatu egressus est, cum de Agrippina referretur, ut memoravi,[2] quodque Iuvenalium ludicro parum specta-

---

[1] epulas *Menagius, Markland:* et vias *Med.,* et epulas *Halm.*

---

[1] The precaution was evidently suggested by the forgery after Lucan's death: see above, chap. 17.

[2] XII. 53.

[3] XIV. 12.

sophy, but light songs and frivolous verses. Some of
his slaves tasted of his bounty, a few of the lash. He
took his place at dinner, and drowsed a little, so that
death, if compulsory, should at least resemble
nature. Not even in his will did he follow the routine
of suicide by flattering Nero or Tigellinus or another
of the mighty, but—prefixing the names of the
various catamites and women—detailed the imperial
debauches and the novel features of each act of lust,
and sent the document under seal to Nero. His
signet-ring he broke, lest it should render dangerous
service later.[1]

XX. While Nero doubted how the character of
his nights was gaining publicity, there suggested
itself the name of Silia—the wife of a senator, and
therefore a woman of some note, requisitioned by
himself for every form of lubricity, and on terms of
the closest intimacy with Petronius. She was now
driven into exile for failing to observe silence upon
what she had seen and undergone. Here the motive
was a hatred of his own. But Minucius Thermus, an
ex-praetor, he sacrificed to the animosities of
Tigellinus. For a freedman of Thermus had brought
certain damaging charges against the favourite,
which he himself expiated by the pains of torture,
his patron by an unmerited death.

XXI. After the slaughter of so many of the noble,
Nero in the end conceived the ambition to extirpate
virtue herself by killing Thrasea Paetus and Barea
Soranus.[2] To both he was hostile from of old, and
against Thrasea there were additional motives; for
he had walked out of the senate, as I have mentioned,[3]
during the discussion on Agrippina, and at the
festival of the Juvenalia his services had not been

THE ANNALS OF TACITUS

bilem operam praebuerat; eaque offensio altius
penetrabat, quia idem Thrasea Patavi, unde ortus
erat, ludis † cetastis [1] a Troiano Antenore institutis
habitu tragico cecinerat. Die quoque, quo praetor
Antistius ob probra in Neronem composita ad mortem
damnabatur, mitiora censuit obtinuitque; et cum [2]
deum honores Poppaeae decernuntur,[3] sponte absens,
funeri non interfuerat. Quae oblitterari non sinebat
Capito Cossutianus, praeter animum ad flagitia
praecipitem iniquus Thraseae, quod auctoritate eius
concidisset, iuvantis Cilicum legatos, dum Capitonem
repetundarum interrogant.

XXII. Quin et illa obiectabat, principio anni
vitare Thraseam sollemne ius iurandum; nuncupa-
tionibus votorum non adesse quamvis quinde-
cimvirali sacerdotio praeditum; numquam pro
salute principis aut caelesti voce immolavisse; ad-
siduum olim et indefessum, qui vulgaribus quoque
patrum consultis semet fautorem aut adversarium
ostenderet, triennio non introisse curiam; nuperri-
meque, cum ad coercendos Silanum et Veterem
certatim concurreretur, privatis potius clientium
negotiis vacavisse. Secessionem iam id et partis
et, si idem multi audeant, bellum esse. " Ut
quondam C. Caesarem " inquit " et M. Catonem, ita

---

[1] cetastis] vetustis *R. Seyffert*, cetariis *Nipperdey*.
[2] cum] dum *Heinsius*.
[3] decernuntur] decernerentur *Agricola*.

---

[1] Padua.
[2] Virg. *Aen.* I. 242 sqq.; Liv. I. 1.
[3] XIV. 48.　　　[4] XIII. 33.　　　[5] I. 72 n.

conspicuous—a grievance which went the deeper
that in Patavium,[1] his native place, the same Thrasea
had sung in tragic costume at the . . . Games
instituted by the Trojan Antenor.[2] Again, on the
day when sentence of death was all but passed on the
praetor Antistius for his lampoons on Nero, he proposed, and carried, a milder penalty;[3] and, after
deliberately absenting himself from the vote of
divine honours to Poppaea, he had not assisted at her
funeral. These memories were kept from fading
by Cossutianus Capito. For, apart from his character
with its sharp trend to crime, he was embittered
against Thrasea, whose influence, exerted in support
of the Cilician envoys prosecuting Capito [4] for extortion, had cost him the verdict.

XXII. He preferred other charges as well:—
" At the beginning of the year, Thrasea evaded the
customary oath;[5] though the holder of a quin-
decimviral priesthood, he took no part in the national
vows; [6] he had never offered a sacrifice for the welfare
of the emperor or for his celestial voice. Once a
constant and indefatigable member, who showed
himself the advocate or the adversary of the most
commonplace resolutions of the Fathers,[7] for three
years he had not set foot within the curia; and but
yesterday, when his colleagues were gathering with
emulous haste to crush Silanus and Vetus,[8] he had
preferred to devote his leisure to the private cases
of his clients. Matters were come already to a
schism and to factions: if many made the same
venture, it was war! ' As once,' he said, ' this
discord-loving state prated of Caesar and Cato, so

6 IV. 17 n.   7 See XIII. 49.
          8 Chaps. 7 and 10 sq. above.

nunc te, Nero, et Thraseam avida discordiarum civitas loquitur. Et habet sectatores vel potius satellites, qui nondum contumaciam sententiarum, sed habitum vultumque eius sectantur, rigidi et tristes, quo tibi lasciviam exprobrent. Huic uni incolumitas tua sine *cura*,[1] artes sine honore. Prospera principis respuit:[2] etiamne luctibus et doloribus non satiatur? Eiusdem animi est Poppaeam divam non credere, cuius in acta divi Augusti et divi Iuli non iurare. Spernit religiones, abrogat leges. Diurna populi Romani per provincias, per exercitus curatius leguntur, ut noscatur, quid Thrasea non fecerit. Aut transeamus ad illa instituta, si potiora sunt, aut nova cupientibus auferatur dux et auctor. Ista secta Tuberones et Favonios, veteri quoque rei publicae ingrata nomina, genuit. Ut imperium evertant, libertatem praeferunt: si perverterint, libertatem ipsam adgredientur. Frustra Cassium amovisti, si gliscere et vigere Brutorum aemulos passurus es. Denique nihil ipse de Thrasea scripseris: disceptatorem senatum nobis relinque."

[1] <cura> *Lipsius.*
[2] respuit *Fisher*: respernit *Med.*, prosperas . . . res spernit *vulg.*

---

[1] One of the passages of Tacitus which, used as ammunition against the *Loi des Suspects*, cost Camille Desmoulins his life : —"Était-il vertueux et austère dans les moeurs ? Bon ! nouveau Brutus qui prétendait par sa pâleur et sa perruque de jacobin faire la censure d'une cour aimable et bien frisée. *Gliscere aemulos Brutorum vultus rigidi et tristis qui tibi lasciviam exprobrent.* Suspect !" (*Le Vieux Cordelier* n⁰ IV., 30 frimaire an II).

now, Nero, it prates of yourself and Thrasea. And
he has his followers—his satellites, rather—who
affect, not as yet the contumacity of his opinions, but
his bearing and his looks, and whose stiffness and
austerity are designed for an impeachment of your
wantonness.[1] To him alone your safety is a thing
uncared for, your talents a thing unhonoured. The
imperial happiness he cannot brook : can he not even
be satisfied with the imperial bereavements and
sorrows ? Not to believe Poppaea deity bespeaks
the same temper that will not swear to the acts of
the deified Augustus and the deified Julius. He
contemns religion, he abrogates law. The journal
of the Roman people,[2] is scanned throughout the
provinces and armies with double care for news of
what Thrasea has not done ! Either let us pass over to
his creed, if it is the better, or let these seekers after
a new world lose their chief and their instigator. It
is the sect that produced the Tuberones and the
Favonii [3]—names unloved even in the old republic.
In order to subvert the empire, they make a parade
of liberty : the empire overthrown, they will lay hands
on liberty itself. You have removed Cassius to
little purpose, if you intend to allow these rivals of
the Bruti to multiply and flourish ! A word in
conclusion : write nothing yourself about Thrasea—
leave the senate to decide between us !' " Nero

[2] III. 3 n.
[3] Q. Aelius Tubero, pupil of Panaetius, jurist, and inter-
locutor in Cicero's *De Republica*, was an opponent of the two
Gracchi : M. Favonius, " ape of Cato," figures fairly promin-
ently, though not too creditably, in the score of years preceding
the battle of Philippi, where he was captured and executed by
Octavian.

Extollit ira promptum Cossutiani animum Nero adicitque Marcellum Eprium acri eloquentia.

XXIII. At Baream Soranum iam sibi Ostorius Sabinus eques Romanis poposcerat reum ex proconsulatu Asiae, in quo [1] offensiones principis auxit iustitia atque industria, et quia portui Ephesiorum aperiendo curam insumpserat vimque civitatis Pergamenae, prohibentis Acratum Caesaris libertum statuas et picturas evehere, inultam omiserat. Sed crimini dabatur amicitia Plauti et ambitio conciliandae provinciae ad spes novas. Tempus damnationi delectum, quo Tiridates accipiendo Armeniae regno adventabat, ut versis [2] ad externa rumoribus intestinum scelus obscuraretur, an ut magnitudinem imperatoriam caede insignium virorum quasi regio facinore ostentaret.

XXIV. Igitur omni civitate ad excipiendum principem spectandumque regem effusa, Thrasea occursu prohibitus non demisit animum, sed codicillos ad Neronem composuit, requirens obiecta et expurgaturum adseverans, si notitiam criminum et copiam diluendi habuisset. Eos codicillos Nero properanter accepit, spe exterritum Thraseam scripsisse, per quae claritudinem principis extolleret suamque famam dehonestaret. Quod ubi non evenit vultum-

---

[1] quo *Nipperdey:* qua.   [2] <versis> *Acidalius.*

---

[1] XII. 4 n.   [2] XV. 45.
[3] In pursuance of the agreement with Corbulo (XV. 29 sqq.).
[4] He was returning from Campania with Tiridates, whom he had met at Naples.

fanned still more the eager fury of Cossutianus, and reinforced him with the mordant eloquence of Eprius Marcellus.[1]

XXIII. As to Barea Soranus, the Roman knight, Ostorius Sabinus, had already claimed him for his own, in a case arising from Soranus' proconsulate of Asia; during which he increased the emperor's malignity by his fairness and his energy, by the care he had spent upon clearing the harbour of Ephesus, and by his failure to punish the city of Pergamum for employing force to prevent the loot of its statues and paintings by the Caesarian freedman, Acratus.[2] But the charges preferred were friendship with Plautus and popularity-hunting in his province with a view to winning it for the cause of revolution. The time chosen for the condemnation was the moment when Tiridates was on the point of arriving to be invested with the crown of Armenia;[3] the object being that, with public curiosity diverted to foreign affairs, domestic crime might be thrown into shadow, or, possibly, that the imperial greatness might be advertised by the royal feat of slaughtering illustrious men.

XXIV. The whole city, then, streamed out to welcome the emperor[4] and inspect the king, but Thrasea was ordered to avoid the reception. He showed no dejection, but drew up a note to Nero, asking for the allegations against him and stating that he would rebut them, if he was allowed cognizance of the charges and facilities for reply. Nero took the note eagerly, in hopes that Thrasea, in a moment of panic, had written something which might enhance the glory of the emperor and sully his own reputation. As this proved not to be the case, and he himself

que spiritus et libertatem insontis ultro extimuit, vocari patres iubet.

XXV. Tum Thrasea inter proximos consultavit, temptaretne defensionem an sperneret. Diversa consilia adferebantur. Quibus intrari curiam placebat, securos esse de constantia eius disserunt;[1] nihil dicturum, nisi quo gloriam augeret. Segnis et pavidos supremis suis secretum circumdare: aspiceret populus virum morti obvium, audiret senatus voces quasi ex aliquo numine supra humanas: posse ipso miraculo etiam Neronem permoveri. Sin crudelitati insisteret, distingui certe apud posteros memoriam honesti exitus ab ignavia per silentium pereuntium.

XXVI. Contra qui opperiendum domui censebant, de ipso Thrasea eadem, sed ludibria et contumelias imminere: subtraheret auris conviciis et probris. Non solum Cossutianum aut Eprium ad scelus promptos: superesse qui forsitan manus ictusque per immanitatem ausuri sint;[2] etiam bonos metu sequi. Detraheret potius senatui, quem perornavisset,[3] infamiam tanti flagitii, et relinqueret incertum, quid viso Thrasea reo decreturi patres fuerint. Ut Neronem flagitiorum pudor caperet, inrita spe agitari: multoque

---

[1] disserunt *Haase*: dixerunt.
[2] ausuri sint *Acidalius*: augusti.
[3] perornavisset] semper ornavisset *Lipsius, Halm.*

took alarm at the looks and spirit and frankness of an innocent man, he ordered the senate to be convened.

XXV. Thrasea now consulted with his closest friends whether to attempt or to scorn defence. The advice offered was conflicting. Those who favoured his entering the senate-house argued that they were certain of his firmness:— " He would say nothing but what increased his glory. It was for the spiritless and the timid to draw a veil over their latter end: let the nation see a man who could face his death; let the senate listen to words inspired, it might be thought, by some deity, and superior to human utterance. Even Nero might be moved by the sheer miracle; but, if he persisted in his cruelty, the after-world at least must discriminate between the record of an honourable death and the cowardice of those who perished in silence."

XXVI. Those, on the other hand, who held that he ought to wait at home, expressed the same opinion of Thrasea himself, but urged that he was threatened with mockery and humiliation: it would be better not to lend his ear to invectives and to insults. " Cossutianus and Eprius were not the only men ready and eager for villainy: there were others besides who, in their brutality, might perhaps venture upon physical violence; and even the respectable might follow through fear. Let him rather spare the senate, of which he had been so great an ornament, the ignominy of such a crime, and leave it uncertain what would have been the decision of the Fathers when they saw Thrasea upon his trial! To touch Nero with shame for his infamies was an idle dream, and it was much more to be feared that he would

magis timendum, ne in coniugem, in filiam,[1] in cetera pignora eius saeviret. Proinde intemeratus, inpollutus, quorum vestigiis et studiis vitam duxerit, eorum gloriam peteret fine.[2] Aderat consilio Rusticus Arulenus, flagrans iuvenis, et cupidine laudis offerebat se intercessurum senatus consulto: nam plebei tribunus erat. Cohibuit spiritus eius Thrasea, ne vana et reo non profutura, intercessori exitiosa inciperet. Sibi actam aetatem, et tot per annos continuum vitae ordinem non deserendum: illi initium magistratuum et integra quae supersint. Multum ante secum expenderet, quod tali in tempore capessendae rei publicae iter ingrederetur. Ceterum ipse, an venire in senatum deceret, meditationi suae reliquit.

XXVII. At postera luce duae praetoriae cohortes armatae templum Genetricis Veneris insedere. Aditum senatus globus togatorum obsederat non occultis gladiis, dispersique per fora ac basilicas cunei militares. Inter quorum aspectus et minas ingressi curiam senatores, et oratio principis per quaestorem eius audita est: nemine nominatim compellato patres arguebat, quod publica munia

---

[1] filiam *Nipperdey* : familiam.
[2] gloriam . . . fine *Madvig* : gloria . . . finem.

---

[1] L. Junius Arulenus Rusticus, also a Stoic; praetor in 69 A.D. (*Hist.* III. 80), and executed under Domitian for composing a life of Thrasea (*Agr.* 2). Plutarch, who had him among his audience at a lecture in Rome, gives an anecdote to illustrate his βάρος (*Mor.* 522 E).

[2] III. 4 n.

[3] The temple to the divine mother of the Julian race, vowed, it was said, by Caesar on the eve of Pharsalia and erected in the centre of his new Forum. That the senate was meeting in it

exercise his cruelty on Thrasea's wife, his daughter, and the other objects of his affection. Therefore, let him seek, unstained and unpolluted, an end as glorious as theirs by whose walk and pursuits he had guided his life!" Arulenus Rusticus,[1] young and ardent, was present at the conclave, and, in his thirst for fame, offered to veto the resolution of the senate; for he was a plebeian tribune. Thrasea checked his enthusiasm, dissuading him from an attempt, futile in itself and profitless to the accused, but fatal to its maker. "His own time," he said, "was over, and he must not abandon the method of life which he had observed without a break for so many years. But Rusticus was at the beginning of his official career, and his future was uncompromised: he must weigh well beforehand in his own mind what course of public life he would embark upon in such an age." The question, whether it was proper for him to enter the senate, he reserved for his private consideration.

XXVII. On the following morning, however, two praetorian cohorts in full equipment [2] occupied the temple of Venus Genetrix;[3] a body of men wearing the toga, but with swords unconcealed,[4] had beset the approach to the senate; and companies of soldiers were scattered through the fora and basilicae. Under their eyes and their menaces the senators entered their meeting-place, and listened to the emperor's speech, as read by his quaestor. Without mentioning any person by name, he taxed the Fathers

seems hardly to be doubted, though the usual place—the *curia Iulia*—lay close at hand.

[4] So that the wearers were easily recognised as guards in the undress uniform normal in the capital.

377

desererent eorumque exemplo equites Romani ad
segnitiam verterentur : etenim quid mirum e longinquis provinciis haud veniri, cum plerique adepti consulatum et sacerdotia hortorum potius amoenitati
inservirent. Quod velut telum corripuere accusatores.

XXVIII. Et initium faciente Cossutiano, maiore
vi Marcellus summam rem publicam agi clamitabat;
contumacia inferiorum lenitatem imperitantis de-
minui. Nimium mitis ad eam diem patres, qui
Thraseam desciscentem, qui generum eius Helvidium
Priscum in isdem furoribus, simul Paconium Agrip-
pinum, paterni in principes odii heredem, et Curtium
Montanum detestanda carmina factitantem eludere
inpune sinerent. Requirere se in senatu consularem,
in votis sacerdotem, in iure iurando civem, nisi
contra instituta et caerimonias maiorum proditorem
palam et hostem Thrasea induisset. Denique agere [1]
senatorem et principis obtrectatores protegere solitus
veniret, censeret, quid corrigi aut mutari vellet:
facilius perlaturos singula increpantem [2] quam nunc
silentium perferrent omnia damnantis. Pacem illi
per orbem terrae, an victorias sine damno exercituum
displicere? Ne hominem bonis publicis maestum,

---

[1] agere] ageret *Agricola, Madvig.*
[2] increpantem *G* : increpatium *Med.*, increpantis vocem
Madvig, Halm.

---

[1] After Seneca and Thrasea, the chief figure in the Stoic
martyrology. For his antecedents and character, see *Hist.*
IV. 5 sq.; for his execution by Vespasian, Suet. *Vesp.* 15;
D. Cass. LXVI. 12).
[2] Less famous than Thrasea or Helvidius, but admired by
Epictetus (*Diss.* I. 1, 28; 2, 12; *Fr.* 21, 22 Schenkl). His
father—see III. 67—was executed by Tiberius, probably for
complicity in the plot of Sejanus (Suet. *Tib.* 61). Of Montanus
little is known (*Hist.* IV. 40, 42).

with deserting the public service and setting the example of indolence to Roman knights. For what wonder that members failed to appear from distant provinces, when many who had attained the consulate and priesthoods preferred to spend their energies upon the embellishment of their pleasure-grounds? —It was a weapon for the accusers, and they grasped it.

XXVIII. The attack was opened by Cossutianus; then Marcellus declaimed with greater violence:— "Supreme interests of state were at issue: the contumacity of his inferiors was wearing down the lenience of the sovereign. Hitherto the Fathers had been over-indulgent, permitting themselves, as they did, to be mocked with impunity by Thrasea, who was meditating revolt; by his son-in-law, Helvidius Priscus,[1] who affected the same insanity; by Paconius Agrippinus,[2] again, heir of his father's hatred for emperors; and by that scribbler of abominable verses, Curtius Montanus. In the senate he missed an ex-consul; in the national vows, a priest; at the oath of allegiance, a citizen—unless, defiant of the institutions and rites of their ancestors, Thrasea had openly assumed the part of traitor and public enemy. To be brief, let him come—this person who was accustomed to enact the complete senator and to protect the slanderers of the prince— let him come and state in a motion what he would have amended or altered: they would bear more easily with his censures of this or that than they now bore with his all-condemning silence! Was it the world-wide peace, or victories gained without loss to the armies, that met with his displeasure? A man who mourned over the nation's happiness, who

379

et qui fora theatra templa pro solitudine haberet,
qui minitaretur exilium suum, ambitionis pravae
compotem facerent. Non illi consulta haec, non
magistratus aut Romanam urbem videri. Abrum-
peret vitam ab ea civitate, cuius caritatem olim,
nunc et aspectum exuisset.

XXIX. Cum per haec atque talia Marcellus, ut
erat torvus ac minax, voce voltu oculis ardesceret,
non illa nota et celebritate [1] periculorum sueta iam
senatus maestitia, sed novus et altior pavor manus et
tela militum cernentibus. Simul ipsius Thraseae
venerabilis species obversabatur; et erant qui Helvidium quoque miserarentur, innoxiae adfinitatis
poenas daturum. Quid Agrippino obiectum nisi
tristem patris fortunam? quando et ille perinde
innocens Tiberii saevitia concidisset. Enimvero
Montanum probae iuventae neque famosi carminis,
quia protulerit ingenium, extorrem agi.

XXX. Atque interim Ostorius Sabinus, Sorani
accusator, ingreditur orditurque de amicitia Rubellii
Plauti, quodque proconsulatum Asiae Soranus pro
claritate sibi potius adcommodatum quam ex utilitate
communi egisset, alendo seditiones civitatium.
Vetera haec: sed recens et quo discrimini patris

---

[1] celebritate] crebritate *Rhenanus.*

---

[1] See above, chap. 23.

treated forum and theatre and temple as a desert,
who held out his own exile as a threat, must not have
his perverse ambition gratified! In Thrasea's eyes,
these were no senatorial resolutions; there were no
magistracies, no Rome. Let him break with life,
and with a country which he had long ceased to love
and now to look upon!"

XXIX. While Marcellus spoke to this and the like
effect, grim and menacing as always, fire kindling
in his voice and look and eyes, there reigned in the
senate, not that familiar sadness, grown habitual
now through the rapid succession of perils, but a
new and deeper terror, as they saw the hands of the
soldiers on their weapons. At the same time, the
venerable form of Thrasea himself rose before the
mind; and there were those who pitied Helvidius
also, soon to pay the penalty of an innocent connection. What had been alleged against Agrippinus,
except the tragic fate of his father; since he, too,
though equally guiltless, had fallen by the cruelty of
Tiberius? As to Montanus, a youth without vice, a
poet without venom, he was being driven from the
country, purely because he had given evidence of
his talent.

XXX. In the meantime, Ostorius Sabinus,[1] the
accuser of Soranus, entered and began his speech,
dwelling upon the friendship of the defendant with
Rubellius Plautus, and upon his governorship of
Asia, " which he had treated rather as a position
conveniently adapted to his own distinction than
with a view to the public interest; as he had shown
by fostering the seditious tendencies of the cities."
This was an old story: what was new, and used for
implicating the daughter of Soranus in her father's

filiam conectebat, quod pecuniam magis dilargita
esset. Acciderat sane pietate Serviliae (id enim
nomen puellae fuit), quae caritate erga parentem,
simul inprudentia aetatis, non tamen aliud consulta-
verat quam de incolumitate domus, et an placabilis
Nero, an cognitio senatus nihil atrox adferret.
Igitur accita est in senatum, steteruntque diversi
ante tribunal consulum grandis aevo parens, contra
filia intra vicensimum aetatis annum, nuper marito
Annio Pollione in exilium pulso viduata desolataque,
ac ne patrem quidem intuens, cuius onerasse pericula
videbatur.

XXXI. Tum interrogante accusatore, an cultus
dotalis, an detractum cervici monile venum dedisset,
quo pecuniam faciendis magicis sacris contraheret,
primum strata humi longoque fletu et silentio, post
altaria et aram complexa, " Nullos " inquit " impios
deos, nullas devotiones, nec aliud infelicibus precibus
invocavi, quam ut hunc optimum patrem tu, Caesar,
vos, patres, servaretis incolumem. Sic gemmas et
vestes et dignitatis insignia dedi, quo modo si
sanguinem et vitam poposcissent. Viderint isti,
antehac mihi ignoti, quo nomine sint, quas artes
exerceant: nulla mihi principis mentio nisi inter
numina fuit. Nescit tamen miserrimus pater et, si
crimen est, sola deliqui."

---

[1] XV. 56, 71.

danger, was a charge that she had distributed money to magicians. That had, in fact, happened, owing to the filial piety of Servilia (for so the girl was called), who, influenced by love for her father and at the same time by the imprudence of her years, had consulted them, though on no other point than the safety of her family and the chances that Nero would prove placable and the trial by the senate produce no tragic result. She was, therefore, summoned before the senate and at opposite ends of the consular tribunal stood an aged parent and, facing him, his daughter, who had not yet reached her twentieth year; condemned to widowhood and loneliness by the recent exile of her husband Annius Pollio,[1] and not even lifting her eyes to her father, whose dangers she seemed to have aggravated.

XXXI. When the accuser then demanded if she had sold her bridal ornaments, if she had stripped the necklace from her neck, in order to gather money for the performance of magic rites, she at first threw herself to the ground, in a long and silent fit of weeping; then, embracing the altar steps, and the altar, exclaimed : " I have resorted to no impious gods, to no spells; nor in my unblest prayers have I asked for anything but that you, Caesar, and that you, sirs, should preserve in safety this best of fathers. My jewels and robes and the emblems of my rank I gave as I should have given my blood and life, had they demanded them. It is for those men, strangers to me before, to see to it what repute they bear, what arts they practise: the emperor I never mentioned except as deity. But my most unhappy father knows nothing; and, if there is crime, I have sinned alone."

XXXII. Loquentis adhuc verba excipit Soranus proclamatque non illam in provinciam secum profectam, non Plauto per aetatem nosci potuisse, non criminibus mariti conexam: nimiae tantum pietatis ream separarent, atque ipse quamcumque sortem subiret. Simul in amplexus occurrentis filiae ruebat, nisi interiecti lictores utrisque obstitissent. Mox datus testibus locus; et quantum misericordiae saevitia accusationis permoverat, tantum irae P. Egnatius testis concivit. Cliens hic Sorani, et tunc emptus ad opprimendum amicum, auctoritatem Stoicae sectae praeferebat, habitu et ore ad exprimendam imaginem honesti exercitus, ceterum animo perfidiosus, subdolus, avaritiam ac libidinem occultans; quae postquam pecunia reclusa sunt, dedit exemplum praecavendi, quo modo fraudibus involutos aut flagitiis commaculatos, sic specie bonarum artium falsos et amicitiae fallaces.

XXXIII. Idem tamen dies et honestum exemplum tulit Cassii Asclepiodoti, qui magnitudine opum praecipuus inter Bithynos, quo obsequio florentem Soranum celebraverat, labentem non deseruit, exutusque omnibus fortunis et in exilium actus, aequitatis deum erga bona malaque documento.[1] Thraseae Soranoque et Serviliae datur mortis

---

[1] aequitatis . . . documento *Jackson*: aequitate . . . documenta *Med. For the appositive documento, cf. XV. 27* (multa Romanis secunda, quaedam Parthis evenisse, documento adversus superbiam) *with Roby, L.G. II. xxxii.*

---

[1] P. Egnatius Celer, a native of Berytus (D. Cass. LXII. 26) and educated at Tarsus (Juv. III. 116 sqq.); indicted in 70 A.D. by Musonius for his part in this affair; defended, on unknown grounds, by the Cynic Demetrius, but sentenced to exile (*Hist.* IV. 10, 40).

XXXII. She was still speaking, when Soranus caught up her words and cried that "she had not gone with him to his province; from her age, she could not have been known to Plautus; and she was not implicated in the charges against her husband. They should take her case separately (she was guilty only of an overstrained sense of duty); and, as for himself, let him undergo any and every fate!" At the same moment, he rushed to the arms of his daughter, who ran to meet him; but the lictors threw themselves between, and prevented both. Next, the evidence was called; and the pity awakened by the barbarity of the prosecution found its equal in the anger caused by Publius Egnatius [1] in the part of witness. A client of Soranus, now bought to procure the destruction of his friend, he affected the grave pose of the Stoic school, trained as he was to catch by manner and by look the very features of integrity, while at heart treacherous, wily, a dissembler of cupidity and lust. Those qualities gold laid bare, and he became an example pointing men to caution, not more against the villain clothed in dishonesty or stained by crime, than against those who seek in honourable attainments a cloak for falsehood and for treason in friendship.

XXXIII. The same day, however, produced also an example of honour. It was furnished by Cassius Asclepiodotus, by his great wealth the first citizen of Bithynia; who, with the same devotion as he had accorded to Soranus in his heyday, refused to desert him when near his fall, was stripped of his entire fortune, and was driven into exile, as a proof of heaven's impartiality towards good and evil. Thrasea, Soranus, and Servilia were accorded free

arbitrium. Helvidius et Paconius Italia depelluntur.
Montanus patri concessus est, praedicto ne in re
publica haberetur. Accusatoribus Eprio et Cossutiano quinquagiens sestertium singulis, Ostorio
duodeciens et quaestoria insignia tribuuntur.

XXXIV. Tum ad Thraseam in hortis agentem
quaestor consulis missus vesperascente iam die.
Inlustrium virorum feminarumque coetum frequentem[1] egerat, maxime intentus Demetrio Cynicae
institutionis doctori, cum quo, ut coniectare erat
intentione vultus et auditis, si qua clarius proloque-
bantur, de natura animae et dissociatione spiritus
corporisque inquirebat, donec advenit Domitius
Caecilianus ex intimis amicis et ei quid senatus
censuisset exposuit. Igitur flentis queritantisque,
qui aderant, facessere propere Thrasea neu[2] pericula
sua miscere cum sorte damnati hortatur, Arriamque
temptantem mariti suprema et exemplum Arriae

[1] coetum frequentem *Ritter :* coetus frequenter *Med.*,
c. frequentē *or* c. frequentes *Med.*[1]
[2] neu] nec *Nipperdey.*

---

[1] Evidently a *persona grata* with the emperor. He has
been naturally identified with the veteran epicure of Domitian's court (Juv. IV. 107; cf. 136 sqq. *noverat ille Luxuriam
imperii veterem noctisque Neronis Iam medias e.q.s.*).

[2] A sort of Cynic friar—*ille seminudus* is the description of
Seneca, who knew him well and admired him without measure
(see, for instance, *De ben.* 7). He was in Rome as early as the
principate of Gaius and seems to have courted the storms without which life became in his view a *mare mortuum* (Sen. *Ep.* 67).
He drew from Vespasian, who ultimately banished him, the
characteristic remark :—Σὺ μὲν πάντα ποιεῖς ἵνα σε ἀποκτείνω,
ἐγὼ δὲ κύνα ὑλακτοῦντα οὐ φονεύω (D. Cass. LXVI. 13).
The allusions in Philostratus, who makes him a friend of
Apollonius, are negligible.

choice of death; Helvidius and Paconius were expelled from Italy; Montanus was spared out of consideration for his father,[1] with the proviso that his official career should not be continued. Of the accusers, Eprius and Cossutianus received a grant of five million sesterces each; Ostorius, one of twelve hundred thousand with the quaestorian decorations.

XXXIV. The consul's quaestor was then sent to Thrasea: he was spending the time in his gardens, and the day was already closing in for evening. He had brought together a large party of distinguished men and women, his chief attention being given to Demetrius,[2] a master of the Cynic creed; with whom—to judge from his serious looks and the few words which caught the ear, when they chanced to raise their voices—he was debating the nature of the soul and the divorce of spirit and body. At last, Domitius Caecilianus, an intimate friend, arrived, and informed him of the decision reached by the senate. Accordingly, among the tears and expostulations of the company, Thrasea urged them to leave quickly, without linking their own hazardous lot to the fate of a condemned man. Arria,[3] who aspired to follow her husband's ending and the precedent

[3] The three generations mentioned in the sentence are as follows :—1. The elder Arria, wife of Caecina Paetus who was involved in the conspiracy of Camillus Scribonianus under Claudius (XII. 52 n.); encouraged her husband to die by stabbing herself and handing him the dagger with the words :— *Paete, non dolet* (Mart. I. 14, etc.). 2. Caecinia Annia, daughter of Caecina and the elder Arria; wife of Thrasea, whom she long survived. 3. Fannia, daughter of Thrasea and the younger Arria, and wife of Helvidius Priscus; relegated, with confiscation of her estate, under Domitian, but returned (with her mother) under Nerva.

matris sequi monet retinere vitam filiaeque communi subsidium unicum non adimere.

XXXV. Tum progressus in porticum illic a quaestore reperitur, laetitiae propior, quia Helvidium generum suum Italia tantum arceri cognoverat. Accepto dehinc senatus consulto Helvidium et Demetrium in cubiculum inducit; porrectisque utriusque brachii venis, postquam cruorem effudit, humum super spargens, propius vocato quaestore, "Libamus" inquit "Iovi liberatori. Specta, iuvenis; et omen quidem di prohibeant, ceterum in ea tempora natus es, quibus firmare animum expediat constantibus exemplis." Post lentitudine exitus gravis cruciatus adferente, obversis in Demetrium. . . .

---

[1] Thrasea's mind must have run back four and twenty years to the day when, dissuading the elder Arria from death, he asked :—*Vis ergo filiam tuam, si mihi pereundum fuerit, mori mecum?* and received the answer :—*Si tam diu tantaque concordia vixerit tecum quam ego cum Paeto, volo* (Plin. *Ep.* III. 16).

set by her mother and namesake, he advised to keep her life and not deprive the child of their union of her one support.[1]

XXXV. He now walked on to the colonnade; where the quaestor found him nearer to joy than to sorrow, because he had ascertained that Helvidius, his son-in-law, was merely debarred from Italy. Then, taking the decree of the senate, he led Helvidius and Demetrius into his bedroom, offered the arteries of both arms to the knife, and, when the blood had begun to flow, sprinkled it upon the ground, and called the quaestor nearer: "We are making a libation," he said, " to Jove the Liberator. Look, young man, and—may Heaven, indeed, avert the omen, but you have been born into times when it is expedient to steel the mind with instances of firmness." Soon, as the slowness of his end brought excruciating pain, turning his gaze upon Demetrius . . .[2]

[2] Here the Mediceus breaks short. There are lost some thirty chapters of this book and the whole of XVII. and XVIII. For their contents, see vol. II. 234[2] and the Chronological Table.

INDEX TO HISTORIES
AND ANNALS

HISTORIES

391

INDEX TO HISTORIES AND ANNALS

INDEX TO HISTORIES AND ANNALS

INDEX TO HISTORIES AND ANNALS

INDEX TO HISTORIES AND ANNALS

INDEX TO HISTORIES AND ANNALS

399

INDEX TO HISTORIES AND ANNALS

INDEX TO HISTORIES AND ANNALS

401

INDEX TO HISTORIES AND ANNALS

ANNALS

INDEX TO HISTORIES AND ANNALS

INDEX TO HISTORIES AND ANNALS

405

INDEX TO HISTORIES AND ANNALS

INDEX TO HISTORIES AND ANNALS

411

INDEX TO HISTORIES AND ANNALS

INDEX TO HISTORIES AND ANNALS

INDEX TO HISTORIES AND ANNALS

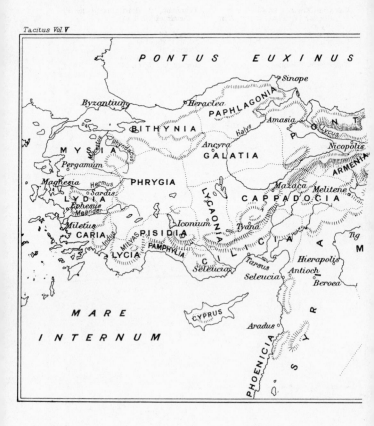

PONTUS EUXINUS

Sinope

Byzantium

Heraclea

PAPHLAGONIA

Amasia

PONT

BITHYNIA

Rhyndacus

Halys

Ancyra

Nicopolis

MYSIA

GALATIA

ARMENIA

Pergamum

PHRYGIA

Mazaca

Melitene

Magnesia

Hermus

CAPPADOCIA

LYDIA

Sardis

Ephesus

Maeander

LYCAONIA

Miletus

Indus

Iconium

Tyana

CARIA

PISIDIA

CILICIA

Tig

MILYAS

PAMPHYLIA

M

LYCIA

C

Seleucia

Tarsus

Hierapolis

Seleucia

Antioch

Beroea

MARE

CYPRUS

S

INTERNUM

Aradus

Y

R

PHOENICIA

A

COLCHIS

IBERIA

ALBANIA

Albana

MARE CASPIUM

Cyrus

Trapezus

MINOR

Satala

Araxes

Artaxata

A R M E N I A

Van

SOPHENE

Amida

MEDIA

ATROPATENE

Gazaca

ranocerta

Zerzis

Nisibis

A S S Y R I A

Ninus

MEDIA

Ecbatana

E S O P O T A M I A

Chaboras

Chala Chalone

Artemita

Nicephorium

Euphrates

Tigris

BABYLONIA

Ctesiphon

Susa

Miles

0   50   100   150   200

Edward Stanford Ltd., London